Analytical Strategies and Musical Interpretation is devoted to music analysis as an interpretative activity. Interpretation is often considered only in theory, or as a philosophical problem, but this book attempts to demonstrate and reflect on the interpretative results of analysis. Two associated types of practice are emphasised: 'translation', the transformation of one type of experience or art object into the musical work, the artistic attempt to persuade us that the new product is equal to, or more truthful than, its origin; and 'rhetoric', the attempt to persuade us, through structure, to accept the signifying power of the work. The unifying theme of the essays is the interpretative transformation of concepts, ideas and forms that constitutes the heart of the compositional process of nineteenth- and twentieth-century music. The repertoire covered ranges from Schumann through Wagner, Mahler, Zemlinsky, Debussy, Schoenberg, Berg, Webern and Stravinsky to Elliott Carter and Harrison Birtwistle.

Analytical strategies and musical interpretation

Analytical strategies and musical interpretation

Essays on nineteenth- and twentieth-century music

Edited by

Craig Ayrey

Goldsmiths College London

and

Mark Everist

University of Southampton

 **CAMBRIDGE**
UNIVERSITY PRESS

Published by the Press Syndicate of the University of Cambridge
The Pitt Building, Trumpington Street, Cambridge CB2 1RP
40 West 20th Street, New York, NY 10011–4211, USA
10 Stamford Road, Oakleigh, Melbourne 3166, Australia

First published 1996

Printed in Great Britain by Redwood Books, Trowbridge, Wiltshire

A catalogue record for this book is available from the British Library

Library of Congress cataloguing in publication data

Analytical Strategies and Musical Interpretation: Essays on
Nineteenth- and Twentieth-Century Music / edited by Craig Ayrey and
Mark Everist.
    p.   cm.
Includes index.
ISBN 0 521 46249 5 (hardback)
1. Musical analysis. 2. Music – Theory – 19th century. 3. Music –
Theory – 20th century. 4. Music – Interpretation (Phrasing,
dynamics, etc.). I. Ayrey, Craig. II. Everist, Mark.
MT75.A62 1996
780'.9'034 – dc20 95-17461 CIP

ISBN 0 521 46249 5 hardback

Dedicated to Arnold Whittall

Contents

Translations

Rhetorics

Preface

When *Theory, Analysis and Meaning in Music*, edited by Anthony Pople (Cambridge University Press) appeared in 1993 it was immediately clear that his contributors' considerations of current music theory had opened the way for a complementary volume of essays devoted to analytical practice. This new project could only be eclectic in subject and approach, but should not lack consistency of purpose. Modelled on the diversity of interests of Arnold Whittall, the doyen of British music analysis, the realisation of this project – the present volume – seeks to maintain a certain communality of attitude to the various topics considered, a communality guaranteed partly by the contributors' professional connections with him. No analyst or theorist in Britain has been more concerned with the interpretative consequences of analysis. Whittall's writing, with its special gift for distilling structural insights in an accessible format without sacrificing interpretative rigour or depth, is valued as a humanising voice in music theory, and as having defined the distinctive character of the British analytical tradition.

We dedicate this volume to Arnold Whittall on the occasion of his sixtieth birthday, in recognition of, and in gratitude for, his critical example and intellectual influence.

Acknowledgements

We thank the contributors for their enthusiasm for this project and the Editorial Board of *Music Analysis* for its encouragement and financial support in the preparation of music examples. Particular thanks are due to Jonathan Cross, James Ellis and Jonathan Dunsby for their help in many ways. We are grateful also for the assistance and support of our colleagues at Goldsmiths College London, especially Anthony Pryer and Benedict Sarnaker, and at King's College London. At Cambridge University Press, Penny Souster has been a constant source of advice, expertise and enthusiastic support.

We gratefully acknowledge copyright permissions for the reproduction of music examples from the following works:

Alban Berg: *Der Wein* and *Lulu*, reproduced by permission of Universal Edition A.G. Wien.

Harrison Birtwistle: *Refrains and Choruses* ©1961, *Tragoedia* ©1967, *Verses for Ensembles* ©1972, *Secret Theatre* ©1991, reproduced by permission of Universal Edition (London) Ltd.

Elliott Carter: Concerto for Orchestra ©1969, reproduced by permission of Associated Music Publishers.

Arnold Schoenberg: *Von heute auf morgen*, reproduced by permission of B. Schott's Söhne and Belmont Music Publishers.

Igor Stravinsky: *Symphonies of Wind Instruments*, *Petrushka*, 'The dove descending breaks the air' ©1962, reproduced by permission of Boosey and Hawkes Music Publishers Ltd. Text of 'The dove descending' by T. S. Eliot reproduced from *Collected Poems 1909–1962*, by permission of the Eliot Estate and Faber and Faber Limited. Facsimiles of *Symphonies of Wind Instruments*, reproduced by permission of the Paul Sacher Stiftung, Basel. 'Sektantskaya', reproduced by permission of Chester Music.

Anton Webern: 'Dies ist ein Lied für dich allein', Op. 3 No. 1 ©1949, reproduced by permission of Universal Edition A.G. Wien.

1

Introduction: different trains

Craig Ayrey

'Interpretation' in music is ordinarily associated with performance. Scholarly and critical work too is always interpretative in some respect. Both types of musical activity play with the two meanings of interpretation: to (re)present or render the work, and to expound or explain meaning.[1] To interpret , we think, is to understand. It is here that clarity ends. How and what do we understand? And, lurking behind this question is another: how do we understand interpretation itself? Are we, as Rilke thought, 'not really at home in our interpreted world . . .'?[2]

The onto-epistemological status of interpretation is a fundamental philosophical question. Similar debate in music has mainly advanced what is called metatheory, and within this, critical evaluation focused on the implicitly interpretative nature of studies conducted in the spirit, if not the letter, of structuralism with either an assumption of disinterested enquiry (often called 'objectivity' or 'neutrality', sometimes a 'limitation on subjectivity') into the autonomous aspects of the artwork (usually called 'structure'), or with the confidence of irrefutable method.[3] But the period of unwitting interpretation is passing: we are all self-aware now (or are presumed to be), sometimes to the extent that our work is hampered by self-conscious control of interpretative practice. Even here, at the heart of what intellectual musicians do, the familiar conflict of theory and practice is present: we can turn our attention to the hermeneutic question itself, a question that provides no ready answer, or continue to work as before, willingly blind to the interpretative traps that our work, valuable

1. See F. M. Berenson, 'Interpreting the Emotional Content of Music', in Michael Krausz, ed., *The Interpretation of Music* (Oxford: Clarendon Press, 1993), p. 61.
2. Rainer Maria Rilke, *Duino Elegies* [1923], 'The First Elegy', trans. Stephen Mitchell (London: Pan, 1987), p. 151.
3. The most influential study of this type is Alan Street, 'Superior Myths, Dogmatic Allegories: The Resistance to Musical Unity', *Music Analysis*, 8 (1989), 77–123. See also Jonathan Dunsby, 'Criteria of Correctness in Music Analysis and Theory', in Anthony Pople, ed., *Theory, Analysis and Meaning in Music* (Cambridge University Press, 1993), pp. 77–85.

as it may seem and productive of significant results, is leading us into. Under such conditions, it is generally agreed that the minimum we should expect of any study is that the strategies of interpretation are acknowledged and clear.

The essays collected in this volume are concerned with praxis, not with the theory of interpretation. Their interpretations are offered, with integrity, as an integral dimension of what the texts they consider might mean. It will be seen as appropriate, I hope, that this first essay in the book explores the boundaries of interpretative praxis in music analysis. First, however, some observations on theory.

When . . .

. . . Nietzsche wrote in 1883–8 that 'Against positivism, which halts at phenomena – "There are only *facts*" – I would say: No, facts is precisely what there is not, only interpretations',[4] he meant that our world is an interpreted world, that our concepts are metaphors, that interpretations constitute the facts as we see them now. *In order to exist for us, phenomena come into being through interpretation.*

But Nietzsche had written in 1882:

> an essentially mechanical world would be an essentially *meaningless* world. Assuming that one estimated the *value* of a piece of music according to how much of it could be counted, calculated, and expressed in formulas: how absurd would such a 'scientific' explanation of music be. What would one have comprehended, understood, grasped of it? Nothing, really nothing of what is 'music' in it![5]

. . . Susan Sontag wrote in 1964 that 'in place of a hermeneutics we need an erotics of art', she meant that criticism should desist from its preoccupation with the meaning of art ('latent content') and concentrate on what it is, that to rehabilitate the immediacy of art 'we must learn to see more, hear more, feel more'.[6] *In order that their existence be maintained, art works must not be interpreted, simply explained.*

But Sontag also asked:

> What would criticism look like that would serve the work of art, not usurp its place? What is needed, first, is more attention to form in

4. *The Will to Power*, ed. Walter Kaufmann, trans. Walter Kaufmann and R. J. Hollingdale (New York: Vintage, 1968), p. 267.
5. *The Gay Science*, trans. Walter Kaufmann (New York: Vintage, 1974), pp. 335–6.
6. 'Against Interpretation', in *A Susan Sontag Reader* (Harmondsworth: Penguin, 1983), p. 104.

art. If excessive stress on *content* provokes the arrogance of interpretation, more extended and more thorough description of *form*
would silence. What is needed is a vocabulary – a descriptive rather
than prescriptive, vocabulary for forms.[7]

... Adorno wrote that 'interpretive understanding [*Verstehen*] ... both dissolves and preserves the enigmatic quality'[8] of art, he meant that the critical task is to solve the 'riddle' of individual works by 'identifying why it
is insoluble'.[9] *In order to maintain their existence, it must be true of art
works that they cannot be explained, but interpretation is essential to
understanding.*

What is meant here by the distinction between explanation and interpretation? Elsewhere, Nietzsche defines explanation [*Erklärung*] as 'the
expression of a new thing by means of the sign of things already known'.[10]
Explanation is thus a reductive activity, the effect Sontag wants to avoid
('latent content', the preoccupation with meaning). But it also problematises the relation of metalanguage to the work: a highly sophisticated metalanguage will almost inevitably 'reduce' the work to its theoretical
precepts; this is what Jonathan Dunsby has called 'overdetermined' analysis in music.[11] Sontag's 'interpretation' is equivalent to Nietzsche's 'explanation' (new things described in terms of the old). And her 'explanation'
seems equivalent to Nietzsche's 'interpretation' (so much for her title)
which, superficially at least, appears to ask the impossible: attention to
the sensuous surface would be a type of interpretative synaesthesia, as a
translation from one medium to another. The resemblance of Adorno's
Verstehen to Nietzsche's 'interpretation' is partial. The expression of the
'new thing' in Adorno is a limited expression: interpretation goes only so
far as to identify the riddle of, not the (chimerical) solution to, the artwork
– 'chimerical' because it is implied that a solution, if it were available,
would be mere explanation of a necessarily *second-rate* work, one that
was completely explicable. All three theories stand primarily as ideals, as
theories. That is to say, they are at once radical and take risks with praxis.
Large areas of criticism (political, ideological, cultural, allegorical: that
is also to say, everything that Sontag is 'against') are marginalised by

7. *Ibid.*, pp. 102–3.
8. *Aesthetic Theory*, trans. C. Lenhardt (London: Routledge, 1984), p. 178.
9. *Ibid.*, p. 179.
10. *Nietzsche Werke, Kritischer Gesamtausgabe*, ed. Giorgio Colli and Mazzino
    Montinari (Berlin: Walter de Gruyter, 1967), vol. VII, Band 2, Fragment 34.
    Translated in Alan D. Schrift, *Nietzsche and the Question of Interpretation*
    (New York: Routledge, 1990), p. 137.   11. Dunsby, 'Criteria', p. 79.

Nietzsche's dismissal of explanation; while Adorno's *Verstehen* risks not exploring the *achieved* work but treating it as a patient for whom diagnosis is sufficient. The apparent banality of Adorno's actual analyses could be said to demonstrate the practical consequence of this theoretical position. [12]

Extrapolating from Nietzsche, the clear implication is that interpretation must be the expression of a new thing *using new signs*, and thus not a translation from new to old, or to put it differently, interpretation must produce, must *be itself*, a new sign. Interpretation itself, therefore, must be creative; it must match the challenge of the artwork. This position is familiar now as the Barthesian view of criticism:

> The danger of Method (of a fixation upon Method) comes from this: research work must satisfy two demands; the first is a demand for responsibility: the work must increase lucidity, expose the implications of a procedure, the alibis of a language – in short must constitute a *critique* (let us recall once again that to *criticize* means to *call into crisis*); here Method is inevitable, irreplaceable, not for its 'results' but precisely – or on the contrary – because it realizes the highest degree of consciousness of a language *which does not forget itself*; but the second demand is of a very different order: it is the demand for writing, for a space of desire's dispersion, where Law is dismissed. Hence, it is necessary, *at a certain moment*, to turn against Method, or at least to regard it without any founding privilege, as one of the voices of plurality: as a *view*, in short, a spectacle, mounted within the text – the text which is, after all, the only 'true' result of any research. [13]

Here, among Barthes's many themes, there is Method as a 'view', an interpretation. And thus an opposition: interpretation as a spectacle, interpretation as speculation. The nominal difference is the difference between product and process, made famous by Arnold Whittall in the teaching of music analysis. Methods in this formulation are tools (good or bad) in a process that is necessarily speculative. But speculation cannot be conducted in a void: there must be something mirrored, something shown. And therefore, to put it more generally, interpretation must be essentially the perception of relations (within the work, between works, media, within culture). This is one intention of Derrida's *il n'y a pas de hors-*

---

12. On this, see Max Paddison, *Adorno's Aesthetics of Music* (Cambridge University Press, 1993), pp. 169–71.
13. Roland Barthes, 'Writers, Intellectuals, Teachers', in *The Rustle of Language*, trans. Richard Howard (Oxford: Blackwell, 1986), p. 319. Barthes's emphases.

texte. Interpretation installs relations (from wherever) in the text: a new sign, in Peirce's infinity of interpretants.[14]

The space between

Interpretation as a 'relational field' is potentially limitless. Jonathan Dunsby succinctly defines the Scylla and Charybdis of theory, the opposition of decidability and undecidability, of 'over-determined' and 'under-determined' analysis,[15] that is found in Nietzsche's interpretative theory as the conflict of dogmatism and relativism.[16] Interpretation today is indeed, as Dunsby suggests, situated inter-state, in the space between extreme positions.

This field is evident also in my three snapshot citations as the conceptual space opened up within interpretation, 'interpretative space', a space between Nietzsche's conception of interpretation as originary and positional (his famous 'perspectivism') and Sontag's sensuous empiricism, and between Adorno's *Verstehen* and the 'enigmatic' quality that he attempts to hold in balance in a single formulation. Sontag, 'against interpretation', seems to be pleading for criticism as a simulacrum, a doubling of the art work: to be pejorative, a sustained tautology, at best an extended metonymy, a criticism of effects, not causes. Adorno, on the other hand, is concerned ultimately with the causative in art-works, their origins and cultural authenticity. Adorno allows this to emerge through a work's structure (that is, through its content which determines form); but Sontag, too, approaches this position in her approval of criticism that 'dissolves considerations of content into those of form'.[17] Sontag therefore pleads for description (as opposed to 'a prescriptive vocabulary for forms') which Nietzsche finds useless. But are they talking about the same activity? Sontag's 'description' could not, certainly, be neutral: there must be something interpretative (in Nietzsche's sense) in it. (If criticism is 'to serve the work of art' then it must be concerned with meaning.) Nietzsche, on the other hand, is concerned with the relationship of description and value (the latter is clearly an element of meaning). It is obvious that Nietzsche's 'scientific' stands for a type of neutrality: such a method can never lead to understanding because it is essentially uninterpretative. But if *everything* is 'interpretation' in Nietzsche then, since there are no facts, a description will constitute an interpretative act, however involuntary.

14. Although interpretation is relational, this does not bear directly upon the ontology of the work, the identity of which is a separate, though related, problem.   15. Dunsby, 'Criteria', pp. 78–9.

16. See Schrift, *Nietzsche*, p. 190.   17. Sontag, 'Against Interpretation', p. 103.

And so there are tensions (spaces) within each theory. In Nietzsche between the rejection of positivism and the limited value given to the 'scientific' explanation of music (there is *something* that can be 'counted, calculated'); in Sontag between 'immediacy' and descriptive formalism (since it is never clear how description of form would remain empirical, or how it would serve 'an erotics of art'); and in Adorno between the simultaneous 'dissolution' and 'preservation' of the work as 'riddle'. Thus my three theorists circle around the question in the quest for a definite position only to encounter obstacles they do not want to overcome. The retreat from extremes is a common, even necessary, move: the 'space between' is preserved in order to make room for interpretation, to defend the creative aporia without which interpretation is paralysed. Interpretation, by definition (it seems to me), cannot itself be defined. But its boundaries can be indicated or declared by recommending ways of working (as Sontag does) and by identifying attitudes.

Modern proposals of theoretical or practical restraints on the activity of interpretation in music have tended to be modest, defining minimum standards of acceptability. Jonathan Dunsby's suggestion of 'correctness' as a criterion for music analysis is an example: 'a standard that gives us the confidence to publish our work, and the confidence to impede the dissemination of work we don't like'.[18] Dunsby attempts to define the relation of method and interpretation flexibly; but the danger here is that only a limited value is conceded to method – method here is a psychological prop – so that 'correctness' exists between proof and subjective response as a type of protocol of praxis. The definition is therefore more pragmatic rather than practical, with the validity of interpretation, I infer, decided by (upper-house) peer review, an impossible cloning of Umberto Eco's 'model reader'. Any statement of protocol will encounter the same irresolvable difficulty: who or what validates interpretation? Who or what, in the end, decides?

I retreat from these questions, since they seem to be unanswerable obstacles, in order to adopt a new perspective. Stepping back from the 'how?' to the 'why?' of interpretation, from Dunsby's protocols to motivation, the essential, minimal fact of interpretation is that it is an act of appropriation.[19] Interpretation is an appropriation directed towards the work, uniting the two senses of the term, possession and appropriateness, towards making the work one's own. In musical performance (where indi-

18. Dunsby, 'Criteria', p. 77.
19. This term, but not all aspects of its definition, is borrowed from Schrift, *Nietzsche*. See especially pp. 169–98.

vidual expression – interpretation – is advanced *through* the work) it is commonplace to refer, for example, to 'Brendel's Beethoven'; it is not nonsensical to refer similarly, in analysis, to 'Schenker's Beethoven'. To express the point more forcibly, we should not separate interpretation from *desire*: desire as Barthes glosses it, 'the demand for writing' which clears a space for desire's 'dispersion' which may take many forms. The act of appropriation is made out of desire not disinterest. But even the use of a 'disinterested' method (neutral, structuralist, systematic) is already an interpretative act, deliberately or unwittingly: that is to say, an intention (however unexamined) not to impose on the text, but to live with it, allow it to reveal itself, to become hospitable to the interpreter. As Wallace Stevens wrote, 'to impose / is not to discover'.[20] To take only the most superficially resistant example, the discovery procedures of the much-maligned neutral or objective methods could be said to express the most self-effacing desire, simply by intending to allow the text 'to analyse itself', whatever the practical outcome. That such methods impose great restraints on the interpreter, but not (at least by intention) on the work, provides a parallel with performance: whereas the nineteenth-century attitude to performance interpretation is focused on the freedom of the individual performer, the late twentieth-century attitude is characterised by authenticity, the decision to *constrain* interpretation. Objective analytical methods, which occupy one theoretical extremity, also could be said to be defined by the drive towards authenticity, an authenticity of structure (but not – certainly not – of textual interpretation). On the other hand, twentieth-century literary (and, increasingly, musicological) interpretation resembles the virtuoso performance tradition of the nineteenth century, especially in style: the virtuoso flourishes of Derrida, or Dai Griffiths in this volume,[21] are remarkably like the nineteenth-century virtuoso's freedom with the text, a technique or style of interpretation that demands that we do not value what is said far above the manner of its telling.

Interpretation as a concept, therefore, has a history which is not to be confused with the reception history of the work: many problems of definition come from the attempt to consider interpretation *tout court*. We take unnecessary risks if Nietzsche's genealogical perspective is ignored. For this reason debates about the limits of interpretative freedom might strike us as naive, as long as it is remembered that we are at liberty to read the interpretation itself with the same free discrimination that we bring to

20. 'Notes towards a Supreme Fiction', in *Collected Poems* (London: Faber, 1955), p. 403.   21. pp. 301–14.

the work. We are free to accept or reject interpretations: it is not necessary to be told what is acceptable (although we, and our students, could expect to be told what is normative). It is an attitude of interpretative hubris that assumes that the production of interpretants stops with the interpreter: plurality, often taken to be only the sum of as many perspectives as can be mustered, also proceeds exponentially, in an exegetical continuum.

It is possible, however, to determine traces of desire, as the minimal conditions for taking an interpretation seriously. Respect for the text is one condition, another is the creative interplay of interpreter and work, the act of bringing something to the work (not extracting a conceptual object from it): an informing rather than an exploitative attitude. Beyond these, all other prescriptions are more or less dogmatic. Interpretation, we may provisionally conclude, will have something to do with intention, within which 'good intentions' towards the text are only a part. Nietzsche's problematic, the status of description as involuntary interpretation, is eased by the notion of intention: descriptive interpretation can be described as 'unintentional'. The interpretative content of a description can be observed, but not, perhaps, taken entirely seriously since a sense of responsibility is lacking. That is to say, we do not know what is the status of the interpretative fallout of a description: an 'intentional' interpretation, on the other hand, contains clues to its significance in its precepts.

All this pre-echoes a theory that might be expected to find favour with music analysts and theorists, Eco's theory of interpretation constructed on three types of intention (author, interpreter, text). These help define the mixture of intentions in the theories of Nietzsche, Sontag and Adorno, a mixture (played down by Eco) that will be present in any interpretation. Nietzsche's 'only interpretations' is the intention of the interpreter, the diatribe against 'scientific' explanation of music is, at least implicitly, *against* the intention of the interpreter (Nietzsche's rage is occasioned by the presumption of the 'scientist' who dares *not* to interpret). The 'truth' for Nietzsche is a personal truth ('This – is now *my* way: where is yours?'[22]). Set against this liberalism (the freedom to be wrong, or useless) is the plurality of Sontag (the freedom to be subjective), concerned above all with the intention of the text ('the sensuous surface of art') which she attempts to protect by regulating the intention of the interpreter. And Adorno sides fundamentally with the work (the intention of the text), *as long as* it is largely predicated on the authority of the author

22. Friedrich Nietzsche, 'On the Spirit of Gravity', *Thus Spoke Zarathustra*, trans. R. Hollingdale (Harmondsworth: Penguin, 1961), p. 213.

or composer. It is not surprising, then, that in an interpretative climate
defined by plural perspectives, much contemporary debate about the relative demerits of analytical and cultural approaches to music springs from
an insecure grasp of the type of intentionality in play in any given
instance. The situation is not ameliorated by the fact that intentions are
frequently implicit, shifting or confused, out of a (sometimes defensive)
desire to expand the terms of a study beyond its theoretically defined limits. (Hence the ritual, extraneous reference to the 'sensuous surface' of a
work in a structural analysis, or the fragmentary, partially applied, analytical methods encountered in musicological work.)

Eco's preference for the 'intention of the text' should provide a corrective. It is, in Bernard Williams's reading, another term for the Model
Reader who is 'the location of constraints on interpretation', though, crucially, this does not imply that 'the idea [the Model Reader] provides a
criterion for acceptable interpretation': 'there is no criterion of acceptable reading', Williams writes, 'only plausible or implausible readings,
and the idea of the Model Reader offers a focus or frame for assembling
the constraints that seem appropriate'.[23] 'Appropriate constraints' is the
variable to be established by praxis, but it seems to me that it could be at
least indicated in theory. No Reader (interpreter) is 'model', no interpretation is 'focused', I would suggest, that does not exhibit a sense of
methodological decorum, an awareness of the limits of method, limits
that have more than a coincidental correspondence to the limits of interpretation itself. While it seems appropriate, timely, now to accept Alan
Street's influential articulation of one manifestation of interpretative
plurality, that plurality can be installed within method, we should treat
cautiously his suggestion that we do away with the 'convenient conceptual props' that distinct methodologies have provided.[24] A collage,
piquant though it may be, is not *ein Gemälde* (that my metaphor would
collapse in the face of a *work* demonstrates baldly the difference between
interpretation and art): interpreters' desire can be expected by their readers to be directed, channelled.

This is Barthes on Theory:

Simply, a day comes when we feel a certain need to *loosen* the theory
a bit, to shift the discourse, the ideolect which repeats itself,

23. 'The Riddle of Umberto Eco', *The New York Review of Books*, 42/2 (2
February 1995), 34.
24. Street, 'Superior Myths', p. 121. See also Craig Ayrey, 'Debussy's Significant
Connections: Metaphor and Metonymy in Analytical Method', in Pople, ed.,
Theory, pp. 130–1.

becomes consistent, and to give it the shock of a question. Pleasure is this question.[25]

And 'pleasure'?

> *Pleasure of the text*. Classics. Culture . . . Intelligence. Irony. Delicacy. Euphoria. Mastery . . . The pleasure of the text can be defined by *praxis* . . . This pleasure can be *spoken*: whence criticism.[26]

The discipline without aporia

'The pleasure of the text can be defined by *praxis*.' Reading this twenty years on, Barthes's definition still offers a challenge to music analysts: to justify their products, in which there often seems to be precious little evidence of pleasure, to their readers. In 1994, hardly an issue of the *Musical Times* failed to contain a complaint about the concern of analysis with the autonomy of works or of its discipline, its formalism: 'music analysts, performers and critics', Anthony Pryer wrote, 'have long felt that they could put history away in a box when they confined their responses to something which they are fond of calling "the music itself"'.[27] And hardly a fresh publication in contextually-aware musicology (the 'new musicology') fails to contain a condemnation of, or challenge to, analysis as traditionally practised.[28] But it has long been recognised, even by music analysts , that music analysis is a formalism, and that this brings with it aesthetic risks. Commenting on the work of Carolyn Abbate in particular and the new musicology in general, Derrick Puffett writes:

> there is no less need for precision, or exactitude, in analysis than there was before [the new musicology]. . . . Analysis, in other words, needs to maintain its own internal logic, its aims and its sense of purpose – which may be described as *formalist* aims and purposes, in the best sense of the word. This does not mean that analysts can afford to ignore everything else that is going on in the world.[29]

---

25. Roland Barthes, *The Pleasure of the Text*, trans. Richard Miller (New York: Hill and Wang, 1975), p. 64. Barthes's emphasis.
26. *Ibid.*, p. 51. Barthes's emphases.
27. Anthony Pryer, 'Re-thinking History', *The Musical Times*, 135/1821 (November 1994), 682.
28. For example, Carolyn Abbate, *Unsung Voices* (Princeton University Press, 1991), p. 176, and Susan McClary, *Feminine Endings: Music, Gender, and Sexuality* (Minneapolis: University of Minnesota Press, 1991), p. 109.
29. 'Editorial: In Defence of Formalism', *Music Analysis*, 13 (1994), 4–5.

This confrontation of perceptions is the tip of a much larger iceberg, the sustained critique of analysis and theory (pejoratively, and largely inaccurately, called 'positivism') begun by Joseph Kerman and Leo Treitler in the early 1980s.[30] But the siege of analysis produced a sea-change in the way the discipline was viewed by its practitioners: the 'positivistic' blindness to aporia[31] was relieved, and the concreteness of 'over-determined' theory fractured. As Puffett indicates, the critical legacy presented a methodological problem for analysts: how to achieve the Barthesian 'loosening' of theory while preserving, *faute de mieux*, analytical tools and procedures that remained of unrivalled efficiency and refinement.

One solution is suggested by Carolyn Abbate and Roger Parker's critique of formalism in their introduction to *Analyzing Opera*:

> All too often, practitioners of music analysis labor doggedly to discover the hallmarks of autonomous structure, or coherence, or organic unity in a work. By doing so, they may ignore a hundred rich contexts for their object, including those we might regard as historical: the conditions of its invention, its intertextuality . . . they end up producing a kind of New Criticism writ small.[32]

The message is clear: acknowledge ambiguity, contextualise the analytical focus, and (as they argue later) don't sacrifice the aporia of a work to analytical rigour. Abbate and Parker's main complaint is the formalist obsession with unity. Opera, of course, poses generic problems, but it would be fair to say that the message has been received: music analysts today find themselves in the 'operatic' situation whatever the object of study. Except, that is, for the formalist, for whom a minimum of ambiguity is the benchmark of interpretative success and theoretical validity.

This formalist–contextualist confrontation is dramatised by Susan McClary within the polarity 'excess and frame':

> As music theorists, we are so compelled to find order in all these traumatic pieces [the repertory 'between Schenker's tonality and Schoenberg's serial music'] that we sometimes resort to the correc-

30. See, for example, Joseph Kerman, *Musicology* (London: Fontana, 1985), especially pp. 60–112; and Leo Treitler, '"To Worship that Celestial Sound": Motives for Analysis', *Journal of Musicology*, 1 (1982), 153–70.

31. The term 'aporia' has come to mean a gap or empty space, but I use it here also more literally, to indicate the location of the analyst in a confusing situation in which one does not know which way to proceed.

32. Carolyn Abbate and Roger Parker, eds., *Analyzing Opera: Verdi and Wagner* (Berkeley: University of California Press, 1989), p. 3.

tive surgery of pitch-class amoebas – to drawing loops around groups of pitches in order to demonstrate that they are actually arranged rationally. Atonal compositions – like patients through most of psychiatric history – are usually silent during the process of analysis, for it is only apparently in the absence of those coils of seductive or demented sound that order can be detected and objectively charted. . . . If – as is so clearly the case – a fascination with madness and transgressive behavior motivates much of the music we care about, then surely we need to take that into account before we jump in with our graphs. Otherwise, what precisely are we doing? Whose rationality are we attempting to establish, and why?[33]

McClary's sample repertoire is astutely, if conventionally, selected: who has not felt the tension between the descriptive interpretation of set theory ('pitch-class amoebas') and the intensity of an Expressionist musical surface? There can be no leap to an idealised conclusion though. Fine distinctions (Nietzsche's genealogy) must be made between genres and within genres. Schoenberg's *Erwartung* and Berg's *Wozzeck*, for example, are generically similar but quite distinct structurally: an analysis of the one may inspire its rejection as 'corrective surgery', an analysis of the other using the same technique will be a revelation. The demands of structure in these two masterpieces are of different orders and status, yet both are 'excessive', even structurally: for Schoenberg motivically, for Berg, careful with derivation, cyclically and formally. Expressive excess is conveyed by structural excess in this style (the same is true of Strauss's Expressionist operas): 'framing' is therefore a compositional tension as well as a theoretical, analytical 'anxiety' (McClary's term).

The theorist today, however, is obliged to have a 'sense of history', to use Arnold Whittall's phrase,[34] an awareness of historical conditions, a sensitivity to cultural contexts and aesthetic intentions: in short, an intuitive grasp of the work as a *composition* beyond the notes. This has long been Whittall's consistent 'humanist' position, but it has a particular timeliness now. The 'way out' for analysis is not necessarily, as Joseph Kerman suggests, through a complex of contexts (applying the analysis *to* contexts or situating it *in* contexts, resulting in a fundamentally divided discourse), but through the awareness of contexts as installed in the composition, an awareness that directs the analyst's work. Whittall's complementary term,

---

33. McClary, *Feminine Endings*, p. 109.
34. 'The Theorist's Sense of History: Concepts of Contemporaneity in Composition and Analysis', *Journal of the Royal Musical Association*, 112 (1987), 1–20.

'contemporaneity', encapsulates this view: it is his term for the appropriateness of analytical interpretation, for Eco's 'intention of the text'. From this established position Whittall can both describe himself as 'an upholder of a strand of the formalist tradition within the new pluralism', and say that 'a composition can never be plausibly interpreted as self-contained, and can never be understood (experienced, enjoyed) "in its own terms"'.[35] Interpretation here includes analysis ('thinking about a composition as a construct'), which must exist, Whittall says, in relation to 'theoretical' and 'cultural' contexts. As I understand him, Whittall intends 'contexts' to mean strategies of interpretation rather than, conservatively, discrete intellectual environments. His position, as a position, has a present rightness about it, a contemporaneity. The issue, though, is its perpetual re-invention as practical realisation, the praxis that cannot be defined 'in theory'. A modern praxis, as Whittall allows, is open to, and may even embrace, aporia: I would add that theory can be loosened by resisting the urge to fill in the gaps in analytical discourse, by paying attention to what is being said, and the reasons for saying it.

How? (to read a letter)

Reading the *Berg–Schoenberg Correspondence*,[36] I became fascinated by the complex of issues surrounding Berg's interest in Schoenberg's opera *Von heute auf morgen* (1928–9), and by the possibility that Schoenberg's study of Berg's new compositions might explain the intertextual correspondences in both composers' creative work during the period 1926–30. This presented itself to me as an interpretative problem: there is very little documentary proof, or possibility of proof, available for this (or any other type of) intertextuality, yet the relations so strongly suggested in the letters seem too important to be left in the limbo of common-room speculation. The speculations below are offered as a staging of the interpretative questions that arise in any study of structural meaning, as my own 'notes towards a supreme fiction' (to borrow Wallace Stevens's famous title)[37] and as an investigation into the significance of an inaudible opposition of (typographical) cases: just what sort of correspondence is a Correspondence?

35. 'Experience, Thought and Musicology', *The Musical Times*, 134/1804 (June 1993), 319.
36. Juliane Brand, Christopher Hailey and Donald Harris, eds., *The Berg–Schoenberg Correspondence: Selected Letters* (London: Macmillan, 1987).
37. 'The "essential poem" which is the full union of imagination and reality', Frank Kermode, *Wallace Stevens* [1960] (London: Faber, 1989), p. 88.

George Perle writes that in *Der Wein*

> as in *Lulu*, and possibly influenced by the example of the one act
> opera *Von heute auf morgen*, that Schoenberg had just completed,
> Berg employs piano and saxophone as integral components of the
> orchestra and for episodes in the standardized timbre of commercial
> popular music.[38]

Compare two extracts (Ex. 1.1). Obviously, the resemblance goes beyond
instrumentation and timbre: the generic tango rhythm is present in both,
but the pitch organisation of the melodic line is similar too (Ex. 1.2a). The
melodic resemblance may be a happy intertextual accident: or is it influence? Perle suggests the latter, but this is not supported by a careful reading of the chronology of the *Berg–Schoenberg Correspondence*:

> Berg to Schoenberg, 4 April 1929
> . . . it strikes me that in this libretto [of *Von heute auf morgen*] the
> *clarity* of *action*, without which theater isn't theater, is achieved
> *solely by what happens on the stage* and by *the way* it happens. *So
> much so* that I even fancy that I have an inkling of the accompanying
> music. In saying that, however, I only mean to indicate something
> about the strength of the text, not about my imaginative powers,
> which must certainly fail, in the face of such *unheard* music, music,
> that is, that until now only you have heard, and that I'll only under-
> stand entirely when I have known it for years.[39]

Soon after writing this letter, which seems to me to be of central importance, Berg composed *Der Wein*, between May and 23 July 1929 (the full
score was completed on 26 August), but did not hear *Von heute* until 27
February 1930 (by which time he had received a full score).[40] *Der Wein* was
premiered on 4 June 1930 in Schoenberg's presence.[41] Berg cannot therefore have been influenced by *Von heute* unless either the libretto specified
the form of the musical numbers (unlikely), or there was a further
communication between 4 April and 23 July 1929 describing or demonstrating the composition process of *Von heute*.

Why does this matter? *Prima facie*, because we desire proof of influence,
at least for the type of direct correspondence Perle describes. But, on reflection, in what respect would this be convincing? It will do nothing to confirm

---

38. George Perle, *The Operas of Alban Berg: Vol. 2 Lulu* (Berkeley: University
   of California Press, 1985), p. 29.
39. *Correspondence*, p. 385. Berg's emphases.
40. *Ibid.*, p. 385.   41. *Ibid.*, p. 402, note 3.

Example 1.1

(a) *Von heute auf morgen*, bb. 64–72

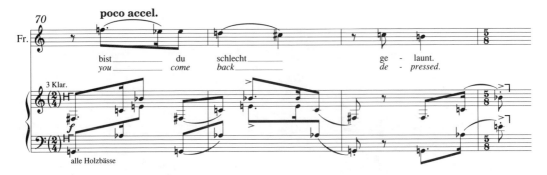

Example 1.1

(b) *Der Wein*, bb. 39–51.

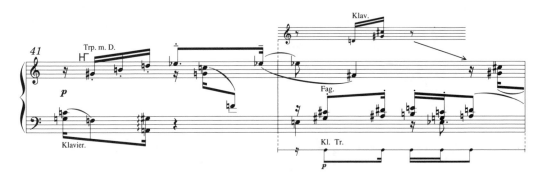

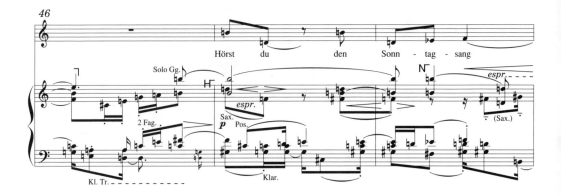

Example 1.1(b) *cont.*

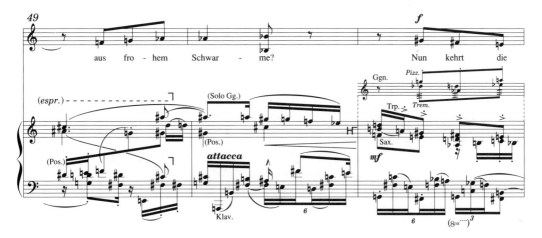

the self-evident similarities in Exx. 1.1 and 2, and in fact it will marginalise an essential dimension in Berg's letter. We may be better off, less constrained, without documentary proof. Berg refers, in an odd, memorable turn of phrase, to '*unheard* music' (note the emphasis) before which his imaginative powers 'must certainly fail'. Yet they do not fail entirely. The complete sentence is turned in on itself, dramatising Berg's groping for the inexpressible, and – possibly – for a formulation that will not offend Schoenberg's compositional dignity. The repetition 'music, music' stands as a 'performance' of 'unheard music' (here I have faith in the reliable translation). As I read it, the structure of Berg's prose is indicative of his intuitive power.

The question is, therefore, what is the 'reality' lying behind contradictions of the passage? What was the 'unheard music' that Berg could not imagine but of which he had 'an inkling'? Let us assume that it was something like the Tango, suggested by the similarity of subjects (the representation of 'modern life') in the libretti of *Von heute*, *Lulu*, and the text of *Der Wein*, all of which Berg was occupied with at the time. The common ground of the extracts in Ex. 1.1 is relaxation, *relâche*: in Schoenberg, 'einem vergnügten Abend', in Berg (ironically) a reference to the 'Sonntagsang' (Baudelaire's ironic 'refrains de dimanche' suggests hymns but implies its opposite, the secular – perhaps even the demonic – not the sacred).[42] That this should have called up the same generic image in Berg

42. The secular implication is unambiguous in the reprise of the Tango in *Der Wein* (bb. 181–90). Stefan George's translation of Baudelaire, the version used by Berg, reads in English as follows: 'The last coin at the gambling table, / a shameless kiss from Adeline, / the strained song of the violin . . .' (trans. Mari Pračkauskas).

Example 1.2   *Von heute auf morgen, Der Wein*: serial similarities
(a) *Von heute auf morgen*
(b) *Der Wein*

and Schoenberg is not surprising: but how did the similarity of the melodic line originate? Since both extracts are serial, surely there must be some similarity in the series of the two works (see Ex. 1.2b)? Clearly, though, this is not a simple correspondence. Berg uses his series strictly, whereas Schoenberg is working with a trope, the scalic hexachord derived from P0 at the beginning of the opera, bars 1–6 (Ex. 1.3a,b).[43] If

43. Schoenberg's trope is based in the hexachordal combinatoriality of P0 and I5. This is evident in the sketches for the work; see *Arnold Schönberg: Sämtliche Werke, Von heute auf morgen*, ed. Gösta Neuwirth (Mainz and Vienna: Schott and Universal Edition, 1972), Abteilung III, Band 7, Teil 1, p. 67. Presumably, the sketches are the unacknowledged source of Luigi Rognoni's similar derivation in *The Second Vienna School: The Rise of Expressionism in the Music of Arnold Schoenberg, Alban Berg, and Anton von Webern*, trans. Robert W. Mann (London: Calder, 1977), pp. 196–7. Now that we have detailed knowledge of Berg's troping techniques in *Lulu*, inaccessible to Schoenberg in the late 1920s, this combinatorial derivation appears interpretatively excessive.

Example 1.3
(a) *Von heute auf morgen*: series
(b) *Der Wein*: series
(c) *Lyric Suite*: series
(d) *Moses und Aron*: series

Schoenberg's *troped* series is now compared with Berg's, the relationship is clarified. Schoenberg's hexachords are similar to the scale that begins the *Der Wein* series, and it contains trichord relations (p,q) of a type that seem today more characteristic of Berg and Webern than of Schoenberg. In *Von heute*, these relations associate the scales and their derivatives. Stylistically, of course, this reveals a general difference between

Schoenberg and Berg: the former conceives a series for its melodic contour and combinatorial properties (as in the opening bars, where P0 and I5 are stated together), while Berg is usually more concerned with tonal formations (triads, scales) and internal symmetries.

However, since *Der Wein* post-dates *Von heute*, Schoenberg could hardly have used *Der Wein* as a reference in deriving the scalic solution to the formal problem that confronted him: the generation of subsidiary musical material to give impetus and direction to the serial surface; and to make this a sufficiently generalised, background figure to exist in the composition as structural bedrock, yet not appear foreign to the structure (either serially or melodically). Schoenberg, like Berg, had to rethink the 'idea' of a scale serially. The *Correspondence* suggests that Berg was the first to alert Schoenberg to this necessity:

> Berg to Schoenberg, 1 September 1928
> Your interest in my new opera [*Lulu*] also makes me happy, and I take your suggestions no less seriously than those you gave me 20 years ago. I believe I am following them in that I'm not restricting myself to a single row, but have from the outset derived from it a number of other forms (scale forms, chromatic, fourth and third forms, progressions of triads and tetrachords, etc., etc., etc.) . . .[44]

Schoenberg's scalic 'inspiration' in *Von heute* is much more likely to have come from the series of Berg's *Lyric Suite* (1926–7) about which Berg wrote him a long technical letter on 13 July 1926.[45] Much has been written about this series and its special properties, but compare it now with the *Von heute* series (Ex. 1.3c). The troped versions correspond closely. Such relations may be factitious, but this is not the only instance. Schoenberg's series for *Moses und Aron* (1930–2) is structured symmetrically, similarly to that of the *Lyric Suite* (Ex. 1.3d). But it is common knowledge that Schoenberg had experimented earlier with symmetrically structured series. In the series of the Wind Quintet, Op. 26 (1924) the second hexachord is almost the literal transposition of the first, and in the Suite, Op. 29 (1926–7) the series is almost palindromic. The latter structure may be simply a by-product of the construction of the series in thirds and sixths that Berg commented on in a letter of 16 May 1927.[46] In addition to its tonal content though, it is possible that Berg recognised the near-palindrome, and exploited this structure exactly in the *Lyric Suite* (completed in early October 1926[47]), thus completing an intertextual circle.

44. *Correspondence*, p. 373.   45. *Ibid.*, pp. 348–51.
46. *Ibid.*, p. 363. Berg first received a score of the Suite on 11 May 1927.
47. *Ibid.*, p. 354, note 4.

Berg shows a preference for strict serial symmetries, while Schoenberg habitually prefers 'defective' pre-compositional structures. (The slightly defective palindrome in the *Moses* series is surely designed to indicate the impossibility of a perfect human representation of God, now an unquestioned fact in *Moses* interpretation.) Note, too, that all three series begin with the semitone, and that Schoenberg's two begin with the same trichord (x). In fact, two trichords (x,y) of the *Von heute* series are the same as that of *Moses*: could this indicate that Schoenberg's two 'operas' are oppositionally related, beyond the obvious sacred/secular genres?

If my interpretations are 'correct', the common source of *Der Wein* and *Von heute* is probably the *Lyric Suite* since the latter contains properties exploited differently in the other two. The correspondence between *Von heute* and *Der Wein* is therefore established as indirect. Of course, this does not constitute a claim that Berg influenced Schoenberg, only that both were concerned with similar structural issues (and were perhaps concerned to conceal their mutual influence).

Other aspects of *Von heute* also struck Berg:

Berg to Schoenberg, 4 April 1929
. . . there is naturally a subjective interest in my capacity as my own librettist, if I may call myself that on the basis of the fact that I am transforming an enormous drama like *Lulu* into a libretto. And there [in *Von heute*] I was struck above all, indeed fascinated, by the librettist's absolutely brilliant solution for texting the ensembles towards the end of the opera. I refer to the passages where two or more characters – as in the old opera – are given the same text (with only the pronouns altered). Only *thus* is intelligibility possible – even in ensembles – and thus the action – despite closed forms (which otherwise tend to retard things) – need never stand still.[48]

Here Berg seems to have had another 'inkling', this time of Schoenberg's 'solution' to a formal problem. The reference to 'closed forms' is strange. Why did Berg think of this, having seen only the libretto? Schoenberg's *musical* 'solution' to the 'problem' of the *buffa* ensemble finale is to set it canonically (bb. 940ff.), one of the most obviously 'closed' forms, used here in response to the 'closed', imitative text. This is probably the object of Berg's reference. Berg, though, had already reached this solution in Act I of *Lulu*.[49] Berg's canon (Ex.1.4b) is thematic, Schoenberg's (Ex.1.4a) merely

48. *Ibid.*, p. 385.
49. In the letter of 1 September 1928, Berg states that he had completed 'over 300 measures' of the score by this date (*Correspondence*, p. 373).

Example 1.4

(a) *Von heute auf morgen*, bb. 941–9

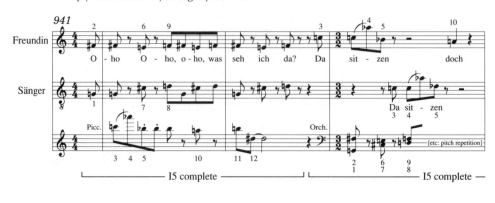

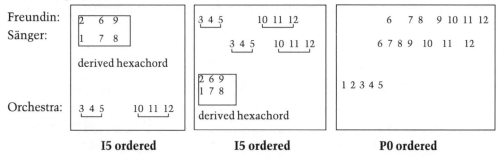

Schoenberg, *Von heute*

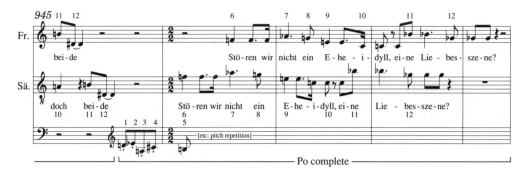

| | I5 ordered | I5 ordered | P0 ordered |

Example 1.4

(b) *Lulu*, Act I, bb. 156–68

Lulu

Lulu's series

Sie be - kom - men mich noch lan - ge nicht. Ich ver - ste - he al - les.

P3: (2) 1 2 3 4 5 6 7 8 9 10 11 (10 11) 12

P4: 3 4 5

Maler

Sie be - kom - men [as Lulu]

P3: (2) 1 2 3 etc.

Lulu

Las - sen sie mich frei! Mit Ge - walt___ er - reich - en Sie

(P4:) (3 4 5) 6 7 8 9 P10: 1 2 3 4 5 10 11 12

Maler

Gnä - di - ge [etc]

P4: 3 4 5 6 etc.

Lulu

gar nichts bei mir Ge - ben Sie an Ih - re Ar - beit. Da - zu

(P10:) 6 7 8 9 I6: (2) 1 2 3 4 5 6 7 8 9 10

Maler

So - bald ich Sie - be -

I6: (2) 1 2 3 4 5

Lulu

müs - sen Sie mich a - ber erst ha - ben Hän - de weg! Gu - te Nacht...

I5: 3 4 5 6 (5 6) P0: 4 5 I0: 6 7 8 P8: 6 7 8

(I6): 11 (10 11) 12

Maler

straft [etc]

(I6:) etc.

Vn2

P0: 1 2 3 4 5 6 [9 7 9]

P8: 1 2 3 4 5 6 7 8

Berg, *Lulu*

Lulu: **P3**: (2) 1 2 3 4 5 6 7 8 9 10 11 (10 11) 12

P4: 3 4 5 (3 4 5) 6 7 8 9 10 11 12

P10: 1 2 3 4 5 6 7 8 9 **I6**: (2) 1 2 3 4 5 6 7 8 9 10 11 (10 11) 12

I5: 3 4 5 6 (5 6) **P0**: 4 5 **I0**: 6 7 8 **P8**: 6 7 8

Violin 2: **P0**: 1 2 3 4 5 6 (9 7 9) **P8**: 1 2 3 4 5 6 7 8 serial: the rotation of pitch classes in the series means that there is always a certain imitative 'canonicity' going on in the pitch structure of a serial work.[50] Did Schoenberg not recognise the technical problem inherent in using imitative counterpoint as a *form* in serial music? Was he unaware of the tension between canonic form and the canonic technique basic to serial style? Schoenberg's many serial canons from this period are, as far as I can discern, traditional in structure: all use row segments allied with phrases of the text, maintaining the identity of serial structure and verbal syntax. The exception is 'Am Scheideweg', the first of the *Three Satires*, Op. 28 (1925) where there is serial elision between the first and second clause.[51] Perhaps Schoenberg had something to learn from Berg who seems to have recognised that the canon must transcend a simple rhythmic imitation – which is what Schoenberg's canon amounts to, adding rhythmic imitation to the (serial) pitch imitation.

In Ex. 1.4a Schoenberg contrives motivic correspondences from disjunct trichords (for example, the pc sequences [3,4,5] and [10,11,12] in I5) and uses segments of the series, or hexachords derived from it, as pitch ostinati. But none of these techniques has a canonic specificity in serialism: the only conceptual additions are rhythmic imitation of trichords or hexachords, and, when Schoenberg wants to bring imitation into the foreground (as in bb. 946–8), a literal, linear presentation of the series. This seems to me to be symptomatic of a structural blindness in Schoenberg: when canon, a fundamental feature of serial technique, is to predominate in the work, Schoenberg's serial technique becomes almost naively simple. Of course, this may be the dramatic point here (satiric characterisation), but my point is that there seems to be little distinction between Schoenberg's technique in *Von heute* and that of the other non-dramatic canons. No doubt what I have called 'naive' has something to do with Schoenberg's respect for the integrity of the series as the 'first creative

50. Perle goes so far as to say: 'The appearance of strict canonic forms in a twelve-tone work is in itself no indication of any remarkable ingenuity on the part of the composer, since the relationships that define these forms are automatically provided by the pre-compositional operations of the twelve-tone system. The exploitation of these relationships is meaningful, therefore, only to the extent that rhythmic, motivic, textural, and harmonic elements function as additional criteria of association and contrast.' George Perle, *Serial Composition and Atonality*, 4th edn (Berkeley: University of California Press, 1977), p. 119. Perle is evidently thinking entirely serially. There is no mention of melody as the basis of canon: motivic imitation is not canonic unless the imitation of entire themes is present.

51. Berg was familiar with the piece. See the letter of 30 May 1926, *Correspondence*, p. 345.

thought'. Berg's attitude to the series is less dominated by its conceptual-isation as structural essence, and thus his canon is 'thematic', in the sense that it is not absolutely determined by strict series. Inevitably, and problematically for my argument, Berg's canon (Ex.1.4b) is in fact more linearly conceived than Schoenberg's. This shows that Berg too under-stands linearity to be the essential distinction between canon as a form and canon as technique (and, *pace* Perle, that canon is not simply provided by the 'pre-compositional operations' of serialism: there is no law or prin-ciple of serialism that demands linearity either pre-compositionally or compositionally; linearity is a stylistic feature). Berg's ordering of the series is freer than Schoenberg's strict sequences, and (except for bb. 162 and 166–8) the canon is serially complete in both voices. Furthermore, the motivic character of Schoenberg's series is absent in Berg, except in the serially-incomplete bars: each voice takes the theme, a *melody*, rather than a sequence of motives, and where non-serial motivic imitations are required, they are generated through the overlapping of series or by bor-rowing pitches from more complete forms in the orchestral part (bb. 166–9). Motivic organisation supersedes serial organisation in these sec-tions, serving the higher purpose of creating a melodic form. Schoenberg's motivic imitations, on the other hand, are produced by *excluding* part of the series of the vocal-line structures. The difference could therefore be said to be between Schoenberg's distribution of motivic correspondences through reduction, and Berg's integral, composed melodies in which motivic correspondences arise from the series itself. Which is to say, as we know, that Berg's inventions are habitually more luxuriant that Schoenberg's.

Thus, the selection of canon as a solution to a problem of operatic composition seems to have occurred independently to both composers. In his 4 April letter, Berg's apparently intuitive understanding of the best musical solution to the problem of ensembles is in all likelihood a tacfully self-effacing indication that he had already solved the problem. The similarity of Schoenberg's actual solution is tantalising: perhaps Berg's hint inspired it?

In the absence of proof, perhaps my interpretation of the correspon-dences above involves reading too much into the texts (reading one into the other)? If documentary proof were found my interpretation would be altered to become an interpretation according to the 'facts' (a change of status), but an interpretation all the same, to be accepted or disputed (no change of validity) in the open-ended contest of interpretations. If it seems outlandish now, it would seem to me no less outlandish if the 'facts' emerged to fit it. While I seem to be arguing for a unrestrained interpretative free play, in fact what I have proposed for Berg is a hypothesis. But unlike the scientific hypothesis open to disproof, a hypothesis in the criticism of any art is only an interpretation. No power of denial can sensibly claim that the relations are not present: it is only the significance of the relations, of the interpretation, that can be discussed.

Extravagantly enough, without my interpretations so far it is scarcely possible to understand the structural significance of a small, neglected, occasional piece by Berg, *Alban Berg an das Frankfurter Opernhaus*, the canon he composed in 1930 for the fiftieth anniversary of the Frankfurt Opera House (Ex. 1.5). The text, by Berg, quotes the title of *Von heute* and, in the coda, a phrase associated with *Moses und Aron*.[52] Why this reference? First, because the opera was premiered at the Frankfurt Opera House on 1 February 1930;[53] secondly, Berg's letter of 4 April shows that *Moses* was habitually associated in Berg's mind (and of course in Schoenberg's) with *Von heute*.[54]

The Idea of the text is formally instantiated: the *all'inverso* occurs in the second 'stanza', to embody the notion of eternity through inversion (a function of the 'unity of musical space'): *plus ça change...* ('was wert war, bleibt wie's beschert war'), from one day to the next ('Von heute auf morgen'), for all eternity ('in aller Ewigkeit'). But more than this, the canonic form itself has demanded a special disposition of the pitch content. The first six notes (soprano) quote the *Von heute* series at I10, while the remainder of the theme contains a quotation of the pitch content of the phrase that ends the opera and quotes the title (Ex. 1.6). There is one important alteration:[55] the A♮ in Schoenberg (b. 1126, Frau) becomes A♭ in Berg (b. 2, soprano). This is unlikely to be an error, since it is clear that Berg is avoiding the A minor triad that A♮ would produce. But it has a much more significant dimension. In Schoenberg the A♮ is a transformation of the *Von heute* series, as a detail of the non-serial transformations characteristic of the final *Sprechstimme* section of the opera. This structural fact is itself expressive of the text, representing the transformation in consciousness of the two protagonists (Frau, Mann), although nothing has changed physically:

52. In the letter of 4 April 1929, Berg quotes Schoenberg's 'von Ewigkeit zu Ewigkeit' which the editors gloss as probably taken from an early draft of *Moses* (*Correspondence*, p. 385, note 2).

53. *Correspondence*, p. 394, note 1.   54. *Ibid.*, letter of 4 April 1929, p. 385.

55. The other is the reordering of F♯ and D♮ which becomes D♮, F♯ in Berg. This change seems to be of a different, purely internal significance in the Canon, to achieve an appropriately expressive line.

Example 1.5

(a) Berg, Canon

Example 1.5
(b) Text and translation

Alban Berg an das Frankfurter Opernhaus Sommer 1930	From Alban Berg to the Frankfurt Opera House Summer 1930

[Kanon]

In deines Lebens fünfzig Jahren
hast du erfahren
viel Freude und Sorgen;

[*All'inverso*]
s'war nicht vergebens;
denn, was wert war,
bleibt wie's beschert war,
von Heute auf Morgen.
(In aller Ewigkeit.)

(Willi Reich, *Alban Berg* (Vienna: Herbert
Reichner Verlag, 1937), supplement, p. 16)

[Canon]

In your fifty years of life
you have experienced
many joys and sorrows;

[Inversion]
it was not in vain;
for what was of worth,
remains as it was given,
from one day to the next.
(For all eternity.)

(Translated by Craig Ayrey)

> Frau: Also there's this difference too,
> their play is produced by fashion,
> but ours by ... love. (bb. 1121–4)

Schoenberg presents his rather ironically, but it is touching too. Berg, not a slave to quotation, and apparently aware of the demands of intertext, restores the A♭ dictated by the series, partly, I suggest, because he recognised that the A♮ has no significance outside *Von heute*. The meaning of A♮ is unique to Schoenberg and cannot be transferred to another work, even one that quotes its context.[56]

56. Since all published versions of *Von Heute auf morgen*, including the full score in the Collected Works, are unreliable, it is possible that Schoenberg's A♮ is a misprint. Nevertheless, because Berg follows Schoenberg's pitch series G♮ E♭ D♮ E♮ C♮ A♮ F♯ D♮ (see Ex. 1.6) with only the minor alterations I have discussed, the issue of the correctness of Schoenberg's text as printed is not vital to my interpretation of intertextual relationship. It would be reasonable to assume that Berg's score of *Von heute* also contained the errors perpetuated in subsequent editions. For the passage under discussion see Stephen Davison, 'Of its Time, or Out of Step? Schoenberg's *Zeitoper, Von heute auf morgen'*, *Journal of the Arnold Schoenberg Institute*, 14 (1991), 271–98, especially Ex. 5, p. 277. See also Alan Street, this volume p. 261.

Example 1.6   Berg, Canon: derivation of the theme from *Von heute auf morgen*

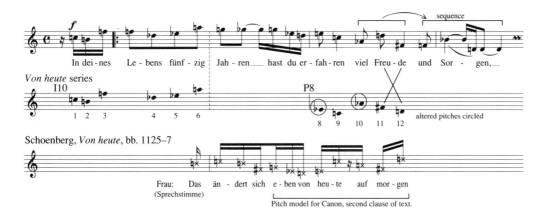

In fact, after the first six notes of the soprano voice, Berg does not simply follow the *Von heute* series. As he had demonstrated in *Lulu* , a canon identified with the series will be distinguishable from the structural norm of serial composition only weakly, by its linearity. He must therefore compose a *theme*, which ingeniously uses material from the beginning and the end of the opera (again, one day to the next, all eternity). This type of thinking which attempts to unite oppositions is built into the text and its musical setting: (1) *Freude/Sorgen* (falling minor sixth); *Heute/Morgen* (rising minor sixth); (2) the somewhat strained, extravagant representation of eternity (as similarity) in the alliteration of the voiced and unvoiced consonants *v*, *w* and *b* that begins the second clause: *s'war nicht vergebens, denn, was wert war, bleibt wie's beschert war*. The organisation of the text is neither accidental, nor (as it may appear) maladroit. Berg had paid close attention to Schoenberg's own texts, particularly the text 'Requiem' (1919). In a letter of 30 May 1926, Berg describes it as containing sentences 'that are surely among the most sublime in the German language':

> For example the verse:
>> Dem Herrn sind 1000 Tage wie ein Tag.
>> Solch einen, so oft sie einander verlieren
>> Schenkt er Liebenden,
>> sich wieder zu sehn,
>> sich immer wieder zu finden.
> and the way it interweaves and grows in intensity from line to line;
> the way it *sounds* (the many *i*'s) as if it were the most precise *rhymed*

poetry, whereas it actually possesses the absolute freedom of the most expressive prose. . . . How long before the professionals, the poets and writers, realize what stylistic wonders lie hidden here?![57]

Complementing Berg's textual alliteration, there is also a larger function of repetition: repeating the entire canon highlights the inversional relations it contains. The second time the theme is explicitly placed in inversion to its I10 version, so that the relation of Berg's theme to the *Von heute* series (I10) is present also in the two forms of the dux (P0, I10) in the canon itself (Ex. 1.7). Appropriately, given the occasion of the piece, Berg is not entirely serious: the canon ends on a C major triad, 'in aller Ewigkeit', which cannot fail to recall 'Am Scheideweg', this time explicitly. For all the changes in musical style (atonality/serialism), Berg suggests to me, tonality remains a possibility (again, 'Von heute auf morgen').

Example 1.7   Berg, Canon: I10 relations

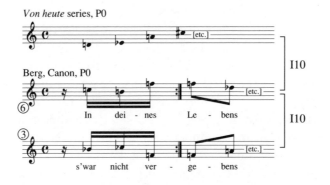

Thus it seems that the canon is as much a tribute to Schoenberg as to the Opera House, a tribute that demonstrated obliquely to Schoenberg how Berg had handled two compositional issues: how to compose a serial canon, here in a quasi-serial context; and how to integrate pre-existent pitch formations, as he had with the scales of *Lulu* which Schoenberg had not yet seen or heard.[58] Intertextual relations, the most explicit form of the correspondences essential to any interpretation, are always structural

57. *Correspondence*, pp. 346–7. Berg's emphases.
58. Acknowledging the canon in a letter of 12 September 1930, Schoenberg's only unambiguous reference to its quality was 'musically extremely polished and it should sound good'. But it is tempting to read his enthusiastic 'When did you suddenly develop such skills?' as referring beyond Berg's diplomatic riposte (contained in the text of the canon) to the management of the Opera House which Schoenberg had sued. See *Correspondence*, p. 409.

in some respect, because, as Arnold Whittall writes, 'all interpretation can be regarded as inherently analytical'.[59] A detail, a Tango, dances beyond the single work.

Arrival?

The essays collected in this volume traverse, though not always inter-textually, territory similar to that indicated in my foray into the Berg–Schoenberg intertext. More specifically, they variously reflect on the praxis of others or demonstrate particular strategies, which are broadly defined in two fields: Translations and Rhetorics, in an extended sense of both terms. This editorial contextualisation of the essays is intended to bring out two associated types of praxis: as 'translation', the transforma-tion of one type of experience or art object into a musical work, the artistic attempt to persuade us that the new product is equal to, or more truthful than, its origin; and as 'rhetoric', the attempt to persuade us, through structure, to accept the signifying power of a work. Both are therefore con-cerned with questions of representation, presence/absence, persuasion, and the conditions through which correspondences arise.

The creative translation from one medium or state to another pro-duces a transformation of an original or 'background' source in the achieved work. Stephen Walsh explores Stravinsky's *Symphonies of Wind Instruments* through the versions (1921, 1947) and sketches in a quest for the identity of the work, while Derrick Puffett's analysis of the neglected topic of transcription reveals the creative consequences of this type of translation (re-writing) in Zemlinsky's Maeterlinck Songs (1910–13). The dimensions of a *vécu* (lived experience) in Schumann's 'Rhenish' Symphony (1850) are analysed by Michael Musgrave, a topic sustained in an aesthetic context in Jonathan Dunsby's interpretation of the cultural and intertextual content of Debussy's *En blanc et noir* (1915). Dunsby's concern with poetry broaches the issue of the translation from one medium to another, an essential dimension of Jonathan W. Bernard's analysis of Elliott Carter's Concerto for Orchestra (1969) in which the existence of the 'absent' poem is analysed as 'non-verbal text'.

'Rhetorics' is used here also to mean the presence of a discursive structure in a work or analysis that directs the organisation of the musical material or the strategies of the analytical procedure. Jonathan Cross's analysis of the dramatic and poetic rhetoric of Birtwistle's *Verses for Ensembles* (1969) and *Secret Theatre* (1984) is close to Bernard's focus. Kofi Agawu explores a larger topic, the rhetoric of narrative in Mahler's

59. Whittall, 'Experience', p. 318.

Symphony No. 7 (1904–5) which introduces the theme of narrativity that underlies the essays by Alan Street, on Schoenberg, and by Anthony Pople, on Stravinsky: both are concerned with the rhetoric (as meta-theory) of interpretation and analysis. Pople teases out the interpretative implications of an analysis by Arnold Whittall, the dedicatee of this volume, of Stravinsky's anthem 'The dove descending breaks the air' (1962). Interpretative rhetoric, as structural self-commentary, is probed by Carolyn Abbate on presence/absence in Wagner; and finally, rhetoric as structural allegory is demonstrated in Dai Griffiths's staging of Webern's song 'Dies ist ein lied für dich allein' (1908) as a psychoanalytic session.

The essays' concern with interpretative praxis is advanced through the demonstration of, or reflection on, the interpretative results of analysis. Beyond this, though, there is a common focus on the re-interpretative ('translation') or structural strategies ('rhetoric') in the works analysed. That is to say, a recurrent theme of the essays is the interpretative transformation of concepts, ideas and forms that (as Whittall has always reminded us) constitutes the heart of the compositional process. Composition both employs interpretative strategies of its own and is located in an interpretative context. Music analysis seeks to reveal these dimensions, with which it begins and ends.

Translations

2

Stravinsky's Symphonies: accident or design?

Stephen Walsh

In memory of Sheila McCrindle

> There is no problem about the 'Sacre' for any moderately intelligent
> musician; but to every musician the 'Symphonies [of Wind
> Instruments]' presents a problem that we shall probably not be able
> to solve until we can get the score for prolonged study. The problem
> is, what happened to Stravinsky's mind in the interval between the
> 'Sacre' and the 'Symphonies'?[1]

Newman's question, unkindly meant, hit the nail squarely on the head. In
the seven years between the first performance of *The Rite of Spring* and
the composition of the *Symphonies of Wind Instruments*, Stravinsky's
music had indeed undergone a change. From a comprehensible madness it
had proceeded to an incomprehensible incoherence, and nobody seemed
to have the slightest idea how it had got there.

One can well understand, certainly, the bewilderment caused by the
Symphonies at its first performance, in the Queen's Hall, London, in June
1921. At that time few of Stravinsky's crucial intermediate works were
known: *Les Noces* and *Renard* still awaited their first hearing in any form,
The Soldier's Tale had had only a single complete performance, in
Lausanne, though the suite was done in London in 1920, three months
after the Aeolian Hall premiere of the tiny and baffling *Ragtime*, and six
weeks after the London opening of the other major new Stravinsky work,
Pulcinella. No wonder Newman pleaded for 'someone who knows the
whole of Stravinsky's work . . . [to make] an attempt at a really judicial
estimate of it'.[2] Performances tended to suffer from the general puzzlement. Koussevitzky, conducting the premiere on a mere two rehearsals for
a whole concert programme, clearly botched all three of the work's essential elements: tempo, instrumental balance and expressive phraseology.
Even a sympathetic musician like Eugene Goossens could do little better,
at least if we may judge from Ansermet's report of his London rehearsal in

1. Ernest Newman, 'Stravinsky and Criticism', *The Sunday Times*, 9 March
   1924.   2. *Ibid.*

December 1921.[3] But was the problem that 'a temporary cloud [had] come over Stravinsky's mind',[4] or was it just another, albeit extreme, case of the innovative artist outrunning his public?

This is not a question to be answered lightly. There is plenty of evidence that the *Symphonies* were born in uncertainty and suffered a deprived and loveless childhood, making few friends and rarely going outdoors. They were played by Stokowski in Philadelphia and New York in late 1923 and early 1924, and by Arthur Prévost[5] in Brussels in January 1924; Ansermet was a good and attentive uncle, but Stravinsky himself rarely if ever performed them before the war, was apparently equivocal about their publication, and soon allowed them to languish under an embargo which denied access to them by everyone but himself and Ansermet. The cloud was not even temporary. When Robert Craft wrote to Stravinsky after the war enquiring about performance materials, the composer could not so much as remember whether the score had been published or not.[6] Much later, when Craft himself conducted 'both the 1920 and the 1947 [versions] in Los Angeles in September 1968, side by side in one concert, Stravinsky did not like anything in the old version'.[7] Of course, Stravinsky's preference for his revised scores was a form of cupboard love; they paid royalties. But this favourite horse-sense argument will not wash in the present case. Already in the sketches, in the manuscript scores, and above all in the work's pre-war publication and performance history, it is plain to see that the *Symphonies* puzzled their composer, for a time almost as much as they puzzled his admirers and critics. This puzzlement can be traced, from the first 'unexpected elements' (as Stravinsky later called the chance beginnings of his works[8]) to the revised score of 1947, which perhaps did, but more probably did not, resolve the many questions and uncertainties surrounding the work.

Several scholars and critics have described the manuscript sources of the *Symphonies of Wind Instruments*, and some have published facsimiles.[9]

3. See his letter to Stravinsky of 20 December 1921, in Claude Tappolet, ed., *Correspondance Ansermet–Strawinsky (1914–1967)*, vol. I (Geneva: Georg, 1990), p. 205.
4. Newman, 'Stravinsky and Criticism'.
5. Not his brother Germain, as given by most authorities.
6. Letter to Craft of 29 August 1947, in Robert Craft, ed., *Stravinsky: Selected Correspondence*, vol. I (London: Faber, 1982), p. 330.
7. Robert Craft, private communication (1985).
8. Igor Stravinsky, *Poetics of Music*, trans. Arthur Knodel and Ingolf Dahl (Cambridge, Mass.: Harvard University Press, 1947), p. 53.

But none of these accounts are complete, and where they support theoretical observations about the work's poetics or aesthetics, the results are mostly anecdotal: suggestive rather than exhaustive. It is, however, possible to use the large amount of source material as the basis for a quite systematic investigation of the genesis and evolution of this astonishing work, and even as a clue to the solution of certain textual conundrums, though it needs to be said at once that Stravinsky's whole empirical approach to composition often seems to deny the possibility of once-and-for-all right answers to questions of this kind, and indeed the very existence of two identifiable 'versions' of this particular score (to say nothing of the myriad other alternatims implied by the variant texts of the original version) should warn us against the romantic notion of a definitive state. The scores 'are so different from each other . . . that the two versions will doubtless continue to be played as two different pieces'.[10]

Before we consider the detailed biography of individual ideas and sec-

9. The most important such publication is the superb facsimile of the autograph full score and particell, or short score draft, issued by the Paul Sacher Stiftung: André Baltensperger and Felix Meyer, eds., *Igor Strawinsky: Symphonies d'Instruments à Vent. Faksimileausgabe des Particells und der Partitur der Erstfassung (1920)* (Winterthur: Paul Sacher Stiftung/Amadeus, 1991). This volume also contains three sketch-page facsimiles, a source list, excerpts from reviews of the first performance and from Koussevitzky's notorious letter to the *Sunday Times* disclaiming responsibility for the fiasco, and a valuable introductory commentary. See also Volker Scherliess, 'Zur Arbeitsweise Igor Strawinskys dargestellt an den "Symphonies d'Instruments à Vent"', in H. Danuser and G. Katzenberger, eds., *Vom Einfall zum Kunstwerk* (Laaber: Laaber Verlag, 1993), pp. 161–85, for another description of the sketchbooks and sketch-leaves and several facsimiles; Vera Stravinsky and Robert Craft, *Stravinsky in Pictures and Documents* (New York: Simon and Schuster, 1978), plate 9 (facing p. 240), for a facsimile; and Craft, ed., *Stravinsky: Selected Correspondence*, vol. II (London: Faber, 1984), pp. 452–8, and vol. III (London: Faber, 1985), pp. 370–81, for many details and transcriptions. Stephen Walsh, *The Music of Stravinsky* (London: Routledge, 1988), p. 282, contains a preliminary account of the work's early textual history.

10. Igor Stravinsky, *Themes and Conclusions* (London: Faber, 1972), p. 39. This brief note includes one or two precise details about the sketch-draft stage of composition, but they look more like documentary research than reminiscence. All the materials under discussion were of course in the composer's hands until his death. Moreover, the opinion expressed differs sharply from his view of the matter in the late forties. See his telegram to Ansermet of 16 January 1948, in Tappolet, ed., *Correspondance Ansermet–Strawinsky*, vol. III, p. 88: 'Why use old instrumentation Wind Symphony when new one technically superior.'

tions of the *Symphonies*, the scene needs to be set and some general
conclusions drawn.

The earliest identifiable sketch for an idea in the finished score, a
double notation of the opening 'bell' motive, is found in a sketchbook of
1917–19, among sketches for the *Piano Rag Music* and between the draft
conclusion of *Ragtime* (dated 5 February 1918) and the initial draft of the
song 'Syelezen' ('The Drake') (28 December 1918).[11] Later in the same
book, among sketches for the *Concertino* for string quartet, is an already
accurate version of the compound-time quaver figure at Fig. 13 (2),[12] followed, after a further page of *Concertino* sketches, by a more inchoate
sketch (for two violins) of the winding, serpentine music at Fig. 15, and a
further group of sketches, partly for string quartet, developing this last
idea alongside another 'monometric' quaver motive not at first apparently
related to either the *Concertino* or the *Symphonies*. These later sketches
probably belong to the summer of 1919, since they follow a fairly
advanced draft of the *Piano Rag Music*, a work Stravinsky was composing
in June 1919 and completed on the 27th.[13]

The striking thing about these sketches, to anyone with experience
of Stravinsky's general working method, is the way in which a number
of different works seem to have become confused in the mind of a composer usually so sure of his creative aims. This is apparent, for example,
in the emergence of *Symphonies* material, in string scoring, from
material intended for a string quartet. The confusions, though, run deeper.
For instance the nearby sketches for the song 'Sektantskaya' draw attention to a marked similarity between the vocal line at the words 'Bogu
slava' and the 'serpentine' passage of the *Symphonies* (Fig. 15) first
sketched a few pages later (Ex. 2.1). The curious thing about this
particular resemblance is that it is precisely at the start of this passage
that, in the final version of the song, Stravinsky adds an obbligato flute –
the eventual lead instrument in the corresponding section of the

11. Sketchbook V in the Paul Sacher Stiftung classification. See Scherliess, 'Zur
    Arbeitsweise Igor Strawinskys', pp. 171 and 184 (n. 33), and Baltensperger and
    Meyer, *Faksimileausgabe*, p. 28, for detailed descriptions of this document.
    Baltensperger and Meyer, p. 39, plate 1, is a facsimile of this sketch.
12. Rehearsal numbers are throughout given as in the '1947' score (actually
    published in 1952). The bracketed figure is the bar number within the section
    starting from the rehearsal number in question.
13. Alfred Pochon's letter to Stravinsky commissioning the *Concertino* for the
    Flonzaley Quartet, now in the Paul Sacher Stiftung, is dated 17 August 1919.
    There is nothing in its tone to suggest that the possibility had already been
    mooted or discussed.

Example 2.1
(a) 'Sektantskaya', bb. 41–5
(b) Sketchbook V: early sketch for music at Figs. 15(3)–16(3) (first viola line
only)

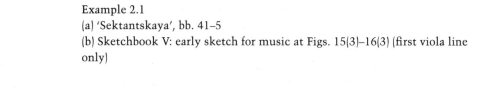

Symphonies.[14] Similar resemblances exist between the *Symphonies* and
the *Concertino*.[15] They would of course be less striking, at least in terms
of poetics, if it were not for the visible confusion of these works in the
sketchbooks, which reveals that, at the very end of the First World War,
and particularly just after the Bolshevik Revolution in Russia, the exiled
Stravinsky was generally in a state of artistic uncertainty, sketching
material with little clear idea of its destination, transferring ideas
between pieces of very different character, and even discarding material
that had already been quite fully worked. None of these practices was
normal with him.

The main body of 1919 sketches is in another book, classified as
Sketchbook VII by the Paul Sacher Stiftung.[16] Here the first intimation
of the chorale idea of the *Symphonies* suddenly appears in the middle of
work on the *Piano Rag Music* (see below, Ex. 2.4a), just as the 'bell'
motive had previously surfaced between the *Piano Rag* and 'Syelezen'.
Later in the book there begins a large block of twenty-six pages of
sketches preceded by the legend: '1ers brouillons pour mes SYMPHONIES
d'INSTR. à VENT'. For various reasons, it is tempting to date this block of

14. But the flute comes in earlier and plays more in the original version with
cimbalom. See Craft, ed., *Stravinsky: Selected Correspondence*, vol. I, pp.
421–9, for a reconstruction of the original song from facsimiles of its
sketches.
15. See Walsh, *The Music of Stravinsky*, pp. 100–2.
16. See Scherliess, 'Zur Arbeitsweise Igor Strawinskys', pp. 172ff. and 184
(n. 34); also Baltensperger and Meyer, *Faksimileausgabe*, p. 29.

'rough work' (the sense of the French word 'brouillons') to July and August 1919. In the sketch-book it almost immediately follows the dated draft of the *Piano Rag Music* (27 June 1919); moreover the first series of sketches includes about ten with registration marks for a harmonium, an instrument that Stravinsky had just incorporated in the second version of *Les Noces*.[17]

Although every essential ingredient of the *Symphonies* (as well as the two other main ideas that were associated with it but eventually discarded) figures in these 'brouillons', there is little evidence that Stravinsky saw them clearly at the time as belonging to a single work, and almost no evidence that he envisaged a work for wind. The title heading will have been a later addition. By far the majority of the sketches carry no instrumental indication at all. Apart from the harmonium group, some of the later sketches revert to the idea of a string quartet, so belong presumably to late August or early September, while a handful introduce mixed groupings, in one case flute, bassoon, harp and double bass). But wind markings as a whole are few, and there is hardly a single case of an unmistakable *Symphonies* sketch carrying indications *only* for wind. Some very elaborate loose sketches for the (as it ended up) flute and clarinet music at Fig. 15 – sketches which belong either to the later stages of the *brouillons* or the early closing stages of composition the following summer – maintain a combination of strings (for the serpentine music) and wind (for the interpolations).

Strings were still the original medium for the crucial 'bell' motive on the page before the one on which Stravinsky drafted his final chorale for the *Revue musicale* Debussy memorial in June 1920 (though the initial string attributions were later scratched out). About the 8th of that month, the composer and his family had moved from Morges to the village of Carantec, on the north Brittany coast. On the 20th he completed (or perhaps fully composed) the piano score – as one assumes it to be – of the chorale which would eventually conclude the

---

17. See Robert Craft, *Stravinsky: Glimpses of a Life* (London: Lime Tree, 1992), p. 375. The registrations in the *Symphonies* sketches can hardly have been made away from an actual instrument, and according to Craft Stravinsky had a harmonium at Morges in the summer of 1919. A note on harmonium registration, in Stravinsky's hand, survives in the Paul Sacher Stiftung on the back of a draft of his telegram to Ansermet of 11 May 1919. Craft also points out that there is a gap in Stravinsky's working 'chronicle' between the completion of the *Piano Rag Music* at the end of June 1919 and the start of work on *Pulcinella* in September.

Symphonies.[18] Twelve days later, on 2 July, he completed the short-score draft, or particell, of the whole work, placing the chorale draft – apparently unaltered – at its end.

The final draft stage of the work, mainly carried out in the twelve days between the completion of the *Revue musicale* score and that of the particell, shows that the *Symphonies* was eventually compiled from back to front, starting (after the chorale) with the section from Fig. 46(4) to Fig. 65, then continuing with the sections at Figs. 41, 13(2), and the start of the work, in that order. But from intermediate sketches, it appears that Stravinsky already had a good idea of the opening music, and perhaps also its position in the work. The very next thing he sketched after the chorale draft was the music from Fig. 4(3) to Fig. 12, with its chorale elements plainly based directly on the chorale draft itself. In fact every ingredient of this music comes from existing material – a striking and significant reversal of the usual concept of derivation in a piece of music; but the very fact that it follows the drafted *end* of the work in the way it does suggests inescapably that Stravinsky was at this moment glimpsing its beginning, even if the actual opening pages had not yet appeared.[19]

One other important group of sketches seems to show that Stravinsky had begun to compile large sections of the eventual score even before writing up the chorale. This is a pair of extended working drafts of the music between Figs. 15 and 37. Exactly where these come in the composition sequence is hard to establish. They are certainly later than the various related sketches in Sketchbook VII, but probably earlier than the chorale draft itself, since they preserve an earlier pitch level (a tone

18. The only actual keyboard indications in the *Revue musicale* publication (December 1920, supplement: 'Tombeau de Claude Debussy') are a pair each of 'm[ain]. g[auche].' and 'm[ain]. d[roite].' markings. Nevertheless Stravinsky probably did mean to imply performance on the piano. The rest of the particell is only on as few as two staves when the texture is very light or when the music is derived from the chorale. And while big hands – like Stravinsky's – are needed, the chorale is perfectly playable two-handed, though it necessitated the omission of important middle-register notes in the final chords. Prunières's letter to the composer of 20 June 1920 ('Do not feel that it is necessary to make a piano reduction . . . you are not obligated to do as the others' – quoted in Stravinsky and Craft, *Stravinsky in Pictures and Documents*, p. 226) proves that piano score had been part of the commission, and as Stravinsky actually finished the chorale on the 20th the letter's release from that condition will have come too late.

19. Baltensperger and Meyer have shown that the particell itself originally preserved a similar order, the pages having been subsequently reassembled and repaginated. See *Faksimileausgabe*, pp. 33–5.

down from the final version) which was corrected at the end of the rough draft that follows the chorale draft. My guess is that this is work Stravinsky did in Morges between the completion of *Pulcinella* in April 1920 and the move to Carantec in June.[20]

The compilation process, which I discuss in detail below, is advancing rapidly and visibly, but there are still primitive features (quite apart from the wrong pitch): for instance, the last of the drafts is still for viola with (presumably) violin, though the wind idea is beginning to emerge in the compound-time quaver interpolation figure as at Fig. 21, already marked 'dyerevo' ('wood[wind]'). We can't be certain exactly when Stravinsky realised he was writing a work for wind. The chorale draft carries no such indication, though the 'quick' draft which immediately precedes it has 'myed' ('brass') and 'dyerevo' for the chords at Fig. 67(5–6) – a dialogue idea that was slightly differently applied in the final score. The first sketch of any kind that leaves a pure wind scoring beyond reasonable doubt is the draft of Fig. 46(4), which has markings only for wind, and enough of them to imply that nothing else was going to be called for – though the indicated scoring is not yet that of the full score.[21] But we can hardly deduce from this that Stravinsky only decided on a 'wind' symphony after drafting the chorale, any more than we can assume that it was only in drafting the chorale that he formed the idea for the work itself. There is, as we have seen, plenty of earlier evidence, at least of an anecdotal kind, that he was looking for ways of assembling the scattered ideas of the sketchbooks into a single work other than the string quartet he *knew* he was writing, and some of these assemblages carry wind markings. His problem seems to have

20. These loose sketches were apparently all made on paper taken from a small landscape format drawing-book, whose remains form an unbound block on which Stravinsky wrote the composition drafts. This does not, of course, prove that the work concerned was contemporary, but it is obviously suggestive. See Stravinsky and Craft, *Stravinsky in Pictures and Documents*, plate 9, facing p. 240, for a good colour facsimile of the earlier draft, and Baltensperger and Meyer, *Faksimileausgabe*, p. 40, plate 3, for a superb one of one page of the later draft. Scherliess, 'Zur Arbeitsweise Igor Strawinskys', pp. 179–80, Facsimiles IV–VI, are a monochrome reproduction of the complete later draft. See also Plate 2.3 in the present essay for the first page of this draft.

21. See Scherliess, 'Zur Arbeitsweise Igor Strawinskys', p. 178, Facsimile III, for a monochrome of this draft. The horn music at Fig. 47(3) is as yet missing, and the following figure for oboes is given to clarinets. But the idea of bassoons is well in place; in fact a bassoon marking for an early version of this motive is one of the few unmistakable wind-scorings in Sketchbook VII.

been to make up his mind which material belonged in which work, and it may well be that it was the *Revue musicale* commission which forced a decision on this by impelling him to write up the non-quartet before the quartet. In the event the *Concertino* itself was finally composed after the particell of the *Symphonies*. It was completed on 24 September in time for the first performance in New York early in November, and only then did Stravinsky return to the *Symphonies* and compose the full score.[22]

From this point on, the textual history of the work becomes confused. At the time of its completion, Stravinsky's music was being published by J. & W. Chester in London, who in 1919 had acquired the rights to the as yet incomplete *Les Noces* as well as various completed wartime scores, some but not all of which had already been published in Switzerland. Chester also brought out the piano score of *Pulcinella* (but not the full score, which eventually went to Editions Russes). But they resisted the two instrumental works of 1920. The *Concertino* was brought out in 1923 by the Danish firm Wilhelm Hansen, but they too declined Stravinsky's offer of the *Symphonies*,[23] and when he signed a new contract with Editions Russes (ERM) in September 1923 the *Symphonies* was among the works they acquired.

At that precise moment, the performance materials for the work were in, or on their way to, the USA, where Stokowski had requested them for his American premiere in November, and as a result ERM's first service to the *Symphonies* was to produce a fresh set of parts for Prévost's Brussels performance in January 1924.[24] Neither of these two sets of MS parts seems to have survived, and one assumes, reluctantly, that both

22. The autograph full score is dated 30 November, by which time Stravinsky was installed with his family in Coco Chanel's villa in the Paris suburb of Garches.

23. See his correspondence with Hansen in the Paul Sacher Stiftung. There seems little doubt that Stravinsky would have liked Hansen, and later Editions Russes, to publish the *Symphonies*, though he may of course have intended to revise it before publication. I find no support in the correspondence for Scherliess's suggestion that the composer hesitated to publish the work at this time (see Scherliess, 'Zur Arbeitsweise Igor Strawinskys', p. 169). All the hesitation seems to have been on the publishers' side, though it may be true that Stravinsky did not press the work as hard as he might have done if he had been happier with it and more convinced of its publishability.

24. See Stravinsky's letter to Paul Collaer of 29 November 1923, in the Paul Sacher Stiftung. In early May 1924, Stokowski had still not returned the original set. Stravinsky wrote to him on 3 May requesting its return. See Craft, ed., *Stravinsky: Selected Correspondence*, vol. I, p. 433.

were destroyed by the bomb which hit ERM's Berlin offices in the closing days of the war. Meanwhile ERM seem to have been in no hurry to publish such a difficult, heterodox and – in the context of Stravinsky's contemporary work – old-fashioned score. In his letter to Stokowski of 3 May Stravinsky refers to the 'many difficulties' surrounding its publication, but I have found no equivalent references in his correspondence of the time with ERM. They did issue, in 1926, a piano reduction of the work by Arthur Lourié (plate no. RMV 423). But no plate number was assigned to the orchestral score and parts until late 1928 or early 1929, and even then at least another three years elapsed before any engraved material emerged.[25]

If a decision was taken in 1928 to go ahead with publication, it may have been prompted by a flurry of performances under Ansermet in the spring of that year, including the work's Russian premiere in Leningrad on 28 March, and a pair of performances in Brussels in April. Did Ansermet himself put pressure on ERM's Paris director, Gabriel Païchadze, on the strength of his Leningrad success with the work, or even at the urging of the Soviet musicologist Boris Asaf'yev, who, as Ansermet wrote to Stravinsky, 'threw himself on the score of *Mavra* and the *Symphonies*, which he knew only in piano transcription'?[26] If so, Ansermet may then and there have undertaken to proof-read the work. In May 1932, according to a letter from Stravinsky to Païchadze, 'Ansermet managed to call about the *Symphonies of Wind Instruments* before his departure for Switzerland. He asks that you immediately send the proof sheets, which he will soon have corrected for you.'[27] Despite subsequent reminders, more than a year seems to have elapsed before proofs finally reached Ansermet. His work on them can be dated from a pair of questioning letters which he wrote to Stravinsky, in Voreppe, on 27 and 30 June 1933, and which the composer characteristically returned to him with his answers scribbled in the margins.[28] Read in conjunction with the marked-up proof

25. The plate number of the full score is RMV 459 and that of the parts RMV 460. The fact that these numbers are consecutive makes it likely that they were assigned in due sequence, not spare numbers that were used up later. I am grateful to Malcolm Smith of Boosey & Hawkes Ltd for this and other information on the publishing practice of the time.

26. Letter of 10 April 1928, in Tappolet, ed., *Correspondance Ansermet–Strawinsky*, vol. II, pp. 145–6.

27. Letter of 28 May, in Craft, ed., *Stravinsky: Selected Correspondence*, vol. I, p. 330 (n. 7).

28. The letters are reproduced in facsimile in Tappolet, ed., *Correspondance Ansermet–Strawinsky*, vol. III, pp. 31–4.

itself (hereinafter Proof X), a copy of which was sent to Stravinsky from Paris after the war and survived in the archive of Robert Craft, as well as in conjunction with the corrected version of that proof (Proof Y), which is to this day the basis of the material that Boosey & Hawkes rent out as the 1920 version of the work, these letters mark the first textual stage of the *Symphonies* full score after the completion of the autograph in November 1920.

If these proofs were the only pre-war printed material of the orchestral score, they could be regarded as more or less faulty – though ostensibly corrected – versions of the MS full score.[29] But a third ERM proof (Proof Z) also survives which calls in question the whole status of the other two, to say nothing of Stravinsky's attitude to the work at that time.[30] While the first two proofs are simply stages in the publication of the original manuscript, Proof Z is clearly a revision. It incorporates significant changes of orchestration (of which the substitution of bassoons for horns on the very first page is only the most striking), as well as changes of melodic and harmonic detailing, some of which are simply corrections of Proof Y but many of which are actual and quite startling revisions. It also embodies radical changes in phrasing and articulation, some but by no means all of which point towards the work's root-and-branch post-war revision.

What are we to make of this unruly and disconcerting text? When and why did Stravinsky carry out the revision? That it is authentic is placed beyond doubt by the fact that the first-page corrections (including the words 'Aux bassons!' and several alterations to dynamics and articulation) were entered in red ink in the autograph full score by the composer. Unhelpfully, the subsequent changes are – with a few exceptions – *not* in the MS, as if the composer had begun idly revising on the autograph score then been forced to leave off by pressure of other work. It may just possibly

29. Which seems to have been in Stravinsky's rather than the printer's possession at the time. See his marginal note, dated 2 July 1933, to Ansermet's letter of 30 June: 'Faut-il que je vous envoie mon manuscrit ou vaudrait-il mieux que je le fasse parvenir à Païtchadze?' Presumably the printer was working from the copy referred to in the 1923 contract with ERM.

30. All three proofs are now in the Library of Congress. Copies of Y and Z are also lodged by Boosey & Hawkes with the British Library, and a pirated edition of Y was published in 1983 by Edwin F. Kalmus in the USA, where the 1920 version is still in the public domain. Apart from Robert Craft's recent recording (MusicMasters Classics 01612–67103–2), which is based on Z, all published recordings of the so-called 1920 version are of Y. The parts (RMV 460) tally, apart from minor discrepancies, with Y.

be to this score that the composer was referring when he wrote to Craft, in August 1947, that 'all I have of this work is a very dirty proof of the orch. score in the last revision made before the war'. As we shall see, though, the internal evidence supports Craft's view that the proof referred to was 'unquestionably the first' – that is Proof X, even though some general details, like the improvements in articulation on the first page, relate Z obliquely to the later revision.[31]

Proof Z is still, it should be emphasised, an ERM score, but a re-engraving, not a corrected version of Y. Nevertheless, it enjoys an intimate relationship with its predecessor. It uses an identical instrumentation, and the new engraving seems to have been imposed on the existing plates, or at any rate to have treated them as a template (since the music of the two proofs tallies page for page). Moreover, it looks on internal grounds as if the engraver had Y to hand when working on Z; certain mistakes in Z echo mistakes in Y, in ways that could not be coincidental. For instance, the first clarinet's written B (concert G♯) on the first quaver of Fig. 39(5) is misprinted as a D in both versions, a most unlikely mistake musically.[32]

One can invent a scenario to explain Proof Z, but one can't, in the end, prove much about it. It must be later than Y, since it embodies changes imposed on the autograph full score (either at the time or later) and therefore regarded by Stravinsky as superseding the original version represented by Y. Its spirit is that of a revision. But it can't be *much* later than Y, because ERM began to run down in the mid-thirties, and certainly would not have contemplated a new printing of so unmarketable a work in the economic climate of 1936 or later. The last works by Stravinsky they published were *Perséphone* and the tiny *Ave Maria*, both in 1934 (they have consecutive plate numbers). Stravinsky offered them the Concerto for two solo pianos in 1935, but they turned it down and it was given instead to Schott.[33] It looks, therefore, as if the revised proofs were pulled not later than 1934, that is within at most a year or so, and possibly only a

---

31. Craft, ed., *Stravinsky: Selected Correspondence*, vol. I, p. 330, and Craft, *Stravinsky: Glimpses of a Life*, p. 378, respectively. Craft is here explicitly refuting the view of Baltensperger and Meyer (*Faksimileausgabe*, p. 37) that the proof in question was Z. See also Richard Taruskin's review of the *Faksimileausgabe* in *Notes*, 49/4 (June 1993), 1617–21.

32. The error may of course have been in the MS copy used by the printer, and presumably destroyed, along with the parts, in 1944. The autograph full score is unambiguous at this point.

33. See Craft, ed., *Stravinsky: Selected Correspondence*, vol. III, pp. 239–40 (n. 36).

few months, of Proof Y. Bearing in mind that Proof X was corrected, not by Stravinsky, but by Ansermet, one might suggest that the arrival of Y (assuming, as is likely, that it was sent to him) confronted the composer with his problem child for the first time for several years, and moreover at a point of no return, since publication was supposedly imminent. This is certainly the most likely moment for him to have undertaken a lightning revision – probably after completing *Perséphone* in January 1934 – and to have insisted that a further engraving be made incorporating the latest changes. Such a concatenation of events would explain the non-publication of Y, and even of Z, since the delay would have taken ERM almost to the point of extinction, post-*Perséphone*. Perhaps we even have here the final musical document of the relationship between Stravinsky and his Russian publisher.

When Stravinsky left Europe in September 1939 (as it turned out, for twelve years) he 'placed most of his full-score manuscripts in a Paris bank vault. Other manuscripts were stored in the cellar of his apartment at 7, rue Antoine-Chantin.'[34] He was not consciously leaving for more than a few months, and would hardly need valuable manuscripts on a tour that was to combine a Harvard lecture course with a series of conducting engagements. When, therefore, he decided to rearrange the chorale of the *Symphonies* as a make-weight for a New York broadcast of the *Symphony of Psalms* in January 1946, he had to work from a borrowed copy of the *Revue musicale* text.[35] And since the object of this arrangement was to use the available wind complement of the *Symphony of Psalms*, its most striking difference from the 1920 scores is the complete omission of clarinets – admittedly a less crucial sonority in the chorale than in earlier sections of the work. It may have been at least as much because of this renewed contact with an old work as because of Craft's well-documented enquiry about performance materials[36] that Stravinsky finally took the work in hand and made the complete revision in which the score was at last published by Boosey & Hawkes in 1952. This 1947 version is likewise much less clarinet-dominated than the 1920 scores, a fact often taken to reflect Stravinsky's later preference for 'cool' sonorities and hard articulations. It may partly, however, reflect its origins in the opportunistic 1945

34. Craft, 'The Stravinsky Nachlass in New York and Basel', in *Stravinsky: Selected Correspondence*, vol. III, p. 514.
35. See Baltensperger and Meyer, *Faksimileausgabe*, p. 33 (n. 37).
36. Letter of 20 August 1947, in Craft, ed., *Stravinsky: Selected Correspondence*, vol. I, p. 329. Stravinsky informed Craft that he had begun work on the revision in his letter of 7 October (*ibid.*, p. 331).

chorale arrangement, just as the work itself may have come together partly because of the *Revue musicale* commission.

This complicated textual history is confusing and perhaps a nuisance for hard-working musicians and publishers. But for idle musicologists it is a source of joy. It offers a rare opportunity to study a work of the front rank at many stages of the creative process, and this fact has inspired writers like Scherliess to general observations about the composer's idiosyncratic way of assembling his music and from there to conclusions about the actual formal character of the work itself – conclusions which lead us back to the best-known analyses of the *Symphonies*, especially those of Cone, Somfai, van den Toorn and Kramer.[37] None of these scholars, however, has used the sketches or other materials to demonstrate in detail, stage by stage, how Stravinsky actually got from his first idea for a particular passage to its subsequent printed forms, or to shed light on why those forms vary so unpredictably. Questions like why did Stravinsky alter the chords at Fig. 1 or the flute figure at Fig. 15 have been asked rhetorically,[38] but scarcely answered, even speculatively – though the materials to hand offer ample encouragement. And what about the notorious mistakes and misprints, the inconsistencies that may or may not have been intentional; what, finally, about the composer's own obfuscations and prevarications, like his insistence in a letter to Ansermet that 'you are wrong; there was never an F on the first quaver of the third bar of 45'?[39] Never mind the *bons mots* about not composing but juxtaposing. What is really interesting about the way Stravinsky wrote the *Symphonies* is that he could change

37. Scherliess, 'Zur Arbeitsweise Igor Strawinskys', it will be noted, was a contribution to a volume on how initial inspiration leads to finished works of art. See also Edward T. Cone, 'Stravinsky: the Progress of a Method', in B. Boretz and E. Cone, eds., *Perspectives on Schoenberg and Stravinsky* (Princeton University Press, 1968), pp. 156–64; László Somfai, 'Symphonies of Wind Instruments (1920): Observations on Stravinsky's Organic Construction', *Studia Musicologica Academiae Scientiarum Hungaricae*, 14 (1972), 355–83; Pieter van den Toorn, *The Music of Igor Stravinsky* (New Haven: Yale University Press, 1983), pp. 337–44; and Jonathan D. Kramer, *The Time of Music* (New York: Schirmer, 1988), pp. 221–85. Taruskin's review in *Notes* (see above, n. 31), an interpretation of the *Symphonies* as an abstract representation of the Orthodox *panikhida* service, is a refreshing change from the now-standard accounts of the work's 'montage' character.
38. Particularly by Craft. See, for example, *Stravinsky: Selected Correspondence*, vol. II, p. 456.
39. Letter of 26 January 1948. See Tappolet, ed., *Correspondance Ansermet–Strawinsky*, vol. III, p. 93, and Walsh, *Stravinsky*, pp. 282–3 (n. 22).

his mind so often about basic details, and be so frequently indecisive and fallible over material that in its origins is so utterly incisive, individual and *sui generis*.

We might usefully begin with the flute figure at Fig. 15, a crucial idea in the piece, and one of those emblematic, signal-like motives characteristic of Stravinsky's so-called Russian period as a whole. It was one of the earliest *Symphonies* ideas to take shape, in the Sketchbook V material of 1919, and was from the start associated with a serpentine, monometric idea similar in drift, if not precise outline, to the running flute/clarinet duet to which it belongs in the finished work.

The various forms of this figure are given in Ex. 2.2. It will be seen that in all essentials the original figure is already the flute theme as at Figs. 15 and 29 in the 1947 score, though at a different pitch, and with a wrong value for the first note, which ought to be a semiquaver to go with the semiquaver form of the accompanying serpentine theme, and which will eventually, of course, grow a dot into the bargain (see also Ex. 2.3). If we compare this sketch with later forms, we shall notice that it has also not yet acquired the false relation (sharpened versus flattened third), or the triplet version of the mordent in the opening arpeggio. Curiously enough, none of these variants figure at all in the *brouillons*, which are much more preoccupied with the linear and formal aspects of the serpent. When the idea reappears, in the loose draft I have dated to the spring of 1920, it still has the undisturbed form of the original sketch, and the notational mistake is corrected towards a melodic rather than an ornamental value for the arpeggio.[40]

It is only when we turn to formal composition drafts incorporating this material that, like a hitherto innocent adolescent, it reveals its true protean nature. The first composition draft of the music at Fig. 15, while as yet without the structural repeat of this passage, contains no less than three different forms of the signal idea, though it is just possible that in the form at Fig. 22(2) (with the triplet mordent in the minor) the sharp has simply been left off the G by mistake, since this version is not found again in any *Symphonies* text.[41] It looks here as if Stravinsky's idea is 'statement plain then embellished', with the false relation as one aspect of the embellishment and the higher register as another. But the temptation to see the triplet as in some way an expression of the particular personality of the clarinet needs to be treated with caution; the ink draft is clearly

40. See Scherliess, 'Zur Arbeitsweise Igor Strawinskys', p. 179, Facsimile IV.
41. But one has to explain why Stravinsky made the mistake on both notations of this double figure.

50 · Stephen Walsh

Example 2.2 Biography of 'signal' motive

Proof X: as autograph full score. Pencil alterations by Stravinsky eliminate the G♯s at [15] and [29(2)]

Proof Y: as autograph full score.

Proof Z:

marked for flute in both octaves, while the suggestion of clarinet for the second figure is a pencil gloss.

At the next stage, the particell, Stravinsky seems to have become obsessed with the sharpened triplet mordent, which displaces the simpler original figure in every case except at the structural repeat at Fig. 29; here the simple version comes twice in the lower octave, followed by the embellished version an octave up. But at Fig. 15 the lower octave figure takes the triplet form with false relation, the only occasion in any text where this happens. Apparently, when he reached this passage in the full score, Stravinsky was struck by the inconsistency, slashed through the E of the triplet in the particell, and transferred to the full score the simple figure but with the G♯ intact, so that for the first time the false relation is expressed through the two-note mordent.[42] Having discovered this new version, he then applied it to the figure at Fig. 29, but only to the second statement; the first he left intact in its primary form, so that at this point in the autograph full score we now have no fewer than three consecutive different versions of the figure: low minor with two-note mordent (the original form), low false-relation two-note, and high false-relation with triplet. This score, of course, is the first definitive version of the work.

That fact did nothing, however, to halt the process of change. The engraver of Proofs X and Y naturally followed the autograph.[43] But when it came to the revision embodied in Proof Z, Stravinsky took a completely new path, expunged both the triplet and the original two-note figures, and substituted the two-note false-relation at every occurrence (with an articulative rest instead of the dot), while keeping the registral contrasts intact. Suddenly, therefore, the whole idea has changed. Instead of the 'statement plain then embellished', we have a concentrated and invariant motive (apart from register), which certainly reflects an important harmonic idea of the work – the false relation of the 'bell' motive – but in so doing abandons those shapes which had typified the idea in its earliest compositional stages. If we find something essentially un-Stravinskian in this stereo-

42. He may also have feared that the flute would lack the necessary bite on the low E.
43. The two-note false relation figures were corrected in Proof X by altering the G♯s to naturals, but the corrections were ignored in Y. The reason may be that they were made later by the composer himself. Proof X does contain marks in Stravinsky's hand, including some in the same heavy pencil as the deletion marks here (Ansermet's corrections are in ink). Possibly they were made at the time of the 1947 revision, though if so it is curious that Stravinsky used proof-reader's marks, rather than simply altering the offending notes on the stave.

typing, so apparently did the composer, since when he revised the work in 1947 he once again completely eliminated the figure in its Proof Z version, and instead reverted to the simple alternation of low minor two-note and high triplet false relation hinted at in the very first draft of this section but later preserved only in the reprise section (Fig. 29) of the particell. No wonder Ansermet, in preparing to conduct the new version in New York in January 1948, queried the loss of the G♯. But Stravinsky insisted.[44]

　　Not only the figure, but also its harmonisation, varies apparently at random from text to text; but in this case the trajectory is not a return journey from an original version back to that version after numerous adventures, but a one-way trip entailing a gradual process of clarification of an implied, rather than stated, first idea. In the early sketch, the harmonisation is dissonant, with many sevenths and tritones resulting from the undulations of the accompanying serpent theme. But when Stravinsky began composing the figure into a continuity, he used his original combination for its second and third figures, backtracking along the serpent theme for its first, which makes for an altogether smoother, more consonant image for the start of the idea (see Ex. 2.3: my imaginary addition is square-bracketed). It is this arrangement, opening with a perfect fifth, that

Example 2.3　Sketchbook V: initial sketch of 'serpent' theme combined with 'signal'. The square-bracketed addition shows how the harmony on the first beat of Fig. 15 was arrived at.

Stravinsky preferred (at both Figs. 15 and 29) in the 1947 score. But the various 1920 texts all have a minor sixth (D♯/E♭ against the melody B) at Fig. 15, reverting to a fifth at Fig. 29. The reason for this divergence is easy enough to see; correct voice-leading at Fig. 15 required the bassoon's D♭ to lead to a clarinet E♭, whereas at Fig. 29 the progression (from the low bassoon F) calls for a clarinet E♮ – and was no doubt designed with that intention. Presumably the lead into the first statement was more difficult to manipulate because the new theme cuts in directly on the preceding passage, with its characteristic parallel sixths. But eventually Stravinsky must have decided that the

44. See Ansermet's letter of 23 January 1948 and Stravinsky's reply of 26 January, in Tappolet, ed., *Correspondance Ansermet–Strawinsky*, vol. III, pp. 90 and 93.

fifth relation was more important than the voice-leading; the 1947 score goes unceremoniously to a clarinet E♮ at Fig. 15 and even, one might feel, makes a virtue of the resulting dislocation of line.

The question of harmony and chord-voicing takes us to the heart of Stravinsky's difficulties with the early version of the *Symphonies*. This is presumably because the work is so heavily characterised by a handful of rather dense chords which originate, nevertheless, in a simple combinatorial idea. Each of the main chords in the chorale sections has its own specific gravity, and nothing in any of them can be excused by voice-leading as such, even though voice-leading remains a factor in chord-linkage. This ambiguity cost Stravinsky many pains, as the sketches of the 1947 revision confirm.

As we saw earlier, the first chorale notation appears among sketches for the *Piano Rag Music*, and well away from other *Symphonies* material. Even so, it already displays features that were to remain characteristic of the chorale music to the bitter end. The melodic outline of the sketch (Ex. 2.4a) corresponds to the music at Fig. 70(2), while the harmony, with its parallel triads (alternating major and minor) and interfering lower seventh (B♭ against A), also remains essentially the same, though much embellished, through all the many vicissitudes of the idea. Subsequent *brouillons* soon establish the correct tonality – G not A; they also explore rhythmic patterns of ones and twos which, in augmentation, were to form the basis of the *Revue musicale* chorale; and, most importantly, they discover the idea of the sympathetic bass, with the addition of a low D to resonate the D component of the upper G major triad, thereby achieving the pivotal harmony of the eventual chorale (Ex. 2.4b).

The remaining chorale sketches in the *brouillons* are mainly concerned with the closing chord sequence, and with a separate, somewhat inchoate triad idea that was to be used briefly in the particell before being discarded in favour of the first adumbration of the chorale theme itself (at Fig. 42).[45] Only at the draft stage does Stravinsky seem to give any thought to the chorale elements in the earlier part of the work. A casual sketch on the same page as the main chorale draft apparently derives the chord sequence at Fig. 4(3) in the final work from a fusion of the sequences at Figs. 66 and 67 (themselves only clearly differentiated in a pencil alteration to the ink draft). But this casual sketch was no doubt made a few days later, when the opening itself was being composed. The crucial discovery was, of course, the chord at Fig. 1, a transposition up a minor third of the chorale chord, but with fuller scoring and more irregular articulation.

45. See Baltensperger and Meyer, *Faksimileausgabe*, pp. 34–5, for a discussion of this substitution, clearly detectable on p. 11 of the particell.

Example 2.4

(a) Sketchbook VII: initial chorale sketch

(b) Sketchbook VII: *brouillons* (some erasures and bracketings omitted)

(cf. Fig. 70 in the work)

(c) Resonance in the two versions (rehearsal figs. as 1947)

The subsequent history of this chord is of considerable interest, and in particular it reveals the importance Stravinsky attached to the element of resonance in thematic chords of this kind. As in the chorale chord, the upper triad – here B♭ major – is 'interfered with' by the lower seventh (C♭ = B), while its upper fifth is resonated by the F at the bottom of the chord. But later, at the equivalent of Fig. 4(3) in the draft, the resonating F is lowered a semitone, unexpectedly producing a pure F♭ major triad below the B♭ one (Ex. 2.4c). This is the first chord in the casual sketch referred to above, and it looks as if it may have been suggested by the bass descent to C♯ in the chorale itself at Fig. 66(3). But Stravinsky later disguised this whole derivation by relocating the descent to F♭. In the particell it falls one chord sooner, at Fig. 4(2), and that timing is preserved in the autograph full score and all printed 1920 texts. However, in 1947 Stravinsky once again rethought this striking and emblematic moment, and in the revised score the descent to F♭ is delayed even longer than in the sketch, until Fig. 5(1) – the final chord before the link into the flute theme at Fig. 6.

Whatever the motive behind this shift, it is by no means the most dramatic revision Stravinsky made to these chords in 1947. He also drastically revoiced and rescored them, weakening some elements and strengthening others. This is not mere tinkering, but has clear aims. In the first chord, at Fig. 1 (Ex. 2.4c), he seeks to strengthen the upper B♭ at the expense of the 'interfering' B♮, not only scoring up the 'right-hand' B♭ itself while significantly reducing the low B, but also adding B♭ resonance in the form of an added bass B♭ and F in the bassoons and double bassoon respectively, far below the interference element. With the F♭ chord, however, the resonance shifts to the new root, with the bassoon B♭ rising to C♭, while the double-bassoon F♭ now resonates a new F♭ in the baritone register (clarinet and horn) – a note which has no equivalent in the preceding chord. The great gain in richness of sound may or may not be intended to emphasise some voice-leading tendency in the descending bass. But all the signs are that Stravinsky was mainly interested in the shifting sonorities of the chords themselves. As we saw, the idea of resonance was built into the chorale chords at an early stage, but the composer may well have felt that in the 1920 scores the effect was not fully realised. The 1947 score not only adopts a more systematic approach to resonance, but does so through a fuller and enriched scoring.

A thorough account of the changes to voicing and layout in the 1947 score would rapidly inflate the present study to the size (and readability) of a telephone directory. Much of this is frankly textural recomposition, and does not necessarily reflect the original image of the music, though it does suggest that it was *tutti* passages like Fig. 54 which Stravinsky felt particularly ill at ease about in the original version. His letter to Ansermet of 26 January 1948 records the conflicting claims of harmony and line which arise here: 'the progress of the trombones (with the tuba and bassoons) is now in major thirds against the trumpets' minor thirds, the G *natural* of the first trombones in the old version being less important'.[46] But this neat constructivist test is far from consistently applicable (or applied) even in 1947. Take the trio for two clarinets and bassoon at Fig. 62 (Ex. 2.5). The bassoon's E♭ minor arpeggios both are and are not a construct, in the sense that they follow a statable rule, but one which is not quite as mechanical as it looks. Even so the

46. Tappolet, ed., *Correspondance Ansermet–Strawinsky*, vol. III, p. 94.

Example 2.5
(a) Particell: the original form of Fig. 62(4) etc.
(b) Proofs X and Y: the misprinted form of Fig. 62(4) etc.
(c) 1947: the 'definitive' form of Fig. 62(4) etc.

(a)

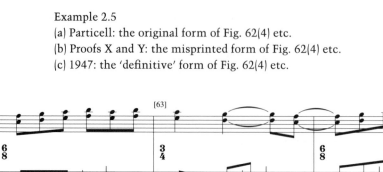

(b)

(c)

tied B♭ (instead of E♭–B♭) at the end of the first bar of Fig. 63 breaks nearly every pattern of note sequence, metre and articulation, and is surely a mistake. But if so, it is a mistake with an ancestry. In all the sketches, the particell and the autograph full score the simple arpeggio pattern is unbroken, but in Proof X there appears a random mutation, in the form of a misprinted C for the E (already flat) on the last quaver of Fig. 63(1), with a C (flat) also on the next quaver, instead of B♭. For some reason Ansermet corrected this double error not to E♭–B♭ (according to the pattern) but to a pair of tied B♭ quavers. However, the correction was never carried forward to Proof Y or Z, yet reappears, like some bizarre throwback, in the 1947 score. Such a coincidence is hard to explain, except by Craft's assumption that it was this proof, rather than Proof Z, that the composer had in front of him when revising the work.[47] In itself it hardly amounts to a likely, or even plausible, reading of the original idea.

There is further support for Craft in this passage. 'Le passage des clarinettes en quartes', Stravinsky told Ansermet in his letter of 26 January 1948, 'n'est plus staccato.' But neither composer nor conductor seems to have been aware of a more substantial question about the 'clarinets in fourths'. In all the sketch material up to and including the particell this is a typical Stravinsky piano white-note-against-black-note pattern (Ex. 2.5). The 'right hand' (clarinets) is mostly in perfect fourths but with F♯s yielding augmented fourths against the passing B♮s: all white notes on the piano. The 'left hand' (bassoon) plays a black-note arpeggio. This is a common separation in pre-twenties Stravinsky.[48] But in writing up the full score he made a mistake of transposition in the alto clarinet part, writing C♯ = F♯ instead of C♮ = F♮, and this error was duly transferred to Proof X, was understandably left uncorrected by Ansermet, and so remains to this day in Proof Y – the version of the 1920 score that is routinely performed by revisionist conductors. How do we know it was a mistake and not a change of mind? Because Stravinsky himself subsequently corrected it in the autograph full score, presumably when making the revision represented by Proof Z, where the F♮ is also reinstated.[49] However, the F♯ still survives in the 1947 revision, now in the form of a written G♯ for the second B♭ clarinet. With Ansermet's unaltered Proof X in front of him, Stravinsky might well have forgotten about this mistake. Or did he simply now prefer the smooth fourths to the more prismatic – not to say pragmatic – original, with its pungent clashes of F♮ against the bassoon's G♭?

This question has a wider significance than the mere equivocation over an accidental. It bears on the whole creative method and intention by and out of which the *Symphonies* came into being in the first place. There was, as we have seen, little early planning in the work's conception. Ideas were noted down, in some cases worked over and developed, and occasionally combined. But the *brouillons*, though quite extensive, give no clear proof of a single intention and no evidence at all of a wind piece as such.

47. *Stravinsky: Glimpses of a Life*, p. 378. See also note 31 above. In his recording based on Proof Z, Craft restores the original pattern here.
48. The *Petrushka* C major/F♯ arpeggios and the start of the 'Jeu du rapt' in *The Rite of Spring* are well-known examples.
49. 'Supprimez tout [*sic*] les ♯-ut chez la Cl-Alto.' The mistake was easy to make. The combination of the B and F clarinets gives the same written notes when, as here, they are playing in fourths, so it would have been virtually automatic to write a C♯ = F♯ in the lower voice against the upper part's C♯ = B♮. Craft's recording surprisingly retains the F♯, despite the F♮ in Proof Z.

There is, on the other hand, a definite feeling that the rapid drafting of the work in late June 1920 was a piece of creative opportunism masquerading, no doubt, as the crystallisation of a previously dormant impulse. We can only guess how much of the work Stravinsky had already assembled in his mind as he drafted the chorale for Prunières's Debussy *tombeau*. There is, though, one section whose composition *can* be traced from start to finish; and here, it may even be, lies the beginning of an answer to that peevish enquiry of Newman's with which this essay began.

The section in question is the long passage for flute and two clarinets beginning at Fig. 15, starting with the 'signal' motive whose protean shape we have already examined. This motive, as we saw (Ex. 2.3), began life as a violin counterpoint to the serpent theme but was then discarded, and the two elements were only reunited at a much later stage. The original version of the serpent theme itself consists mainly of a sequential form of b. 2 of the second clarinet part in the finished work: quite a nondescript figure, with little of the usual Stravinskian incisiveness. On the other hand, the just preceding *Symphonies* sketch – an almost accurate notation of the compound-time quaver theme at Fig. 13(2) – suggests that these various ideas were already linked in Stravinsky's mind, notwithstanding their incompatible-looking nature, and despite the fact that they first appear, separately, among sketches for another work, the *Concertino* for string quartet. A linked *Concertino* sketch is a curious chromatic quaver ostinato worked first as fives against fours, then as fives against sixes, fours, threes and twos – like a proto-minimalist experiment in phasing. This idea has no direct counterpart in the *Symphonies*; but Stravinsky did try, in one sketch, to combine it with the compound-time theme, and since these two ideas recur in tandem late in Sketchbook VII it looks as if he either had this in mind as a *Symphonies* combination, or (much more likely) still had no idea what the *brouillons* were leading to. The combination in Sketchbook VII even attempts the quodlibet effect as in the final version at Fig. 23(3), but with the chromatic quintuplets instead of the serpentine theme as countersubject to the compound-time quavers (Ex. 2.6).

Meanwhile, Stravinsky had already tried out the 'quodlibet' treatment with expanded versions of the serpent idea, evolved originally as a string duet, first for viola and cello, then violin and cello, then violin and viola – broadly in the form of the flute/clarinet duet from Fig. 15(4). Against this flowing music, he has the idea of a marcato interruption, as at Fig. 21, but still without thematic shape (Plate 2.1); then two pages later, having apparently written out an extended version of the duet, he expands it from within by splicing in an extra phrase complete with the marcato

Example 2.6 Sketchbook VII: the final *brouillon*. Only the upper part of the second half was retained.

figure, so that the interruption seems to have been composed literally – not just metaphorically – as such (Plate 2.2).

That seems to be as far as he got with this interruption idea at the time of Sketchbook VII (presumably July/August 1919). But at some stage between these *brouillons* and the final drafts he made further substantial sketch-drafts, gradually working the music towards its final form.[50] These drafts have been much cited as an example of Stravinsky's scissors-and-paste method. But detailed discussion has been lacking. What Stravinsky seems to have done first is copy out literally and at pitch (that is, a tone below the eventual pitch) the two 'interruption' sketches shown in Plates 2.1 and 2.2. This copy already reveals the inherently rotational, repetitive structure of the idea, and Stravinsky at first, mistakenly, underlines this property by adding more 'interruptions' (still on the single note D). Only then (perhaps) does he see the need for more specific, thematic interpolations, in the shape of the compound-time quaver figure (here semiquavers), which he apparently dumps on the duet music, at two points, in an existing form also copied out of the sketchbook from the very same page as the first of the two duet sketches. At the same time he further expands the duet itself by splicing in an additional phrase of the closing music (as at Fig. 24).[51]

The music is still far from its final form. There is no sign of the 'sig-

---

50. These are the loose sketches I speculatively dated to Stravinsky's final weeks at Morges (April–June 1920). More important than their dating, however, is the fact that they seem to be the only surviving composition drafts for the *Symphonies* apart from the final drafts themselves.

51. The sketch is reproduced in facsimile in *Stravinsky in Pictures and Documents*, plate 9, facing p. 240. The seemingly empirical character of this whole procedure is graphically shown by the different writing materials Stravinsky used: black ink for the original duet, red ink for the interpolations, pencil for the splicing. Was this a conscious visual aid? It appears so, since in the next draft he again uses red ink for the interpolations and pencil for the splicings.

Plate 2.1 Stravinsky, *Symphonies of Wind Instruments*, page from Sketchbook VII showing serpent theme and 'interruption' idea

nal' theme which really defines the passage in the *Symphonies*, the opening part of the duet (before the first interruption) is much too short, the music is a tone down, and the unit is still the semiquaver, as it was in Sketchbook VII.[52] Moreover, the scoring is still implicitly for violin and cello, with woodwind for the interruptions. Some but not all of this is corrected in the next draft (Plates 2.3 and 2.4). The unit is now the quaver, perhaps because the draft follows on immediately from an accurate draft of the quaver music from Fig. 13(2). But the linkage is still unclear. The quaver-music draft (rough and in pencil) ends, as in the work, with three statements of the 'signal' theme, but the jointure into the serpent theme is still only made as a 'cue' on a stave above, even though the appropriate inner voice-leading looks unmistakable, and even though the fact that the music is a tone below its already established (and eventual) pitch seems to indicate that its presence here is specifically for linkage purposes. It also seems incredible that Stravinsky only came back to the 'signal' theme in this passage as an extension of the quaver music, even though it had first seen the light, in Sketchbook V, in conjunction with the serpent theme.

The new draft of the serpent passage itself is neat, in ink, and much more complete, but still a tone down and still for strings (the lower line is in the alto clef and marked for viola). This time the basis is the preceding draft (with splicing), played twice. Once again Stravinsky adds the 'interruptions' in red ink, positioned as before, but in the second playing only.[53] Meanwhile there are further splicings. But this time the inserted material consists of statements of the 'signal' theme, apparently lifted clean from the end of the preceding quaver-music sketch, and, as the final composition draft shows, spliced in with hardly any ceremony; the serpent music simply stops, then restarts after the splicing, with minimal dovetailing of inner voices. The finished draft regularises these various additions, but it makes little attempt to suture them in. The pitch is now as in the final version (established, apparently, by the compound-time quaver music's reverting to its original level), and the scoring is at last for wind. But there

52. The unit had varied. In the earliest sketch, in Sketchbook V, the unit is a semiquaver at crotchet 63, appreciably faster than the eventual quaver at crotchet 108. Other early sketches have a quaver unit. Stravinsky's reversion to the semiquaver for this present draft and its two predecessors in Sketchbook VII suggest that he had still not noticed the link between the serpent theme and the compound-time theme, which is always hitherto in quavers. Does this also prove that the combination here – in semiquavers – was an afterthought?

53. See Baltensperger and Meyer, *Faksimileausgabe*, p. 40, plate 3, for a facsimile of one page of this draft.

Plate 2.2   Stravinsky, *Symphonies of Wind Instruments*, page from Sketchbook VII showing later version of 'interruption' idea

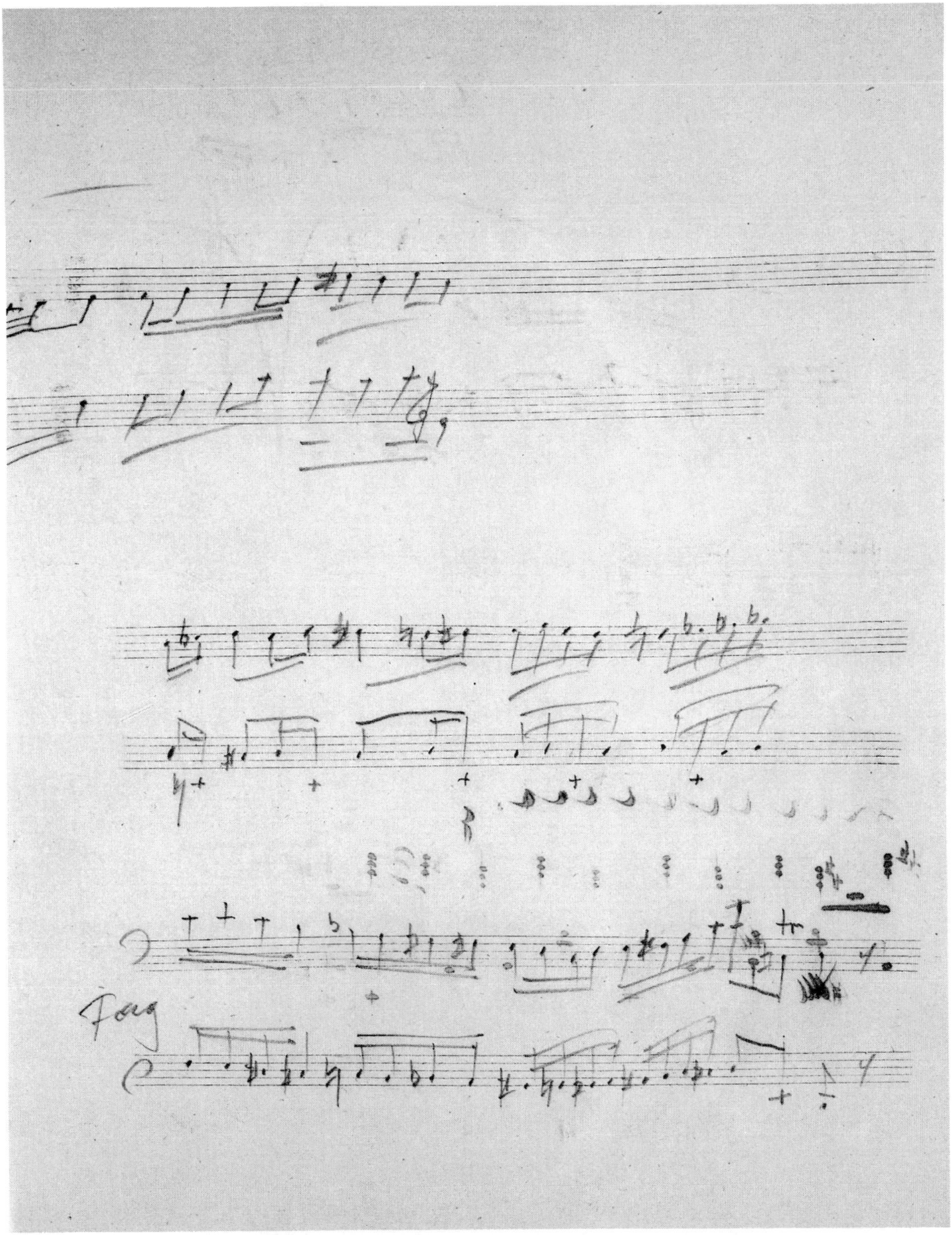
Fag

Plate 2.3 and 2.4 Stravinsky, *Symphonies of Wind Instruments*, later drafts of serpent theme, with 'interruption' idea in red ink (Plate 2.4, right)

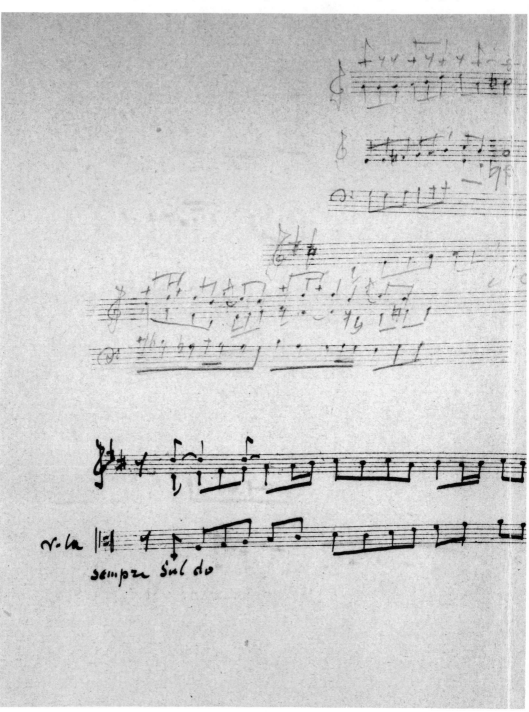

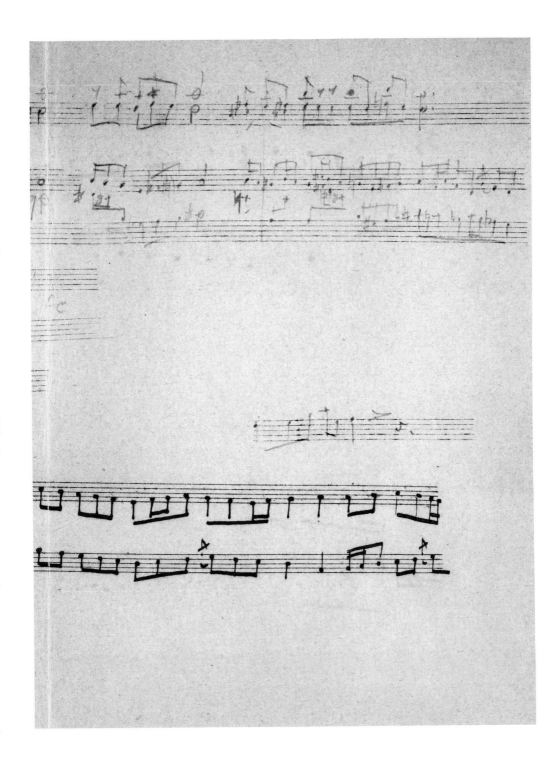

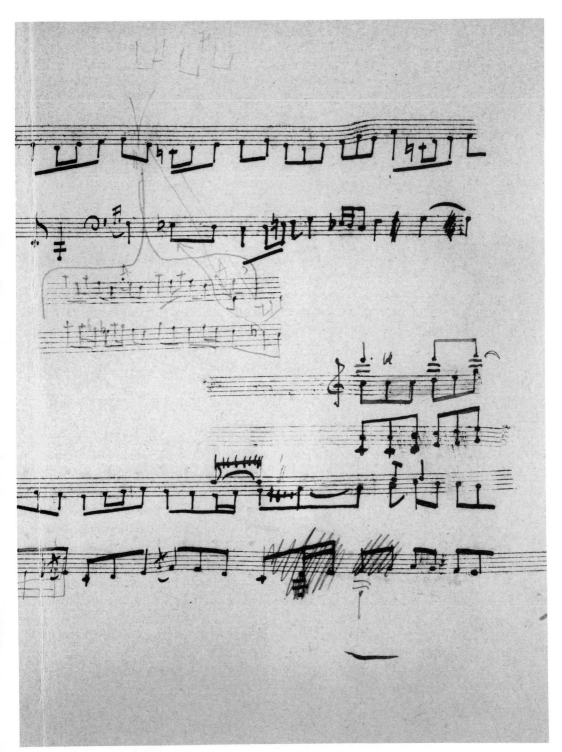

is as yet no sign of the major sectional repeat, from Fig. 29.[54] Only with the particell does the music achieve its full extension.

We are so used to Stravinsky's style, with its abrupt formal montages, that it is easy to overlook the unusual aspects of this compositional method. But it is also easy to misinterpret them, especially in a work as devoid as the *Symphonies* of what one might call continuity mechanisms. Here ostinato, so important to *Petrushka*, *The Rite of Spring*, *Les Noces*, *The Soldier's Tale*, plays little part; transitions, where they exist at all, are mere gestures; repetition, though fundamental, often goes no further than the minimum needed to establish formal recall. With all its variety of ideas, the piece lasts less than nine minutes. Above all there is no trace of those symbolic continuity devices soon to invade Stravinsky's style under the guise of neo-classicism.

But this does not mean that the music has no logic or pattern. In the passage just described, for instance, the splicings and overlayings may look arbitrary. But they do somehow obey a creative logic, as is evident from the fact that the three apparently unrelated elements began life in combination or as consecutive ideas, while two of them – the serpent and the compound-time quavers – continued to enjoy a symbiotic relationship throughout the sketches, cropping up side by side like romantic lovers mysteriously drawn together without hope of union. Naturally the solution to this problem is unromantic and modernist. But it is not for that reason arbitrary.

Similarly, the different versions of the 'signal' motive itself, or the experiments with chord voicings and resonances, show that Stravinsky himself found it difficult to ascertain the true character of his materials – detached as they were from known and suggestive contexts. There are other examples, some curious. The fragmentary theme in fifths at 3, for instance, presents such an essentially brisk and perfunctory image (doppio movimento, in effect) that it comes as a shock to discover that it originated in tempo with the 'bell' motive, that is at semiquaver = quaver in terms of its eventual notation (Ex. 2.7). Moreover this ratio survived into the particell, where the alteration is still visible. But the original tempo there for both motives was 108, not 72 as it became. There was a new speed for the chorale motive (down to 72). But in changing the main 'bell' motive tempo to 72 in the particell, with a *stesso tempo* for the chorale, Stravinsky must have felt this to be too slow, and 108 too awkward a ratio, for the 'fifths' fragment, so he doubled it (in effect) to 144 by halving its

---

54. Because of the way the transitions work, the actual missing section is Figs. 26 to 37.

Example 2.7   Sketchbook VII: sketch showing the initial integration of the two themes at [3].

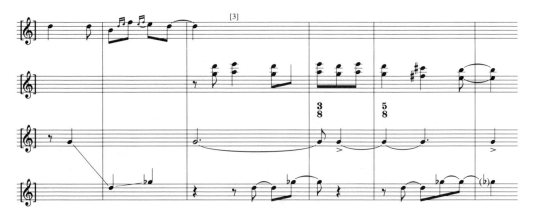

values. The result is a drastic last-minute change in tempo alignment which affects the whole work. And yet proportional tempo seems the very essence of the finished score.[55]

The composer's first thoughts on the texture of the flute solo at Fig. 6 survived even longer. In all the 1920 texts the accompaniment is a smooth crotchet 'ghosting' of the main melody, for flute and alto flute, constructed out of four-note patterns which form, usually, major sevenths but occasionally octaves. But this was completely recast in 1947 into a fluid texture of held and mobile chords based on sevenths and ninths and studiously avoiding octaves.[56] Still more bizarre, the passage varies in length, being three whole crotchets longer in the revised score (the abbreviated recurrence of this theme at Fig. 40 is the same length in both versions). This may be partly for harmonic reasons, since the new accompaniment seems to need longer to 'resolve'; but it's just as likely that the new harmonies were thought out in terms of the already lengthened theme.[57]

One consequence of this hesitation over detailing was a plethora of mistakes, some of which survive to this day in the printed (1947) score.

---

55. Notice that the harmony, as well as the tempo, was originally continuous through the 'bell' and the 'fifths'. This, too, seems to have been altered in the particell.
56. 'I hate octaves,' Stravinsky is supposed to have told Lawrence Morton, 'octaves are a *Schwindel.'*
57. The 1947 sketches, however, suggest that the new texture was worked out for the reprise, then transposed back for the earlier section. Stravinsky wrote out the old texture above the stave at Fig. 40 as a guide, then wrote out Fig. 6, stopping when he reached the extent of the theme at Fig. 40.

Take the notorious double-bassoon and low brass E♭ on the last beat of Fig. 67(1). Harmonically, if not melodically, it looks plausible. Yet its pedigree is suspect, to say the least. The note is E♮, moving to D♯ on the next beat, in every autograph source (including the full score, where the second note is spelt E♭), but suddenly a tied E♭ in the *Revue musicale* print. Why? Did Stravinsky alter it, or merely (more probably) overlook it? Whichever is the case, the mistake was duly carried into the 1926 piano reduction and from there (presumably) into Proof X, where it was corrected in the tuba but not in the double bassoon. Proof Y thus has E♮ in the tuba but a tied E♭ (for some reason bracketed) in the bassoon. Proof Z, however, following the autograph full score, reverts to E♮ all round. Unfortunately, Stravinsky apparently used the *Revue musicale* print as the basis for his 1945 arrangement, with the result that both parts now revert to E♭, while 1947 – based presumably on these same texts plus Proof X – naturally does the same.[58] Yet when Ansermet queried this note in his letter of 30 June 1933, Stravinsky expressly corrected it to E♮. One can hardly doubt that E♮ is right. But the significant point in the present context is that the composer ever ratified such an error, thus turning a printer's slip into a creative decision. Yet if the *original* choice had been E♭, it would hardly have attracted debate, whatever the contextual reasons (and they certainly exist) for preferring E♮. Consistency is a poor guide in music so essentially governed by moment-to-moment testing rather than by rules of procedure.[59]

Empiricism certainly lay deep in Stravinsky's nature. The readiness to find by testing and comparing may belong philosophically to a middle-aged work like *The Poetics of Music*, but it is already the creative powerhouse of the composer's youth, in *Petrushka* and *The Rite*. The *Symphonies of Wind Instruments* is simply the extreme case. Speaking the language of the *Poetics*, one might say that if you grub around in a forest, the things you find will be forest things, though you may not know how they grew or how they belong together. You can press them in a book, or put them together in a glass case, and one day their logic may strike you. But it may not be so obvious to other people, who haven't lived with

58. This also tends to refute Baltensperger and Meyer's claim that it was Proof Z that Stravinsky had to hand in 1947. See note 31 above.

59. The second trumpet A♮ on the first beat of the same bar is quite a different case, but it supports the argument. Stravinsky never clearly approved Ansermet's alteration of this note to an A♯ in Proof X. Ansermet queried the natural in his letter of 30 June 1933, precisely – it seems – on grounds of consistency, but Stravinsky omitted to answer the point. He restored the A♮ in the 1945 arrangement, however, and so it remains in 1947. All autograph sources concur. The figure simply is inconsistent.

them as you have and perhaps don't know where you found them. Worse – or better – still, you may yourself go on looking at them and seeing new details that hadn't struck you before. Finally, a tableau of *objets trouvés* from the forest may take on the appearance of a work of art, an immutable portrait of woodland life rather than a mere tray of specimens.

'The true creator,' Stravinsky wrote, 'may be recognised by his ability always to find about him, in the commonest and humblest thing, items worthy of note . . . The least accident holds his interest and guides his operations. If his finger slips, he will notice it; on occasion he may even draw profit from something unforeseen that a momentary lapse reveals to him.'[60] The neo-Thomist elements in the *Poetics* are mainly concerned with the image of the artist as artisan, honest craftsman, *homo faber*. The idea that such 'making' could benefit from chance discoveries or even mistakes is a somewhat less orthodox extension of Maritain's exhortation to artists 'to abandon the immense intellectual disarray inherited from the nineteenth century, and rediscover the spiritual conditions of an honest labour',[61] but it is nevertheless part of the same rejection of inspiration as a function of the higher brain, in place of a faculty more akin to the humble ability to recognise the virtue of whatever may happen to turn up. This, clearly, is already the creative context of the *Symphonies of Wind Instruments*, a work composed – as chance would have it – in the very year of publication of Maritain's *Art et scolastique*. It isn't just that, in the long textual career of this strange work, mistakes were (in fact) made which today are embalmed in the published score and which are by no means demonstrably – musically – 'wrong'. It's that the whole work – in its pragmatic, experimental being – seems to inhabit a world of variable possibilities, of observation and testing, a world in which right and wrong look like the mere arbitrary choice between one accident and another. No wonder Ernest Newman, already the author of two books on Wagner and one of the leading contemporary students of late Romantic music, found *The Rite of Spring*, with its paragraphs and sequences and climaxes, comprehensible (if disagreeable), but the *Symphonies* unintelligible.

The fact that it is, for all that, a profoundly traditional artefact – an icon, stern, glowing and in its own way immutable – is not the least moving aspect of the light this brief and apparently unassuming masterpiece sheds on the creative mind.

60. *Poetics of Music*, pp. 54–5.
61. Jacques Maritain, *Art et scolastique*, third edition (Paris: Rouart, 1935), p. 3. The book first came out in 1920.

3

Transcription and recomposition: the strange case of Zemlinsky's Maeterlinck songs]

With a note on the 'Skandalkonzert' of 31 March 1913

Derrick Puffett

> Transcription. 3.*Mus.* The arrangement, or (*less properly*) modification, of a composition for some voice or instrument other than that for which it was originally written.   (*OED*: my emphasis)[1]

> I made Diana's manor for you, Nimue . . . It is the Grail Castle. It is Merlin's tomb. It is the esplumoir, the cage of the moulting hawk, the place of transformations. It is the house whose walls are winds. It is my crystal cave.   (Robert Nye, *Merlin*)[2]

I

This essay is about the translation of one work of art into another. The word translation is used advisedly: it represents an attempt to establish a middleground between transcription, or arrangement (the two terms are used interchangeably in so much of the literature that it seems pointless to try to distinguish between them now), on the one hand, and recomposition on the other, recomposition meaning, obviously, the creation of a new work from an old one. The work chosen to exemplify this concept is the *Sechs Gesänge* on texts by Maurice Maeterlinck, Op. 13, by Alexander Zemlinsky, though I should perhaps emphasise that the project started life as a means of getting to know these remarkable songs better, not as the result of a wish to demonstrate some theoretical idea.

Zemlinsky's music has gained some ground, both in terms of the number of performances it receives and in terms of critical appreciation, over the last thirty years or so, partly because of a general growth of interest in the music of turn-of-the-century Vienna and a desire to explore the work

---

1. *The Compact Edition of the Oxford English Dictionary*, vol. II (Oxford University Press, 1971), p. 3349.
2. (London: Hamish Hamilton, 1978), p. 210.

of those composers who were Schoenberg's contemporaries and have hitherto been somewhat overshadowed by him – composers such as Busoni,
Schreker, Korngold and Franz Schmidt – partly, one suspects, because of a
growing reaction against modernism and the rather stifling, not to say
repressive, aesthetic value-judgements associated with it. It would be going
too far, no doubt, to talk of a Zemlinsky 'revival'. But it is true to say that
most of the important works are now recorded, that performances, though
not exactly frequent, are more than just occasional, and that curiosity
really seems to have got beyond the stage where he was valued simply for
having been Schoenberg's brother-in-law. And the work most commonly
performed and recorded is probably the Maeterlinck Songs. Their most celebrated outing was on 31 March 1913, when four of them were presented at
the concert given in the Musikverein, under the auspices of the
Akademischer Verband für Literatur und Musik, the occasion of one of the
most famous riots in musical history and now commonly referred to as the
Skandalkonzert. Of the four works actually performed on that occasion –
Zemlinsky's songs, Schoenberg's Chamber Symphony, Op. 9, Webern's Six
Orchestral Pieces, Op. 6, and two of Berg's orchestral songs on texts by Peter
Altenberg (the concert broke up in disorder before a fifth work, Mahler's
Kindertotenlieder, could be heard) – the Zemlinsky was the only one to
emerge unscathed, indeed the only one to evoke any positive enjoyment in
the critics.[3] Since then, and especially in the last few years, it has become a
minor classic, if not a frequent repertory item then at least an occasional
and welcome alternative to the more hackneyed Mahler song cycles. (That
one could say such a thing must have been unimaginable in 1913!)

II

It is worth setting out the facts about the composition of the *Sechs
Gesänge*, insofar as they are known, both because the information contained in the various published sources is rather sketchy and because they
have some bearing on the 'identity of the artwork', a topic raised in the
last part of this essay. Before doing so, it may help simply to list the songs
as they appear in the voice-and-piano version, the first version to be published (with the exception of No. 3, the titles correspond, as in
Maeterlinck, to the poems' first lines):

1 'Die drei Schwestern'
2 'Die Mädchen mit den verbundenen Augen'

3. See, for example, the review quoted in H. H. Stuckenschmidt, *Schoenberg:
His Life, World and Work*, trans. Humphrey Searle (London: Calder and
Boyars, 1977), p. 185.

3 'Lied der Jungfrau'
4 'Als ihr Geliebter schied'
5 'Und kehrt er einst heim'
6 'Sie kam zum Schloß gegangen'[4]

When, in the following discussion, the songs are referred to by number, the numbering conforms to this list.

The songs were composed in two batches, the first (Nos. 1, 2, 3 and 5) in the summer of 1910, the second (Nos. 4 and 6) in August 1913. The songs of the first batch were premiered, in their voice-and-piano version, on 11 December 1910, orchestrated in early March 1913, no doubt with the *Skandalkonzert* (if not the *Skandal*) in mind, and premiered in that form on the 31st. The two later songs were written on 18 and 20 July 1913 and orchestrated on 4 and 6 August of the same year.[5]

It is when one considers the songs' publication history that things get complicated. All six songs were published, by Universal, in a voice-and-piano edition of 1914. This was of course *after* the first four of them (that is, Nos. 1–3 and 5), as well as the other two, had been orchestrated, but for some unknown reason Zemlinsky chose to publish them in their

4. On Zemlinsky's choice of poems see Horst Weber, *Alexander Zemlinsky* (Vienna: Elisabeth Lafite, 1977), pp. 82–96. Zemlinsky took them from a German translation (referenced below, note 32) of Maeterlinck's *Quinze chansons* (1900). The six texts are: 'Les trois sœurs ont voulu mourir' (No. 14 in Maeterlinck); 'Les filles aux yeux bandés' (4); 'Cantique de la Vierge dans "Sœur Beatrice" [*sic*]' (15); 'Quand l'amant sortit' (10); 'Et s'il revenait un jour' (2); and 'Elle est venue vers le palais' (9). Weber's contention that these poems were originally included in Maeterlinck's plays appears to be true of only 'Quand l'amant sortit', which came from *Aglavaine et Sélysette* (1896), and the 'Cantique de la Vierge' from the 'miracle' *Sœur Béatrice*; the 'Cantique' in fact appeared first in German, then in English and only then in French (1901). See Maurice Maeterlinck, *Poésies complètes*, ed. Joseph Hanse (Brussels: La Renaissance du Livre, 1965), pp. 282–9.

5. Most of this information comes from Weber, *Zemlinsky*, and from Alfred Clayton, to whom I owe most of my knowledge of the composer. Clayton's article 'Was man über Alexander Zemlinsky wissen sollte', in the programme for the ninth concert of the Vienna Philharmonic Orchestra, 1991–2 season (24 May 1992), is an extremely useful gathering of facts. Clayton informs me (personal communication) that there is a Washington MS of song 5 bearing the date 22 August 1910. The catalogue for the Zemlinsky exhibition in 1992, *Alexander Zemlinsky: Bin ich kein Wiener?*, ed. Otto Biba (Vienna: Gesellschaft der Musikfreunde, 1992), p. 74, confusingly attributes the orchestration of song 6 to 1924(!); but there are good reasons to suppose that Zemlinsky wrote the last two songs with their orchestrations in mind, and if so, it is unlikely that he would have put off scoring them for so long.

original, pre-orchestral versions, which do not take account of the changes he made in the process of orchestrating them, and in their original keys. For this reason it is incorrect to refer to the voice-and-piano versions (an ungainly phrase which I keep having to come back to) as a vocal score.[6]

At this time, incidentally, the name Maeterlinck is nowhere mentioned. This is because at the start of the war the Belgian poet had come out with an 'anti-German manifesto' as a result of which Austro-German composers' affection (that of the fiercely nationalistic Webern in particular) for his verse had cooled considerably.[7] It was not until the publication of the orchestral score, ten years later, that Maeterlinck's name appeared on the title-page.

This time, as before, the songs came out in two batches, corresponding to the chronology of their composition. Nos. 1–3 and 5 (now numbered 1–4) appeared first,[8] Nos. 4 and 6 (renumbered 1 and 2) in a second batch.[9] The point to note here is that the *order* of the songs is different from that of the voice-and-piano versions, in which 'Als ihr Geliebter schied' appeared as No. 4, not 5. In other words, Zemlinsky reordered the songs, all of which had been composed by August 1913, for their voice-and-piano

6. Song 3 had already been published in the *Neue Musikzeitung* of 22 June 1911 and was published again, along with No. 5, in *Das moderne Lied: eine Sammlung von 50 Gesängen ausgewählt von Josef V. von Wöss* (Universal Edition, UE 5500, © 1914); No. 3 was also published in the *Musikblätter des Anbruchs*, vol. II (1920). What I have said above concerning the 'original keys' assumes, of course, that it is the keys of the voice-and-piano versions, and not of the orchestral versions (as will soon become apparent, only the keys of the first two songs are different anyway), that are the original ones. I have no positive proof of this; for that one would need to consult the manuscripts, to which I have not had access. But it hardly seems likely that Zemlinsky would publish the voice-and-piano versions in keys established only *after* the orchestrations without also incorporating the changes he had made in the process of scoring.
7. See Hans Moldenhauer, *Anton von Webern: A Chronicle of His Life and Work* (New York: Alfred A. Knopf, 1979), p. 211. The phrase 'anti-German manifesto' is Moldenhauer's.
8. A. ZEMLINSKY / VIER GESÄNGE / OP. 13 [front cover] // VIER GESÄNGE / NACH TEXTEN VON MAURICE MAETERLINCK / FÜR MITTLERE STIMME UND ORCHESTER / von / Alexander Zemlinsky / Op. 13 [title-page]. UE 7066, © 1922 on the title-page, 1923 on the first page of music.
9. A. ZEMLINSKY / ZWEI GESÄNGE / AUS OP. 13 [front cover] // ZWEI GESÄNGE / NACH TEXTEN VON MAURICE MAETERLINCK / Für mittlere Stimme und Orchester / von / Alexander Zemlinsky / aus Op. 13 [title-page]. UE 7066 (NB: the same plate number as the previous volume, even though the pagination starts afresh), © 1924.

publication the following year, and then reverted to their order of composition for their orchestral publication in 1924.[10] This is worth bearing in mind when one considers the cyclic organisation of the two versions, in which tonal structure plays a part. It should also be remembered if one tries to posit a poetic–allegorical 'meaning' for the sequence of songs as a whole ('sequences . . . as wholes'?). Horst Weber, for example, in his book on Zemlinsky, suggests an interpretation for the six songs in the following terms: '(1) The "inner realm" (Weber's interpretation owes much to Novalis); (2) Awareness of life; (3) Intensification; (4) Certainty of death; (5) Leave-taking; (6) Experience of death'.[11] Such an interpretation is not only conceptually rather weak (it could apply, *mutatis mutandis*, to almost any of the great Romantic song cycles), but it assumes a definitive 'state' for the work which is simply not borne out by the facts of composition.[12]

III

The differences between the two versions may be summarised in general terms as follows.

Most obviously, for the orchestral version two of the songs are transposed.[13] These are Nos. 1 and 2, which appear in C minor and F♯ minor in the voice-and-piano score, D minor and G♯ minor in the orchestral. Possible reasons for the transposition are suggested below; meanwhile it is enough to note that the tritone relationship between the two songs has been preserved.

A second obvious difference between the two versions concerns the much wider range of colour available to the orchestra. The forces Zemlinsky deploys are not particularly large (by turn-of-the-century standards): triple rather than quadruple woodwind, only two horns instead of

10. The copyright dates for the first volume have to be discounted, I think. I am grateful to the Hire Library of Music Distribution Services Ltd for the loan of the orchestral scores.

11. Weber, *Zemlinsky*, p. 89. Translations from Cord Garben, 'An Advocate's View of Zemlinsky', in programme note to complete recording of Zemlinsky's songs, DG 427 348-2, p. 16.

12. Nevertheless Weber is the author of the most detailed study of the Maeterlinck Songs and an interesting, if brief, essay on Zemlinsky's orchestration. See 'Zemlinskys Maeterlinck-Gesänge', *Archiv für Musikwissenschaft*, 29 (1972), and '"Figur und Grund": Secessionistic Instrumentation of Alexander Zemlinsky', in Geoffrey N. Moon, ed., *Art Nouveau and Jugendstil and the Music of the Early Twentieth Century* (Adelaide: [University of Adelaide], 1984).

13. But see the proviso entered in note 6 above.

the usual four, a fairly modest array of percussion.[14] But he uses them, as might be expected, to maximum effect: anyone familiar with the *Lyrische Symphonie* (the well-known model for Berg's *Lyrische Suite*, but also another work that has achieved minor-classic status in its own right) will recognise, albeit in embryonic form and with perhaps less than total mastery of the medium, effects of extraordinary delicacy and precision, especially in passages where the music illustrates some idea in the text. The example, from 'Als ihr Geliebter schied' (Ex. 3.1), is an extreme one but can nonetheless be taken as characteristic. Here the combination of solo, pizzicato and tremolando violins, all muted, with fluttertongued flute, high oboe and burbling low clarinet(s)[15] on the one hand and celesta, harp and harmonium on the other (the interaction of staccato harp and offbeat pizzicato first violins is particularly striking) – the whole unified by a *pppp* roll of 'swish' cymbal – provides a much more vivid evocation of the line of text ('I heard the glowing of the light' – shades of *Tristan!*) than the necessarily monochrome piano version. The decorative yet spare character of such orchestration is quite different from the steely counterpoint of Mahler, the sumptuous doublings of Strauss or the elegant heterophonic superimpositions of Schreker, to name three contemporaneous examples; perhaps the closest parallel would be with the Schoenberg of *Erwartung*, though it is not clear that Zemlinsky, who was to conduct its premiere in 1924, even knew the score at this early date, much less that he had studied it.

The third major difference between the two versions, obvious to anyone who has tried to follow the voice-and-piano version while listening to the orchestral, but hard to demonstrate without detailed comparison, is that Zemlinsky has added short introductions and postludes to some of the individual songs (in one case he has even interpolated a bar). This may have been in response to a criticism of Schoenberg, who found the ending of the first song (in its piano version) too abrupt.[16] But in any case it corresponds to a feeling, experienced by many listeners, that the use of the orchestra presupposes a larger scale of operation than voice-and-piano, a feeling summed up by the Swiss composer Othmar Schoeck when, hearing a performance of Richard Strauss's 'Traum durch die Dämmerung' in

14. The exact disposition of Zemlinsky's orchestra is given below in an Appendix.
15. It is not clear from the score whether one or two clarinets should be playing.
16. See letter of 13 March 1913 from Schoenberg to Zemlinsky quoted in Ernst Hilmar, 'Zemlinsky und Schönberg', in Otto Kolleritsch, ed., *Alexander Zemlinsky: Tradition im Umkreis der Wiener Schule* (Graz: Institut für Wertungsforschung, 1976), p. 76.

Example 3.1   Zemlinsky, 'Als ihr Geliebter schied'

its orchestral version, he said: 'The song doesn't lend itself well to orchestral accompaniment; it is too short.'[17] This feeling is difficult to justify in formal/technical terms; it may have more to do with the sense of physical environment, the use of a large hall as opposed to the more intimate surroundings appropriate to the *Lied*. Whatever the truth of the matter, it is a fact that Strauss's songs conceived with orchestral accompaniment, some of them of astonishing originality, such as the rarely-heard 'Notturno', Op. 44 No. 1 (1899), are on a much larger scale than anything he attempted for voice and piano. And Zemlinsky's later orchestral songs, not only the *Lyrische Symphonie* (1923) but also the lesser-known *Symphonische Gesänge*, Op. 20 (1929), are of course symphonic too, though here the word acquires specific technical associations to go along with, and make sense of, the sheer increase in size.

IV

More detailed comparison is probably best effected by taking the songs one at a time. There are so many points to be got over that a *topical* approach – dealing with one technique of transcription after another – would be too complicated (though some sort of synopsis will be attempted later). At the same time, it is not really feasible to take the songs in the order in which they appear in the score (that there are *two* possible orderings does not help matters), since one of the most complex of the songs, in the number and variety of techniques used, is the first. What I propose to do therefore is to discuss the songs in the order in which they appear in the orchestral score, that is, with 'Als ihr Geliebter schied' in fifth place, but putting aside the first song until last-but-one. In that way the reader will get a sense of simple techniques leading to more complex ones, the two biggest songs, which naturally evoke the greatest virtuosity on the part of composer/transcriber, being left till last.

'Die Mädchen mit den verbundenen Augen'

The most immediate difference between the orchestral version and its predecessor is that the former begins with a seven-bar introduction. It is worth noting at this point that *all* of the 1910 settings begin without any introduction whatever (and dispense with a postlude, though there is a two-bar phrase in the piano at the end of the 'Lied der Jungfrau', overlapping with the last bar of the voice part, which should strictly count as

17. Quoted in Werner Vogel, *Othmar Schoeck im Gespräch* (Zurich: Atlantis, 1965), p. 20. My translation.

one). This contributes to the folklike quality of the songs which Adorno admired and Schoenberg disliked.[18] In the case of 'Die Mädchen' the prelude has a particular intensity because Zemlinsky borrows its opening phrase from his setting of the first line of the last stanza, '[Sie] haben das Leben gegrüßt' (they greeted life), the emotional climax of the poem. Not only is this phrase intense in itself, especially in its scoring for divided violas and cellos, but Zemlinsky marks it 'sehnsüchtig' (longingly), an inscription given particular relevance by the no doubt coincidental reference to Wagner's *Tristan* at the entry of the solo cello (see Ex. 3.2).

The introduction has a transitional function too. The previous song, 'Die drei Schwestern', had ended on a D major triad which provided a Picardie-third conclusion to its prevailing D minor tonality. (Keys referred to here are naturally those of the orchestral version.) By taking as the material for his introduction a phrase that begins a tritone away from the tonic of the present song, G♯ minor, Zemlinsky is able to effect a smooth transition from one song to another; it will be remembered that the two songs are in keys a tritone apart. In addition, the prominence of the note D within the introduction – as root of the first chord, as bass to the first chord of the second bar (the apex of intensity for the two-bar phrase), and as melody-note at the beginning of the third bar – creates resonances with the D minor/major of the previous song and, for that matter, the D major of the closing song in the set, 'Sie kam zum Schloß gegangen'. The note D continues to be prominent, in fact, during the four bars of 6/8 that prepare the entry of the voice (Ex. 3.2).[19]

The next few bars set out one of the song's main textures: vocal line doubled by cor anglais, with accompaniment shared between divided violas and lower strings. There is a hint of *Klangfarbenmelodie* (a technique safely in the public domain since Schoenberg had published his *Harmonielehre* two years earlier: no chance of Zemlinsky being given the

18. See Theodor W. Adorno, 'Zemlinsky', in *Quasi una fantasia: Essays on Modern Music*, trans. Rodney Livingstone (London: Verso, 1993), pp. 120–1; letter of Schoenberg to Zemlinsky cited in note 16 above.

19. For this and subsequent examples, I employ a form of orchestral reduction which draws on the 'analytical' layout (much hated by conductors, but potentially useful for musicologists) of Schoenberg's late orchestral scores. The intention is to give as much detail as possible without overloading the score with doublings, transpositions, etc. (certain details have inevitably to be omitted). In these reductions the voice part is left out. The original piano version, transposed where necessary into the key of the orchestral song, is given below, in small notes, with the voice part immediately above; the voice part here follows the *orchestral* version. As in Schoenberg's 'analytical' scores, all instruments are given in C.

Example 3.2   Zemlinsky, 'Die Mädchen mit den gebundenen Augen'

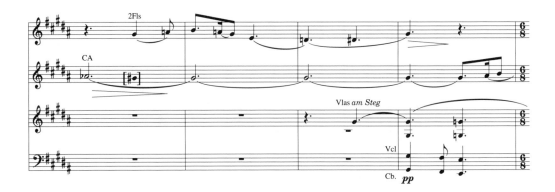

Example 3.3 Zemlinsky, 'Die Mädchen mit den gebundenen Augen'

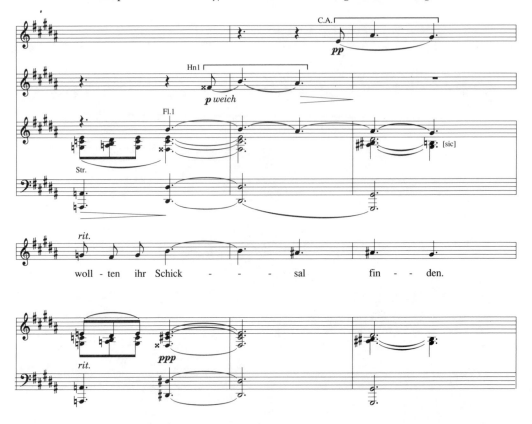

woll - ten ihr Schick - - - sal fin - - den.

credit, like the unfortunate Webern, for coming up with the idea first[20])
in the passing of G♯, the tonic pitch, from cor anglais to violas *am Steg* and
back to cor anglais, a better means of giving the singer her pitch than a
tuning fork. (When the same G♯, and the same mode of instrumentation,
return for the third line of the stanza, the flutes too are involved.) The
splashes of instrumental colour – flutes and divided cellos pizzicato off
the beat – at the end of the singer's first phrase (and corresponding phrases
throughout the song) are a nice touch absent, of course, from the voice-
and-piano version. Later the wind instruments will help to close the
stanza with little snatches of imitation (Ex. 3.3), a suggestion, perhaps,
of the more thoroughly polyphonic treatment of the next song.

These are simple enough devices which any orchestrator might have

20. See Schoenberg's remarks in 'Anton Webern: *Klangfarbenmelodie*' (1951), in
Style and Idea, trans. Leo Black (London: Faber and Faber, 1975), pp. 484–5.
Of course the technique had been used extensively by Wagner and Mahler,
long before Schoenberg got round to describing it.

used – though the snatches of imitation (not to mention the addition of a prelude) already go beyond the *OED*'s narrow definition of transcription. More interesting is the block-like treatment of the orchestra throughout the song. The poem is one of those in which Maeterlinck interpolates a line of a parenthetical nature (here the line is varied slightly on each appearance) with a continuously evolving narrative, a technique which can be regarded as slightly precious, or proto-modernist, according to taste. Zemlinsky underscores such interpolations by giving them to three muted trumpets *wie aus der Ferne* doubled by celesta at the octave, with bass line provided by clarinet and two muted horns, in contrast to the rather spare viola and cello textures of the surrounding passages. It will be noted that such an arrangement introduces an element of (vertical) stratification alongside the (horizontal) block-like treatment: in the voice-and-piano version the 'trumpet and celesta' chords are separated much less obviously from the supporting bass line. This (horizontal and vertical) disposition of the orchestral forces is Zemlinsky's way of responding to the idiosyncratic verse-structure of Maeterlinck's poem.

Zemlinsky treats the material of the second stanza in similar fashion, now dividing it between four-part woodwind (a woozy 'chorale' at 'Haben zur Mittagsstunde') and the trumpet/celesta consort already mentioned. At the word 'Wiesengrunde' – a touch which Adorno might have approved – the chord is enhanced by a low thud of pizzicato cellos and basses on the note D, another possible reference to 'Die drei Schwestern'. The D minor chord left at the end of the bar prompts the return of the opening phrase (its first hearing in the voice-and-piano version, of course) for 'Haben das Leben gegrüßt'. The return of violas and cellos at this point, with their 'sehnsüchtig' motive, makes the phrase even more intense.

There is no need to go through the rest of the song in detail. Zemlinsky creates a reprise by repeating the last two lines of the first stanza (an effect, needless to say, already present in the voice-and-piano setting), while the third stanza itself is devoted to a development and liquidation of the 'Haben das Leben gegrüßt' phrase. One interesting detail is that the addition of a phrase of imitation (flute 1 and clarinet) to a previously chordal bar – the second 'gegrüßt' – allows the composer to present the succeeding *vocal* phrase (doubled, as before, by cor anglais) as an intensification of the (previously non-existent) point of imitation, the voice's C♯ varying the C♮ in flute and clarinet. Along with this piece of imitation goes the introduction of a cross-rhythm not used before (either within the song or in its previous version): the second 'gegrüßt' is accompanied by divided-viola '6/4' triplets, which prepare for the return to 6/8 (the change from bowed tenuto in the violas to mixed arco/pizzicato is another nice touch),

Example 3.4   Zemlinsky, 'Die Mädchen mit den gebundenen Augen'

while the first bar of 6/8 has quadruplets in clarinet and muted horns, as though the latter instruments are reluctant to give up the 4/4 metre of the preceding section. Treatment of metre and theme – the imitation of 'Haben das Leben gegrüßt' in flute and clarinet helping towards its liquidation in violas three bars later – has a bridging function here (Ex. 3.4). The single bar of postlude has the celesta playing a minor triad doubled at the octave, a sonority which anticipates similar sounds in the 'Lied der Jungfrau'.

There is one textual peculiarity in the orchestral version of this song that should not go unnoticed. In the bar following the *first* statement of 'Haben das Leben gegrüßt', the bass note is B♭, creating a fourth-chord among the lower instruments instead of the octave-and-fifth of the piano version. This sonority is so odd that one's first thought is that the B♭ must

Example 3.4 *cont.*

be a misprint. But Zemlinsky has altered the passage to conform with his
'quotation' of the same phrase in the introduction.

'Lied der Jungfrau'

This song uses a reduced orchestra (harmonium, celesta, eight solo
strings) and draws attention to the fact that each song in Zemlinsky's
orchestration has its own individual sound – a feature he picked up, no
doubt, from a study of the Mahler cycles (*Kindertotenlieder*, in particular,
can be seen to have been something of a model for the Zemlinsky work).[21]
    With its thick chordal harmony – another quality Schoenberg dis-

21. See below, p. 115.

liked (though, to be fair, he did praise this song[22]) – there was not much
that Zemlinsky could do with it except to enliven the texture in some
way. This he did by means of a technique which brings to mind a remark
of Alexander Goehr (a remark in turn suggested by a passage in
Schoenberg's *Harmonielehre*): 'Central to Schoenberg's compositional
development is his use of motivic construction, which gives life to the
otherwise still and inexpressive structures of harmony.'[23] In this case it is
not that the harmony is inexpressive, rather that Zemlinsky relies so
much on the expressive, even hyper-expressive, nature of the sonorities
that he tends to neglect other possibilities. But the point is there. And his
solution is the same as Schoenberg's: to *animate* an otherwise almost
completely homophonic texture through the use of motivic development.

This process starts as early as the eight-bar introduction (another new
feature of the orchestral setting), which contains its own liquidation in the
form of the cello and double-bass motives which highlight an interval soon
to become prominent in the vocal line, the semitone C♭–B♭. The motivic
development is at first discreet, with the harmonium – ever-dependable
standby of the Second Viennese School, particularly where transcriptions
are concerned – assuming most of the harmonic support. (There is a noteworthy deviation from the piano version at the end of the first four-bar
phrase, where the two solo violas, introduced to call attention to an otherwise rather ordinary inner part, have D♮ instead of the original D♭; this
seems to be because taking the inner part down to C♮, as is implied in the
piano version, would lead to octaves with the bass in the next bar. C♮ is
omitted from the following harmonium chord accordingly.) But there is an
efflorescence of imitation, caused by the introduction of more solo strings,
in the second half of the stanza. This efflorescence continues in the transition between the verses, with a remarkable double pattern of points of
imitation (the celesta part becomes more active here too) (Ex. 3.5).

The imitation/motivic development continues to animate the bass of
the next few bars but then fizzles out, 'activity' being provided by a (rather
humdrum) repeated-note pattern in the violas. But following the impetus
given by the third-beat pizzicato fifth on double basses at the beginning of
the phrase 'die weinend gefleht' ('that has entreated in tears'), another passage of imitation starts up which carries the music through the link to the
third stanza. This in turn provokes another remarkable burst of counterpoint towards the end of the song. What is interesting here is that

22. See Hilmar, 'Zemlinsky und Schönberg', p. 76.
23. 'Schoenberg and Karl Kraus: The Idea behind the Music', *Music Analysis*, 4
    (1985), 67.

Example 3.5   Zemlinsky, 'Lied der Jungfrau'

Zemlinsky not only continues to develop the motivic material he has relied upon so far but introduces a new series of imitative points, featuring the descending arpeggio of a triad. The new motive is derived from the piano's closing phrase in the original version of the song, but introduced as it is here in the very first bar of the third stanza, and developed contrapuntally in the last five bars, it creates a much stronger conclusion for the song as a whole. This, however, means relinquishing the syncopation of the harmony over the bass in the penultimate bar of the original version (Ex. 3.6).

Zemlinsky makes no use of contrasting orchestral blocks in this song, which is of course texturally much more homogeneous than the previous one, but what he does is in some ways more interesting. The final pizzicato chord in cellos and basses makes a connection with their pizzicato notes in the introduction.

There are two textual peculiarities in this song, one musical, one verbal. In the fifth bar from the end of the orchestral version Zemlinsky omits a (B)♭ sign in the parts for bass instruments (doubles basses and harmonium). Because of the tie across from the previous bar, this B♭ is often played B♮(= C♭), which is not inconceivable in the context (shades of Wagner's Hagen!). However, there is no tie in the harmonium part. (Should there be?)

Example 3.5   *cont.*

Even more curiously, a word in the text (seven bars from the end of the orchestral version) is changed from 'weisen' to 'weinen'. This could well be just another misprint, but given Zemlinsky's penchant for lachrymose effects involving solo violin[24] it is possible that the change was deliberate.[25]

24. See the discussion of 'Als ihr Geliebter schied' below.
25. There is another change of text, from 'Hände' to 'Stunde', at the end of the first stanza. As with the change from 'weisen' to 'weinen', this is linguistically possible but does nothing for Maeterlinck's already rather fragile verse. (The removal of 'Hände' from 'Hände voll Huld' may be considered a positive loss.)

Example 3.6   Zemlinsky, 'Lied der Jungfrau'

'Und kehrt er einst heim'

The poem takes the form of a dialogue, each of the five stanzas being divided into two parts. As with the previous settings, Zemlinsky adds a prelude. Its main function seems to be to open up the registral space above the vocal line: when the voice enters it is doubled by the first violins an octave higher. (One incidental consequence of this doubling is that we get a *variation* of the melody – the g^2 in the bar containing the word 'heim' – before it occurs in the voice. So who is doubling whom?) This means, among other things, that the dialogue effect cannot be rendered through contrasts of instrumental register (one of various possibilities). Instead it is effected through the contrast of instrumental blocks: strings and softer-toned woodwind for the first 'speaker', oboes, cor anglais, horns and tremolo violas *am Steg* for the second. These block-contrasts, though obviously not of the same order as those found in, say, Stravinsky's *Symphonies of Wind Instruments*, are kept up more or less consistently throughout the song.

Another feature of the orchestral version made possible by the opening up of the higher register is the little antiphonies between flutes (in the upper octave) and clarinets and first bassoon (in the lower). These are extended downwards into a third octave in the second stanza ('Sprich als [Schwester]') and into a fourth octave (the cello pizzicato F just before the words 'Mein' Goldring gib') in the third. There are also some striking octave transfers, impossible (and unnecessary) in the voice-and-piano version, between half-stanzas.

Following on from the opening of the higher register, there is a more thorough exploration of the harmonic possibilities, in particular a more daring use of sonorities based on fourths. It is not so much a question of reharmonising the music as of realising the potential inherent in it. Thus the fourths that seem to grow out of the accompaniment in the piano version are here presented starkly as chords – though 'stark' is too harsh a word for the soft-toned flutes and clarinets (Ex. 3.7: note the counter-melody, also doubled at the fourth, in violins 2 and violas, an element absent from the original). When this music returns at the beginning of the fifth verse, the woodwind chords are compressed into the lower octave, almost like a quotation from the Schoenberg Chamber Symphony. The same passage contains a chain of fourth-chords in celesta which is entirely new (Ex. 3.8).

The use of the celesta in this passage suggests that orchestral potentialities as well as harmonic ones are being realised here. Such a sonority would not even have occurred to the composer in the voice-and-piano version. And this leads to a further thought: if the celesta is being employed

Example 3.7   Zemlinsky, 'Und kehrt er einst heim'

for its extramusical associations (adumbrations of the other-worldly were soon to become a commonplace in the music of Schreker, not to mention Bax and Tippett[26]), maybe other instruments too are being used for extramusical reasons – certainly the three notes of the glockenspiel in the third stanza, the only time the instrument is heard in the cycle, sound like a reference to the first song of the *Kindertotenlieder*, just as the tamtam at the end of the next song evokes other, more funereal Mahlerian associations.

For the rest, the song contains many examples of 'animated' accompaniment: the ostinato in bass clarinet, harp and pizzicato cellos, different every time it comes back (another Mahlerian feature), the more conventional doublings of the climax. By the same token, Zemlinsky's

26. See my article 'In the Garden of Fand: Arnold Bax and the Celtic Twilight', in Jürg Stenzl, ed., *Art Nouveau, Jugendstil und Musik* (Zurich: Atlantis, 1980), p. 207.

Example 3.8   Zemlinsky, 'Und kehrt er einst heim'

reluctance to use the double basses for the piano's low E in the middle of the second verse – a marvellous tolling effect in the original, probably unrealisable in orchestral terms[27] – means that he has to 'animate' the texture in another way, evidently by introducing a countermelody on high oboe (Ex. 3.9).

There is one remarkable bit of recomposition in this song (and here Zemlinsky goes far beyond mere transcription). Just before the start of the fifth verse, the repetition of a phrase in the piano (original version) leads to the inclusion of a 3/4 bar. In the orchestral version Zemlinsky not only varies the phrase by inverting it but creates a written-out *ritardando* by replacing the one bar of 3/4 with two bars of 2/4. This makes the original seem pedestrian by comparison (Ex. 3.10). A second, equally telling, bit of recomposition occurs a few bars later, where the composer reduces two

27. Cf. the problematic orchestral 'bells' in *Parsifal*.

Example 3.9   Zemlinsky, 'Und kehrt er einst heim'

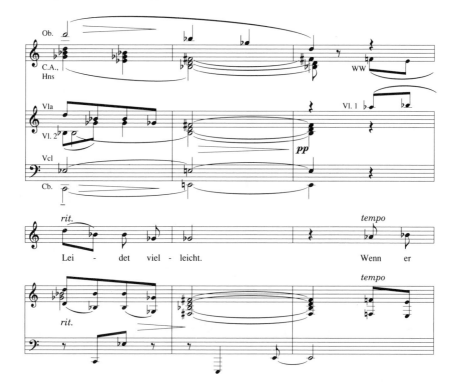

bars of 2/4 plus one of 3/4 to two bars of 2/4 only: here the effect is obviously one of compression. Characteristically even-handed, however, Zemlinsky restores the lost 3/4 bar just before the very end, by introducing a 3/4 bar – another written-out *ritardando* – not present in the original. Even this modification is given thematic relevance by the inclusion of an augmented form of the harp arpeggios from the preceding bars.

'Als ihr Geliebter schied'

This was the first of the songs composed in 1913, after the *Skandalkonzert*, and thus the first to be orchestrated with an already-composed instrumental prelude. That the other 1913 song, 'Sie kam zum Schloß gegangen', also has a prelude is good reason for thinking that these songs were created with their orchestral realisations in mind. Certainly they seem more orchestrally conceived than their predecessors.[28] At the

28. See my remarks on some of the songs in Schoeck's *Elegie* (1921–3), another instrumental cycle which, though it was first written out in a version for voice and piano, seems in many respects orchestrally conceived, in *The Song Cycles of Othmar Schoeck* (Berne: Paul Haupt, 1982), pp. 151–2.

Example 3.10   Zemlinsky, 'Und kehrt er einst heim'

same time, the very 'completeness' of the orchestral realisation reveals a certain thinness, undernourishment even, in the original composition: without the flesh endowed upon them by their orchestral covering they would look distinctly undercomposed.

The block contrasts of the piano part are inherent in the text – another poem with 'parenthetical' interpolations, though this time the interpolations make a sort of progression ('door', 'lamp', 'soul' in Maeterlinck; 'door', 'light' and 'breath' [Hauch] in the German) – and Zemlinsky naturally carries these contrasts into the orchestration. Because the blocks, in both piano and orchestral versions, are projected registrally as well as through the phrase structure, Zemlinsky ensures a connection between the various registral masses by means of voice leading. The orchestral scoring, remarkably, manages to combine

Klangfarbenmelodie and 'motivic' orchestration (the two types of orchestration most readily associated with the Schoenberg school[29]) with block structure all within the space of a few bars (Ex. 3.11).

As before, the texture is 'animated' in ways that make it more suitable for orchestral presentation: see in particular the bass patterns in bb. 11ff.,[30] the solo cello line in bb. 12–14, the 'surging' violas in b. 24 – though, as I suggested earlier, these alterations point to a weakness in the original composition. The *Klangfarben*-like treatment of the chords in bb. 12–14 are another, rather desperate, expedient. Another, more inspired bit of 'animation' is the continuation of the imitation in bb. 21–2 (first violins, b. 23).

The passages that reveal the full extent of Zemlinsky's recomposition are his setting of the 'parenthetical' interpolations. The second of these has already been quoted (Ex. 3.1); the first (bb. 5–6), with its curious colouring of flutes and muted trombones (plus a timpani roll on low E♭ for the last two beats of bar 6), anticipates Webern. (But for the triadic harmony . . . However, this type of orchestration is already present in the Webern of the Six Orchestral Pieces, another of the works programmed in the 1913 concert. Could Zemlinsky have seen the score in advance?) These passages, though, with their 'special effects', are less noteworthy than the rhetorical impetus given to the second half of the song by its scoring. Here the sense of the piano version being only a shadow of its later self is particularly strong: the last five bars, especially, concluding with tam-tam stroke, are much more sharply profiled in the orchestral version.

Once again, two textual matters deserve mention. One is the idiosyncratic squiggly line used to denote a string portamento, a sign found again in the *Lyrische Symphonie* and one quite distinct from the straight line employed by Mahler and others (an indication of their difference in temperament, one is tempted to add). The portamento even finds its way into the last two bars of the vocal line in the orchestral score, though here, disappointingly, indicated by the more conventional straight line.

29. See in particular Carl Dahlhaus, 'Analytical Instrumentation: Bach's Six-Part Ricercar as Orchestrated by Anton Webern', in *Schoenberg and the New Music*, trans. Derrick Puffett and Alfred Clayton (Cambridge University Press, 1987); Joseph N. Straus, 'Recompositions by Schoenberg, Stravinsky and Webern', *The Musical Quarterly*, 72, (1986), a trial run for Straus's book *Remaking the Past: Musical Modernism and the Influence of the Tonal Tradition* (Cambridge, Mass.: Harvard University Press, 1990); also, for a helpful list of orchestration techniques, Malcolm Miller, 'Richard Wagner's *Wesendonck-Lieder*: An Analytical Study' (Diss., University of London, 1990), pp. 45–6.
30. Because this song is the same length in both of its different versions, it is possible to give bar numbers.

Example 3.11 Zemlinsky, 'Als ihr Geliebter schied'

The other textual matter concerns a change of word in the text. Where Maeterlinck has 'Elle avait souri' (she had smiled) at the end of the first verse, Zemlinsky has 'da hab ich sie weinen gesehn' (I saw her weep), completely altering the meaning of the verse (and perhaps of the poem).[31] Whether Zemlinsky himself or his German translator was responsible for the change I have not been able to establish, though since the translator, Friedrich von Oppeln-Bronikowski,[32] was a linguist of huge experience it

31. The meaning of the poems is not always obvious even in English, though to look for rational explanations in Maeterlinck is often to bark up the wrong tree.
32. Zemlinsky used the translation in Maeterlinck, *Gedichte*, trans. K. L. Ammer and F. von Oppeln-Bronikowski (Jena, 1906). This was also the translation used by Schoenberg for his *Herzgewächse* (1911).

Example 3.11   (cont.)

can be assumed that he knew the difference between smiling and weeping.
The change is all the more amusing (in a lachrymose sort of way) as
Zemlinsky takes the opportunity to introduce a chromatic motive on solo
violin, an obvious piece of Mahlerian word-painting, at the same moment
(b. 12) that the solo cello begins its descending phrase *klagend* (Ex. 3.12).

'Die drei Schwestern'

Back to 1910. This is by far the longest of the early settings, and its
orchestration involves Zemlinsky in more new composition than any
other number in the score. By this stage in the discussion – all the main

Example 3.12   Zemlinsky, 'Als ihr Geliebter schied'

da hab ich sie wei - nen ge - sehn,____

techniques of transcription having been introduced – a simple 'chronological' description should suffice.

The new prelude is a fascinating piece of composition in its own right. Above a sustained A on muted trumpet Zemlinsky sets out a pattern of descending chords, each made up of a perfect fourth and a perfect fifth but in different arrangements (let us call them arrangements A and B). From the third bar onwards this pattern is combined with the two-bar bass motive that underlies the first vocal phrase, a motive which is itself coupled with an inner part based on a neighbour-note inflection (A – A – A♭ – A). By the time we reach the third chord in the upper part of the orchestra, the chord now presented in arrangement B, the combination of chord and bass motives produces a fourth-chord which is a clear portent of

Example 3.13   Zemlinsky, 'Die drei Schwestern'

many similar sonorities later in the cycle. It is worth noting that the chord
in the upper parts immediately following, in what would have been
arrangement A, has to be modified in order to accommodate the E♮ in the
bass. (Noteworthy too are the anticipations of the piano's accompanimental figure in muted trombone, another Webernian touch.) (Ex. 3.13)

From now on Zemlinsky lets free fantasy reign, sometimes with
quite zany results. The first bit of new composition within the setting is
the solo violin countermelody (at first doubled by piccolo) at the word
'Kronen' – a pre-echo of Weill's 'Lonely House'? – and the addition, at the
same time, of a new strand in three solo violas leads to a stratification of
the texture in the next bar, in which the three upper parts are played on

muted trumpets (and solo violas), an octave higher than in the piano version, while the rest of the violas provide a new supporting line (the G♭ on the third beat). The word 'Tod' evokes a curious offbeat thump of timpani/low pizzicato strings in the same bar; this is repeated at the same point in the phrase (but without word-painting connotations) two bars later, and is then moved back a quaver, in the next bar again, to give impetus to the upbeat arpeggios before the 'Bewegter'. The semiquaver figurations two bars earlier in the piano, nicely divided 5 – 6 – 7, are new, as are the sextuplet alternations in the viola. Another interesting detail: the upwards transposition of the trumpet chords required by the stratification of the texture leads to the omission of the passing note F♯ (E♮ in the original piano version), which would doubtless sound too vulgar in the upper octave.

Each of Zemlinsky's three stanzas is in three parts, each corresponding to one of Maeterlinck's short verses. The second section of Zemlinsky's first stanza – the sisters' song to the wood – accordingly starts with new material. In the orchestral version this is anticipated in the bar before the 'new' section (horns in the bar beginning 'wohnen'). Violins and woodwind then present the new material in a variety of rhythmic groupings, while the first horn adds a chromatic countermelody à la Strauss. At the end of the vocal phrase ('erben'),[33] horns echo the music of 'Wald, so gib uns' while the strings elaborate the piano's original rising pattern in various heterophonic arrangements. There is even a canon between horns and oboes at the close of the section. The third section, depicting the wood's laughing response to the sisters, presents a most striking 'animation' of the original, rather dull, piano texture, but the amount of fresh composition is actually less than in the earlier part of the stanza.

The second stanza sees the first entry of the harmonium, which presents the chordal accompaniment of the original setting rather more plainly than has generally been the case until now. There is an element of the grotesque in the scoring of the accompanimental figure, here transferred to the bass, on harp and low pizzicato strings. The second section of the verse, portraying the sisters' song to the sea, is another remarkable piece of illustrative writing, with heterophony in the accompaniment, but as in the closing section of the first stanza the amount of fresh composition is actually rather small. Not so, however, in the final section of the verse – the sea's weeping reply – which, as might be expected, evokes a suitably tearful response from the composer; jests apart, this is a splen-

---

33. The phrase 'daß wir [sterben]' is given a syncopation in the orchestral version that it previously lacked.

didly imaginative piece of recomposition, with the wailing semiquaver figures in lower woodwind and trumpet replicated by piccolos in quaver patterns which set up divisions of one and a half bars across the prevailing three-bar phrase. On the merely illustrative level, the glissando figures in cellos and basses, doubtless inspired by Schoenberg's *Pelleas und Melisande*, which was premiered in the same concert at which Zemlinsky conducted his long-to-be-forgotten tone poem *Die Seejungfrau*, are another fine touch. It is a pity that only the last few notes of the violins' pizzicato scale in the third bar are audible (Ex. 3.14).

The descent from the climax includes a rather disconcerting 'quotation' from Mahler's Ninth Symphony, a second-beat crotchet in the horn swelling to a stopped note a semitone below on the third, minim, beat. The first such 'quotation' of many (others will be discussed shortly), it is apt to sound incongruous, nothing more than one of Zemlinsky's forgetful, slightly embarrassing references to a composer whose main criticism of him was that he had so bad a memory he was unable to remember when he was quoting someone else.[34] But there is another way to take such 'quotations', as I shall suggest below. In the meantime the horn's stopped note serves to prepare a passage of Mahlerian grotesquerie, for the third stanza begins with orchestration that in another context one might be tempted to call parodic: two low flutes (doubled by eight violas, half of them tremolando *am Steg*) on the accompanimental figure, muted trombones in octaves on the bass, nothing in the middle. Yet the element of parody, if that is what it is, is wholly in the orchestration: the notes are a literal transcription of Zemlinsky's original piano part, than which nothing could be more serious (indeed the closest parallel is with Brahms's *Vier ernste Gesänge*). Here we have another example of the composer using his orchestration to open areas of sensibility unknown to the earlier version.[35] The orchestration, in other words, performs a transformational function rather than a merely transcriptive one.

The reference, in Zemlinsky's third stanza, to a town on an island evokes a sort of *Inselbildung* – see the two bars before 'Sehr langsam' – that Schoenberg may just possibly have learnt from his teacher.[36] In the next few bars, however, island construction gives way to stratification as

34. Henry-Louis de La Grange, *Mahler*, vol. I (London: Gollancz, 1976), p. 550.
35. The parallel this time is not so much with Schoeck's *Elegie* as with Berg's 1928 orchestrations of his *Sieben frühe Lieder*.
36. On *Inselbildung*, see Walter and Alexander Goehr, 'Arnold Schönberg's Development towards the Twelve-Note System', in Howard Hartog, ed., *European Music in the Twentieth Century* (Harmondsworth: Penguin, 1961), pp. 99–100.

Example 3.14 Zemlinsky, 'Die drei Schwestern'

the upper notes of the piano chords, now scored for heavily divided strings, are separated from the *klagend* appoggiatura figure (first bassoon an octave above low clarinet). The texture thickens in the usual fashion as the sisters finish their song to the town. Then, just before the third section, which describes the town opening its gates, Zemlinsky inserts a single bar for orchestra alone which elicits the most gut-wrenching sonority in the entire cycle (Ex. 3.15).

Horst Weber quotes a chord that the composer jotted down in someone's voice-and-piano score, designed to explain the harmony to the singer/player.[37] Transposed to D minor, the only key in which it has any physical reality, it would read as shown in Ex. 3.16. This is all very elegant and shows the chord to be one of those symmetrical constructions that so fascinated composers around the turn of the century. However, there is a note missing: the B♮ that emerges at the bottom of the harp and piano arpeggios after the bass F has sounded, and acts as a kind of 'subjacent root' to the dominant ninth chord exposed above. According to this interpretation, the chord could then be analysed as the conjunction of two dominant ninth sonorities a tritone apart, one of those tritonal-axis affairs that often underlie early twentieth-century harmonic symmetry (Ex. 3.17). Whatever the explanation, Weber is surely right in arguing that the chord is necessary for reasons of voice leading (though this is not a term he uses), providing as it does a better preparation for the ensuing six-three harmony than did the augmented-sixth chord of the original version. But I think that Zemlinsky was also carried away by his own rhetoric: whether or not the chord stands in need of theoretical justification, voice-leading or otherwise, the momentum generated at this point by the sheer power of the orchestration seems to demand a 'breathing-space' before the beginning of the final, *schwungvoll* section.

This 'rhetorical' power of the orchestra has been mentioned before, and it is worth bearing in mind as we approach the last song. In the meantime, the surging movement thus generated carries the three sisters to their destination, the voice having to rise an octave (and being granted a written-out *ritardando*) to cope with the final swell (Ex. 3.18). This brings us in where we started, at the beginning of the orchestral 'transition' to the second song.

37. 'Zemlinskys Maeterlinck-Gesänge', p. 193, note 24.

Example 3.15 Zemlinsky, 'Die drei Schwestern'

Example 3.15 (*cont.*)

Example 3.16

Example 3.17

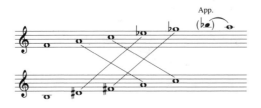

'Sie kam zum Schloß gegangen'

This, the final poem in the cycle, derives its meaning from a play on words which is only possible in the original French, the 'elle' of the first line referring to death (*la mort*); death in German (*der Tod*) is masculine. It is also based on a complicated rhyme scheme which gets lost in the translation. All this apart – and by this point in a performance of the cycle anyone not drained by the claustrophobic intensity of Zemlinsky's music will surely have given up trying to make sense of the poems – the song itself has a fatalistic, world-weary character, suggested partly by the harmony, partly by the funereal rhythms, which puts it in the same class (at least for the duration of the performance) as Mahler's *Der Abschied*.

The orchestration has a part to play in all this too. From the first entry, in b. 4, of the solo violin, which picks out the main notes of the oboe lines and adds little *crescendo–decrescendo* hairpins to them, Zemlinsky evokes a whole repertory of expressive gestures derived from late Mahler, and in particular from the first movement of Mahler's Ninth. The articulation of the bass pattern, first divided among cellos, double basses, harp and horn and from then on constantly redistributed among the same instruments, is another late-Mahlerian device, as is the swaying movement of the solo cello (a variation of the stopped-horn motive from the first song), carried down to a register an octave lower than its appearance in the voice-and-piano version.

Example 3.18 Zemlinsky, 'Die drei Schwestern'

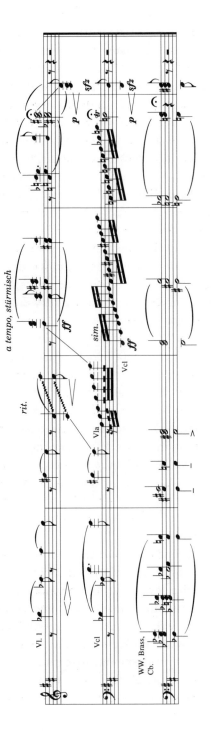

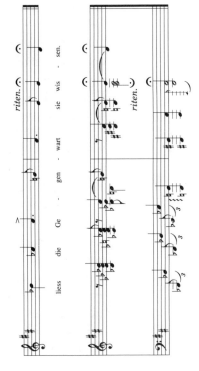

This emphasis on *late* Mahler is necessary as a corrective to the notion, first put about by Adorno and repeated by just about every commentator since, that the song derives principally from Mahler's early *Lieder eines fahrenden Gesellen*.[38] Not that Adorno's observation lacks substance; but the situation is a little more complex, as I shall try to show. Meanwhile, back to the subject in hand. As the voice reaches the word 'gegangen', and the bass instruments start to vary their ostinato for the first time (simultaneously the clarinets introduce a chugging countermelody which is new), violins, woodwind and horns dissect the repeated chords in the original piano part. It is important to be clear about what exactly is happening here. This is *not* a 'motivic analysis' of. the kind practised by Webern in his orchestration of the Bach ricercar and described by Dahlhaus and others in such loving detail.[39] Zemlinsky is not in the least concerned with clarifying the motivic structure, which is quite simple anyway; if anything he obscures it, by breaking up the natural pairing of the crotchets. What he seems to want to do, rather, is to create a sort of impressionistic haze by dividing the music up into its smallest chordal constituents – which, of course, involves separating the crotchet 'pairs' – and scoring each chord in such a way that it appears to overlap with the next. Thus the first chord in the bar is given to *tenuto* flutes, *staccato* first violins with grace note, and celesta in the higher octave; this resonates with the second chord in the bar, given to high bassoon and horns (in notes which are actually shorter than the flutes' but still marked *tenuto*) and pizzicato second violins. The pizzicato notes, far from dying away the moment they are sounded, seem to carry across the space left by the rest on the third beat – and so it goes on, with short notes giving way to sustained ones (minims in flutes, substitution of arco for pizzicato strings) as the phrase continues. The dull repeated chords of the piano version have been 'animated' in a way no pianist could suggest.

One could go on in this vein throughout the entire song. But it seems more interesting to point out Zemlinsky's articulation of the inner parts in the bars that follow, together with a development of the 'swaying' motive in second violins (the move towards B♭ major) and a motivically correct elaboration in the violas, as the texture takes on a 'mysterious' quality largely absent from the piano version. Here the word 'Bangen' (fears) appears to be the catalyst, with its most immediate results in the clarinet skirls and harp arpeggio. This is surely 'recomposition' at its best. At the same time this very improvement in the texture points towards a

38. 'Zemlinsky', p. 120.   39. See above, note 29.

lack of definition in the earlier version: thinness of composition is desperately evident there, presenting a serious challenge to the pianist, who has to make what he or she can of the arbitrarily spaced chords, the desultory voice leading.

Just before the beginning of the second stanza the horn makes its first reference to the *Lieder eines fahrenden Gesellen* – the undulating figure from the opening – its quavers quickly taken up by violins and violas in figuration that seems rather to recall the second song of that cycle. The quavers continue to 'animate' the second stanza (there is no comparable figuration in the voice-and-piano version). Here again the precisely sustained wind chords and clearly notated cello line – no chance of the use of a damper pedal! – draw attention to the vague and inconsistent voicing of the piano original. Orchestrating such an original is more an act of *composition* than of recomposition: there can be no question of 'making a new work from an old one' when the old one is so conspicuously undercomposed. For this reason, among others, the new version seems more artistically consistent, on a consistently higher level, than its predecessor. The succeeding passage, which is one of the work's most inspired, seems less of a jolt – less of a shift to a higher level – in the orchestral version than in the voice-and-piano: the marvellous evocation of the Queen's footsteps (alternating fifths in timpani and harp, an effect absent in the original, as are the 'swaying' neighbour-note pattern from Mahler's Ninth in the violas, the descending chromatic scale for solo violin tremolando *am Steg*, and the *Klangfarben*-like passing of the original piano-right-hand figure between low flutes and second violins) is all the more effective for having been so cogently prepared.

Inspiration remains high throughout the third stanza. The King's question to the Queen, as she walks out to her death (the 'unknown woman' who has come to the palace at dawn) – 'Wohin gehst du?' (Where are you going?) – suggests *Tristan*-like configurations as well as harmonies in the strings (complete with squiggly portamento), while the woodwind (in ascending order: cor anglais, two flutes, oboe) articulate an appoggiatura figure that is only implicit in the piano version. Similarly, the King's anxious warning – 'Gib acht in dem Dämmerschein!' (Take care in this half-light!) – involves a total reorganisation of the piano texture, with a chromatic inner part, rather lost in the original, transferred to very high violins, not to mention various exotic percussion effects.[40] This is, again, 'recomposition' at the highest level, a complete reinterpretation of

40. The orchestration of the final song is so complex that illustration would require quoting the entire texture.

material that could otherwise seem routine. The King continues his anxious questioning: 'Harrt drunten jemand dein?' (Is someone waiting for
you down there?); and the horns answer him with a second reference to
the *Lieder eines fahrenden Gesellen*, this time in the minor ('Yes, the
ghost of old Gustav!'). The approach to the fourth and last stanza
(bb. 38–40) redistributes the material of the former piano part with a
change of register (the transposition up an octave of the oboe melody), a
reversal of the pattern of syncopation between bass and accompanimental
figure, and a clearer articulation of the bass ostinato than was possible
before. Also new is the quaver figure in the second clarinet, a variation
of the 'chugging' pattern from near the beginning.

New material in the last verse includes the falling sixths and sevenths in cellos (another borrowing from Mahler's Ninth) and a related,
dotted figure in second violins. What is more surprising, given the
Mahlerian context, is the *literal restatement*, a few bars later, of no fewer
than four bars from earlier in the song (bb. 46–9 = 12–15). When I say 'literal restatement' I mean just that: this father-figure of the Second
Viennese School, for which avoidance of repetition was almost an article
of faith, has actually sat down and copied out a whole page of full score. I
find this unexpected literalism as revealing as the dog in Sherlock Holmes
that fails to bark in the night. Precisely *what* it reveals is harder to say. But
the function of these bars seems to be to build up a 'head of steam', a
rhetorical momentum, to carry the music through to the climactic passage in which the Queen is embraced by the unknown woman.

There is no such climax in the piano original. Or if there is, it is handled very discreetly – a '*cresc.*', a '*rit.*' and a single '*Sehr zart und langsam*'
marking – with no hint of the emotional saturation that fills the orchestral texture at this point. The descending semiquaver figure, fluttertongued, in the flutes (b. 50) may or may not be a reference to the surging
climax of the first song. Certainly the harp glissandi are new. But the overall effect is that of an apotheosis:[41] the Queen walks to her doom, arm in
arm with her visitor, the texture gradually clears (the squiggly portamento
leading to nothing, as the solo violin fades out simultaneously with the
singer, must present a nice problem of interpretation) and the horns, now

---

41. I may overstate, but the point I want to emphasise is that Zemlinsky's
orchestration performs an act of *transformation*, achieving emotional effects
out of all proportion to any that could be conveyed by the rather thin
original. It is in this sense, as well as the more specific one suggested below,
where the conjunction of references to early and late Mahler creates the
impression that time has been collapsed into a single moment (see note 47),
that the metaphor of Merlin's crystal cave becomes relevant.

muted, intone for the last time, and in the major, their reference to Mahler's *Wayfarer* songs. The final bars are a *locus classicus* of motivic liquidation.

V

What does all this Mahlerising mean? One answer would be to invoke the issue of Zemlinsky's 'eclecticism', on which Mahler's own view – that Zemlinsky's main problem was a bad memory – has already been quoted. His opinion was shared by Alma Mahler and sundry critics of the day.[42] Later Adorno would turn this opinion on its head by arguing that Zemlinsky's eclecticism was the eclecticism of genius, showing a

> truly seismographic sensitivity to the stimuli by which he allowed himself to be overwhelmed. Weakness which never pretends to be creative acquires the strength of a second nature. The unreserved sacrifice of the pathos of personality becomes a critique of personality and hence something intensely personal.[43]

Recently, however, a voice has floated down from the reaches of Higher Criticism, suggesting (in the context of a discussion of Brahms's influence on turn-of-the-century composers) that

> this 'seismographic' receptivity actually prevented Zemlinsky from absorbing the essence of Brahms. He registered the aftershocks, so to speak, but failed to locate the epicenter of the tremor.[44]

The pomposity of this criticism provides its own amusement, as does the ontological language (who can say what 'the essence of Brahms' is?). Adorno seeks to replace a teleological view of history, in which the survivors are the ones who are most original, with a paradoxical inversion of that view. The meek shall inherit the earth. But to invert the paradox yet again, for the sake of a joke about epicentres, seems to trivialise the issue. Historical teleology, for Mahler, Schoenberg and the other 'originals', was

---

42. See, for example, the review of *Die Seejungfrau* quoted in Hilmar, 'Zemlinsky und Schönberg', p. 64. Walter Pass provides a general survey of early Zemlinsky reception in 'Zemlinskys Wiener Presse bis zum Jahre 1911', in Kolleritsch, ed., *Alexander Zemlinsky*.   43. 'Zemlinsky', p. 115.
44. Walter Frisch, *The Early Works of Arnold Schoenberg, 1893–1908* (Berkeley: University of California Press, 1993), p. 40. Frisch's critical method, in this particular case, is to compare two very early Zemlinsky works with a mature Brahms string quartet.

a hard-won position, something they really believed in. If Zemlinsky is not to be counted an original in the same sense, we might at least refrain from returning to a situation in which eclecticism is just a dirty word.

Perhaps there is another way to see all this. Leave value judgments behind; take the music simply for what it is. (As for whether there is anything truly personal in it, Schoenberg's recommendation – repeated listening[45] – would seem to provide the answer.) 'Originality' and 'eclecticism' are labels we put on it ourselves, figleaves for hiding our instinctive likes and dislikes. 'Criticism is the act of finding bad reasons for what we believe upon instinct', Eliot said.[46] The invocation of Eliot is not altogether gratuitous. Listening to a piece by Zemlinsky can be a kaleidoscopic experience, a series of shocks and involuntary memories which we may or may not choose to assemble into a coherent whole. It is a kind of musical travelogue, not unlike listening to a performance of the Berio Sinfonia, though (I believe) on a higher aesthetic level. When we listen to the last of the Maeterlinck songs, especially in its orchestral version, we seem to be hearing all the Songs of a Wayfarer, indeed all the Mahler symphonies, rolled into one, a lifetime's experience collapsed into a few minutes of music.[47]

It is not a question of identifying particular Mahlerian 'quotations', though one could do that (and I have done it, to a certain extent, above). What matters is to recognise the richness of the experience and enjoy it

45. 'Zemlinsky' (1921), in Style and Idea, p. 487.
46. Selected Essays (London: Faber and Faber, 1951), p. 117.
47. A review of Robert Nye's Merlin, quoted on the dustjacket of one of his other novels, comes to mind:

> It is like walking into an illuminated manuscript – the imagery has the beauty of mediaevalism, always at the point where the seasons change, so that all is simultaneously still, held in eternity, and about to crack – and there finding oneself in a world which does not offer a mirror image of reality, but rather a crystallisation of it.
>
> (Allan Massie, The Scotsman (no date given))

This in turn recalls Adorno's comment on the Maeterlinck Songs – 'an inward-turned Middle Ages' ('Zemlinsky', p. 120) – and the fake mediaevalism that informs the Maeterlinck poems themselves. No less than Nye's Middle Ages, where comic pedantry, preposterous anachronism and a Joycean zest for language draw new energy from time-hallowed myths, Maeterlinck's mediaevalism is a fantastical, made-up thing, even though it expresses itself in prettiness, idealisation and mannered verse rather than in ribald prose (Burne-Jones rather than Rabelais). The 'eclecticism' of Zemlinsky's music is perhaps an even more suitable home for it than the perfected originality of Debussy's.

while it lasts. Listened to in this way, Zemlinsky's music becomes a sort of collage, albeit one on a high artistic level, like *The Waste Land*. Who cares (except the copyright holders) if the lines are not by Eliot but by Verlaine, Baudelaire and a hundred others, including Eliot's first wife? It is the juxtapositions that matter, the ability to put one quotation next to another in a way that moves the heart. Zemlinsky's music, similarly, especially a work like the Maeterlinck Songs, moves because it finds new meanings for hackneyed gestures. If a 'postmodern' age can appreciate anything, it should appreciate this. The pity is that Zemlinsky was as much a victim of the prejudices of his time as anyone else; he really *wanted* to be original. And when he achieved originality, as in the late *Sinfonietta* (1934), it was at the cost of his soul. For here synthesis is attained, a 'new' style forged, but without any real meaning. The quotation from the final Maeterlinck song – 'Wohin gehst du?' – that occurs in the slow movement of this work ought to be one of its most moving gestures. Yet it goes for nothing, because the quotation is a quotation without a context. The 'quotations' from Mahler within that final song mean something, as I have tried to suggest, because the meanings inhere partly in the context. Take the Maeterlinck poems away and they would mean little. When Zemlinsky quotes himself he reveals himself, like Peer Gynt, to be an onion without a centre. His 'centre' is always borrowed.

VI

To return, once again, to the subject in hand. Zemlinsky's 'techniques of transcription' can be summarised as follows (with references to the songs in which they make their main appearances):

1. *Transcription* itself, in the narrow sense defined by the *OED*: literal arrangement (parts of the second and third songs)
2. *'Motivic'* orchestration *à la* Webern, and occasional *Klangfarbenmelodie*, to clarify the musical structure and enhance word-setting (songs 2, 4,[48] 6)
3. The use of orchestral *blocks*, to articulate the verse-structure of the poem and the musical form (songs 2, 4, 6)
4. *Stratification* of the texture (a vertical equivalent of the last-mentioned) for the sake of greater clarity and sharper characterisation (songs 1, 2)
5. The *opening up of registral space*, sometimes combined with antiphonal effects and the use of orchestral blocks (songs 1, 5)

48. Numbering of songs 4 and 5 refers, again, to their positions in the voice-and-piano cycle.

6. *Animation* of homophonic textures through motivic development (song 3), including the animation of the bass and inner parts (song 5)
7. The *development of harmonic possibilities* (the fourth-chords in song 4, the prelude to 1)
8. *Textural/orchestral recomposition*, including the use of 'iconic' sonorities (songs 4, 5), the suggestion of parody and the grotesque (song 6), and, in particular, the generation of rhetorical momentum by orchestral means (songs 1, 4, 6)
9. *Recomposition of actual musical material*, or the rewriting of the texture for what appear to be purely musical purposes (song 5)
10. *New composition*, notably the preludes and postludes which provide 'room to breathe' and occasional transitions (songs 1, 2, 3), and, most spectacularly of all, the one-bar interpolation in song 1

There is a continuum here[49] (though not a progression – one technique is not to be considered 'superior' to any other), and Zemlinsky moves up and down it with all the assurance of a master-craftsman. Arnold Whittall's judgement of the composer – that 'at his best, and in a remarkable variety of forms and moods, Zemlinsky, though not a great master, was indeed a composer of many masterly qualities'[50] – seems if anything to err on the side of caution.

VII

Time to sum up. Zemlinsky's Maeterlinck songs exist, or have existed, in three states:

1. The version (four songs only) performed on 31 March 1913
2. The version (voice and piano) published by Universal in 1914
3. The orchestral score published in 1924[51]

It seems unlikely that version 1 will ever be performed again.[52] But versions 2 and 3 present a nice aesthetic problem. When the songs are performed in their original version, as they are in the complete recording of

---

49. I owe my use of this term, and some of the ideas in the following section, to Millan Sachania, whose work on Godowsky set me thinking about the notion of transcription in the first place.
50. Talk on 'Music Weekly', BBC Radio 3, 4 December 1983.
51. Adorno misleadingly ascribes the two volumes of the last to 1922 and 1926. 'Zemlinsky', p. 117.
52. Except perhaps in nostalgic retrospectives of the work of the Second Viennese School. The conference on Expressionism held in Manchester in 1992 included a complete reconstruction of the *Skandalkonzert*.

Zemlinsky's songs,[53] it is in the keys and sequence of the original – and rightly so, as this is what the composer published in 1914. But when the orchestral version is done, it is, so far as I am aware, always in the keys and sequence of 1924. We have, then, a case of a work with two distinct identities. To the best of my knowledge, no one has ever suggested transposing, and reordering, the songs of the voice-and-piano arrangement to match those of the orchestral. But there is at least the basis of a case for performing the orchestral songs in their earlier sequence. (The matter of transposition is more complicated.) In this regard it would be interesting to know in what order Zemlinsky performed the songs when, and if, he conducted the orchestral cycle.[54]

Of course it could be that even he perceived the work as having more than one 'identity'. This might explain why he transposed the first two songs (even before the last two had been written) for their performance in 1913. It is unlikely that this was done for practical reasons, since the range and tessitura of all six songs are roughly the same.[55] But it might be that, in presenting them for orchestral performance, he thought of them as more of a *cycle* than he did the voice-and-piano version. In which case, what would make more sense than to make of them a closed tonal structure, with the first and last songs in D major/minor ('Und kehrt er einst heim', the final song in the 1913 'version', begins in A minor but ends with a consolidation of D), on the lines, perhaps, of Mahler's *Kindertotenlieder*, another work that keeps its heaviest orchestration for the beginning and end? (As does Berg's *Altenberg* cycle: sometimes it seems as if Zemlinsky was making deliberate and systematic reference to every other work on the programme of that unfortunate concert.) The orchestral set in its full form – version 3 – does, in fact, have a more cyclic feel about it than the voice-and-piano version, partly because of its greater end-weightedness:

	1	2	3	4	5	(4)	6[56]
1913	d–D	g♯	e♭–E♭		a–D		
1914	c–C	f♯–F♯	e♭–E♭	d	a–D		D
1924	d–D	g♯	e♭–E♭		a–D	d	D

53. Referenced above, note 11.
54. I know of no evidence on this subject.
55. Weber's point, that the voice comes through more clearly at the higher pitch ('Zemlinskys Maeterlinck-Gesänge', p. 200, note 35), makes little sense, as the *relation* between voice and accompaniment would be the same whatever the transposition.
56. Numbering, again, according to the voice-and-piano version. Upper-case letters refer to major keys, lower-case to minor.

There is also the matter of the 'transition' interpolated in the orchestral versions (versions 1 and 3) between songs 1 and 2, easing the tritone move across the two songs, and – once one starts looking for this sort of thing, the possibilities are endless – the apparent quotation of that transition (the music portraying the sisters' greeting to life) in the 'revised' version of song 5,[57] composed, however, before the 'earlier' version was published!

Of course (again) we shall never be clear about exactly what it was that Zemlinsky wanted. What we can be clear about is that there is no 'definitive' version of the Maeterlinck Songs. Each version has its own distinct identity – an identity corresponding, as is usually the case with transcriptions, to a specific medium of performance[58] – but in this particular instance the transcription (or arrangement, or translation) must be granted a validity equal to that of the original composition. Perhaps an even greater validity – for there are aspects of the work, as I have suggested, that seem imperfectly realised in the voice-and-piano version. (Questions for another article: What does it mean to say a piece is 'undercomposed'? How much new composition, or recomposition, is necessary to turn an 'undercomposed' piece into a 'fully realised' one? And at what point does a piece become 'overcomposed'?) In this respect it is instructive to compare Zemlinsky's reworking of the Maeterlinck Songs with some of the transcriptions made by Schoenberg and others for the Society for Private Musical Performances.[59] But then the various transcribers' aims were quite different.[60] It was, after all, Zemlinsky who had composed the songs in the first place; and in such matters the composer, like the customer, is always right.

57. Cf. Exx. 3.2 and 3.10.
58. Cf. the debate between Peter Kivy and Jerrold Levinson, in Kivy, 'Orchestrating Platonism', paper read at the Central Division Meeting of the American Philosophical Association, May 1987; Levinson, *Music, Art and Metaphysics* (Ithaca: Cornell University Press, 1990), especially pp. 231–5; and Kivy's chapter entitled 'Orchestrating Platonism' in *The Fine Art of Repetition: Essays in the Philosophy of Music* (Cambridge University Press, 1993). Kivy's second contribution (presented as an enlarged and revised version of the first, which I have not seen) is curious in that it purports to answer criticisms of his APA paper made by Levinson at the conference while taking no account of the more detailed (?) criticisms of the paper contained in Levinson's book. Another interesting article is Stephen Davies, 'Transcription, Authenticity and Performance', *British Journal of Aesthetics*, 28 (1988).
59. Schoenberg's transcription of the *Lieder eines fahrenden Gesellen*, or the ensemble version he made (in collaboration with Rudolf Kolisch) of Reger's *Romantische Suite*, are serviceable examples.
60. There is some piquancy in the fact that when Erwin Stein transcribed Zemlinsky's songs 2 and 5 (MS in the Arnold Schoenberg Institute, Los Angeles; recorded on Phillips 6514 134) for the same Society, he used the

Appendix: Zemlinsky's orchestra

	1	2	3	4	5	6
Picc.	2					
Fl.	2	2		3	2	3
Ob.	2			2	1	1
C.a.		1		1	1	1
Cl.	2	1		2	2	2
B.Cl.	1	1		1		
Bsn	2	2		2	2	2
Hn	2	2		2	2	2
Tpt	3	3				
Tbn	3				3	
Timp.	*	*			*	*
B.Dr.	*					*
Tri.	*					
Cym.	*				*	*
Tam.					*	
Harm.	*		*		*	
Glock.				*		
Pno	*					
Cel.		*	*	*	*	*
Hp	*			*	*	*
Solo Vl.			2			
Solo Vla		(12)	2			
Solo Vcl.		(8)	2			
Solo Cb.		(4)	2			
Str.	*	—61		*	*	*

NB.   Songs numbered here according to the orchestral version

orchestral version rather than the original as a basis – and thus denied himself the opportunity, for example, of restoring to the piano the tolling bass notes of No. 5 in its voice-and-piano version.

61. See Solo Str.

A Note on the 'Skandalkonzert' of 31 March 1913

There are several aspects to this concert which have not perhaps received sufficient attention.

In the first place, there seems to be some disagreement, surprising in a concert which occasioned one of the 'best-documented scandals in twentieth-century music history', as the editors of the Berg–Schoenberg correspondence call it,[62] as to the actual order of events in the programme. From the reviews it is possible to establish that the order was indeed Webern–Zemlinsky–Schoenberg–Berg(–Mahler), but it is odd that Carner and DeVoto do not agree with this.[63]

Secondly, it has not been sufficiently noted that the programme as finally presented (it was originally planned to include Wagner's *Tristan* Prelude, but this had to be withdrawn[64]) was extremely short. Even allowing for more expansive tempos than are the custom today, it could hardly have lasted much more than an hour, and this in itself might have been cause for dissatisfaction among those present.

Thirdly, there is the fact that the programme as finally put on was a most oddly balanced one. If the evening had started with the *Tristan* Prelude, as the organisers had presumably intended, there would have been some sort of symmetry with the *Kindertotenlieder* at the end, the two substantial and relatively familiar works embracing the shorter and lesser-known ones. To start the concert with Webern's brief pieces, possibly the most 'advanced' (and to the audience the most difficult) works on the programme, was incautious, if not deliberately provocative. At the very least Schoenberg could have mollified the situation by placing his own Chamber Symphony first: though not exactly a lollipop, this was a longer and more familiar work than some of the others on the programme and would have made a better opener. Then again, it seems incomprehensible that Schoenberg should have programmed just two of Berg's very short songs out of context – a tight, cyclic context, to say the

62. *The Berg–Schoenberg Correspondence: Selected Letters*, ed. Juliane Brand, Christopher Hailey and Donald Harris (London: Macmillan, 1987), p. 166.
63. See Mosco Carner, *Alban Berg: The Man and the Work* (London: Duckworth, 1975), p. 25; Mark DeVoto, 'Berg the Composer of Songs', in Douglas Jarman, ed., *The Berg Companion* (London: Macmillan, 1989), p. 51. The review cited in note 3 above establishes the correct order of the proceedings.
64. See Rosemary Hilmar, *Alban Berg: Leben und Wirken in Wien bis zu seinen ersten Erfolgen als Komponist* (Graz: Hermann Böhlaus, 1978), p. 95. A poster advertising the concert with *Tristan* Prelude is reproduced in the catalogue for the 1992 Zemlinsky exhibition, p. 62; without, in Stuckenschmidt, *Arnold Schoenberg*, p. 186.

least – and to have put them immediately before the *Kindertotenlieder*. It is almost as if Schoenberg *wanted* to cause a riot.[65]

Finally, the point has to be made that it may have been bad performances, as well as the works themselves, that contributed to the uproar. Organisation of the concert seems to have been shambolic in the extreme, with Schoenberg in Berlin until a few days before the concert and Zemlinsky in Prague. Vocal rehearsals were left to the willing but inexperienced Berg (practical music-making was not his forte), orchestral rehearsals to one Martin Spörr. Exactly who coordinated the whole effort is unclear. By 7 March Schoenberg had not even seen the Zemlinsky score, doubtless because the orchestrations had not yet been completed, while Berg's songs had not been tried by the orchestra as late as the 28th.[66] It is hard to see how the concert could possibly have succeeded in such circumstances. Sometimes the Second Viennese School seems to have been the victim of its own collective paranoia, bringing about the very failures through which it felt itself persecuted.

65. On the order of the programme, which went through several changes, see the letter of Schoenberg to Erhard Buschbeck (10 March 1913) quoted in Hilmar, *Alban Berg*, p. 95.
66. See (Ernst) Hilmar, 'Zemlinsky und Schönberg', pp. 76–7.

4

Symphony and symphonic scenes: issues of structure and context in Schumann's 'Rhenish' Symphony

Michael Musgrave

I

Schumann's Symphony in E♭ major Op. 97, the so-called 'Rhenish' Symphony,[1] occupies a symbolic position historically as well as chronologically. Written exactly half way through the century (from November to December 1850), it stands at the parting of the symphonic ways. From around this time, the co-existence between the pictorial, evocative or narrative aspects of the genre, and the purely formal – whether appearing most overtly in the symphonies of Berlioz, or with greater restraint in those of Mendelssohn and Schumann – begins steadily to weaken. On one side, the New German School claims a modern expression of the symphonic spirit through the newly invented 'symphonic poem' of Liszt, a genre which gathers momentum through the 1850s. On the other, Schumann's protégé, the young Brahms, growing to maturity through this decade, holds these works in contempt: waiting until 1876 to release a major purely instrumental symphony, he offers a response that will finally polarise the fundamental debate about the nature of musical progress – that concerning the respective claims of the 'referential' and the 'absolute' in music.[2] For Schumann, however, reaching the end of his instrumental compositions by the early 1850s, the rift was not as yet apparent. The 'Rhenish' Symphony, a five-movement work with clearly

1. Not Schumann's term. The association would certainly have been drawn from the detailed description with examples published in the *Rheinische Musik-Zeitung*, 1 (1850–1), 293ff., reproduced in R. Kapp, ed., *Robert Schumann, Sinfonie Nr. 3, Taschenpartitur, Einführung und Analyse* (Mainz: Goldman/Schott, 1981). But it seems most likely to have emerged from the remark of Josef von Wasielewski in his early biography of Schumann, *Robert Schumann, Eine Biographie* (Dresden: Kunze, 1858), that the work 'may truly be called "The Rhenish"'. See A. L. Alger, trans., *The Life of Robert Schumann* (Boston: Ditson, 1871), p. 173.
2. Dahlhaus characterises the 1870s as the 'second age of the symphony', and thus by implication Brahms's First Symphony as inaugurating it. See Carl Dahlhaus, *Nineteenth-Century Music* (Berkeley: University of California Press, 1989), p. 236.

acknowledged referential associations, yet eventually published as a self-sufficient work, looks back over the symphonic trends since Beethoven's 'Pastoral' Symphony had opened up new vistas of expression and structure. As a highly individual and effective work by a composer whose symphonic claims are still insufficiently acknowledged, it offers a fascinating model for the exploration of some central issues in the development of the nineteenth-century symphony: those of large-scale formal structure and integration, and of the role of pre-existent, or otherwise referential material.

Although Schumann's various comments in support of the value of both purely instrumental composition and of the use of titles and programmes might seem contradictory, they existed in complementary relation in his creative outlook; if he aspired to the former as a compositional ideal, he reserved an equal place for the latter in the process. The deletion on publication of the title which appears above the autograph full score of the fourth movement of the 'Rhenish' Symphony – 'in the style of an accompaniment to a solemn ceremony'[3] – and the suppression by Schumann of other background evidence concerning its stimuli, was by no means unusual or specially significant. Schumann had previously deleted titles from works on publication, as well as sometimes adding or changing them.[4] His attitude towards the role of titles in symphonies emerges in his review of Berlioz's 'Fantastic Symphony' where he shows impatience with the composer's lengthy account of the work's background and programme, observing that Berlioz might have confined himself to headings for each of the five sections. It emerges further in the Berlioz review that he would have dispensed with Beethoven's titles for the movements of the 'Pastoral' Symphony as well, suggesting that they hinder appreciation: 'Once the eye has been directed to a particular object the ear no longer judges independently.'[5] In support of his view, he suggests that 'Beethoven was very well aware of the dangers . . . in the few words with which he prefaced it – "more an expression of emotion than tone painting" – there lies an entire aesthetic for composers'.[6]

3. 'Im Charakter der Begleitung einer feierlichen Ceremonie'. The manuscript resides in Berlin Stadtsbibliothek Preussischer Kulturbesitz, Mus ms autogr. R. Schumann 12, with the heading 'Dritte Symphonie (Es-dur) für grosses Orchester von R.S. Op. 97'.
4. These include the 'Spring Symphony', Op. 38, the Fantasia in C, Op. 17, and the Intermezzo, Op. 2 No. 4.
5. *Neue Zeitschrift für Musik*, 3 (1835), 50, my translation. Schumann's review was of the *Symphonie Fantastique* in Liszt's piano transcription, not the full score.   6. *Neue Zeitschrift für Musik*, 2 (1835), 65.

But Schumann did not always act of the basis of this conclusion. Elsewhere in his writings emerges the seemingly contrary view that titles can help to avoid the danger of misinterpretation of a composer's wishes, which may arise not merely through inappropriate performance, but through the failure to understand the special quality of a great work: he remarks that 'there are certain mysterious moods of the soul [*Seelenzustände*] which can be more readily understood by means of these verbal indications, and we must be thankful for them'.[7] A similar attitude is discernible in the observation that, for the many listeners who appreciate only the most simply differentiated moods and emotions in music, 'it is very difficult . . . to understand masters like Beethoven and Schubert who could translate every circumstance of life into the language of tones'.[8] But Schumann's interest in titles went far beyond the needs of performer or audience to the very conception of a work. As a composer he found great value in attaching titles to musical ideas, as he explains, again in connection with the 'Fantastic' Symphony:

> We must not too lightly estimate outward influences and impressions. Unconsciously an idea sometimes develops simultaneously with the musical image; the eye is awake as well as the ear; and this ever-busy organ frequently follows certain outlines amidst all the sounds and tones, which, keeping pace with the music, may take form and crystallise.[9]

The background to the 'Rhenish' Symphony offers clearer links to the nature of these preoccupations than that of any other orchestral work. Schumann gave ample evidence of inspiration in both general and specific terms such as to encourage a broader reconstruction of the imaginative context for the whole. In addition to the titled fourth movement of the work, we have the statement of his friend and fellow musician Josef von Wasielewski that 'the idea was first conceived . . . on seeing the cathedral at Cologne'.[10] That the symphony was directly associated with the Schumanns' move to the Rhineland from Leipzig, and the consequent optimism Schumann felt, is further confirmed in two letters to his publisher Nikolaus Simrock written on 1 March and 19 March 1851, seeking the work's publication. In the latter especially he expresses his

---

7. *Neue Zeitschrift für Musik*, 15 (1841), 33. Trans. Leon B. Plantinga in *Schumann as Critic* (New Haven: Yale University Press, 1967), p. 119. For further discussion of 'Seelenzustände' see Plantinga, *Schumann as Critic*, p. 120.   8. *Neue Zeitschrift für Musik*, 1 (1834), 10, my translation.
9. *Neue Zeitschrift für Musik*, 3 (1835), 50, my translation.
10. Wasielewski, *Schumann*, p. 173.

great pleasure in producing a symphony in the Rhineland and suggests that 'here and there a piece of life is mirrored'.[11] (The Rhine had long musical associations for Schumann: he had set several poems in which the Rhine was a significant and clearly spiritual image – perhaps most notably the powerful 'Im Rhein, im heiligen Strome' in *Dichterliebe*[12] – and he would later set another Rhenish subject for full orchestra and chorus, the *Rheinweinlied*.) Wasielewski was also the recipient of sentiments as to the work's special associations. He quotes Schumann as saying 'I wished national elements to prevail and I think I have succeeded.'[13] But the desire to allow the work to stand independent of its inspiration is equally clear in his remark that 'we must not show our heart to the world; a general impression of a work of art is better; at least no preposterous comparisons can then be made'.[14] By 'showing our heart to the world' Schumann is probably referring to the movement titles given in the programme of the first performance (which was at Düsseldorf, 6 February 1851), which retained the title of the fourth movement and 'Intermezzo' for the third (the latter is not in the autograph, so it must have come from Schumann), and by an early analytical account of the work, which offered in addition other pictorial suggestions.[15] But Schumann's reluctance to discard his titles and to permit associations to survive until the first performance may well confirm his awareness of the very special nature of the work – a unique blend of the picturesque and associative with a powerfully conceived overall structure, thus blending two distinct principles, that of a narrative sequence of scenes, and a symphonic 'plot archetype'.

Before turning to the special character of the symphonic scheme, the 'referential' dimension may first be explored. Schumann's reflections on the nature of the creative process find echoes in the statements of later composers and the work of theorists. Aaron Copland's reference to the

---

11. H. Erler, *Robert Schumanns Leben aus seinen Briefen geschildert* (Berlin: Ries und Erler, 1886), vol. II, pp. 137–9.
12. The clearly historically inclined contrapuntal idiom of the piano part of this song offers an earlier example of the association of this feature with the visual image of the sacred river Rhine.
13. Wasielewski, *Schumann*, p. 173.   14. *Ibid.*
15. The programme is reproduced in Kapp, *Schumann, Sinfonie Nr. 3*, p. 180. It shows that Schumann also used the designation 'Finale' for the fifth movement, and that the first movement was originally marked 'allegro vivace' (though published as 'Lebhaft'). The analytical article, published in *Rheinische Musik-Zeitung* (1850–1), 293ff., refers to the same titles. See Kapp, *Schumann, Sinfonie Nr. 3*, p. 189.

'usable past' of a particular piece, or of a composer's work in general, prompts Pascall's gloss on the concept of 'intertextuality', that

> the world of the piece combines genesis and structure. The network of relationships between musical differentiations within a piece forms its artistic statement. This statement is at once understand-able yet original ... conditioned by its past yet the result of an imaginatively creative act.[16]

This essay seeks first to explore some aspects of the work's originality through its imaginative treatment of both its referential and the structural dimensions in light of both Schumann's comments and of symphonic precedent.

II

Wasielewski's assertion of the impact of Cologne Cathedral on Schumann's inspiration for the symphony is supported by the facts. Clara's diary confirms the effect the sight of the cathedral had upon Robert and Clara when they visited at the end of their first month in the Rhineland, where, on 2 September 1850, Robert had taken up the position of director of music at Düsseldorf:

> Sunday 29th [September] we made a pleasure trip to Cologne which enchanted us instantly, beginning with the first view from Deutz, and continued with a particularly impressive view of the grandiose cathedral, which on closer inspection surpassed our expectations.[17]

Wasielewski also asserts that, during the composition of the work, Schumann was greatly influenced by the festivities consequent upon the elevation of von Geissel, Archbishop of Cologne, to the rank of Cardinal, and he assumes that the symphony 'probably owes its [fourth] movement originally headed "an accompaniment to a solemn ceremony"' to this.[18] However, the widely drawn inference that Schumann was present at the ceremony is not factually correct. The Schumanns' *Haushaltbuch*, which gives a record of the period of working on the various movements, shows him to have have been working at home on that day, 12 November, 1850 –

16. Robert Pascall, *Brahms: Biographical, Documentary and Analytical Studies* (Cambridge University Press, 1983), p. vii.
17. B. Litzmann, *Clara Schumann* (Berlin: Breitkopf und Härtel, 1902–8), vol. II, p. 227.
18. Wasielewski, *Schumann*, p. 173.

in fact, unwell:[19] attendance would, of course, have required travel from Düsseldorf and would therefore certainly have been noted. Nor does the report of the ceremony itself offer any direct support for a musical connection, indicating only that the psalm 'Lauda Jerusalem' was sung at the beginning and a 'Volkslied' at the end (the likely organ improvisation might well have gone unreported).[20] It must be concluded that the style of the movement represented Schumann's ideal evocation of such an occasion, perhaps conceived as an imaginative complement to it rather than a musical recreation. The images that would have formed part of a major religious ceremony were quickly provided by the first analytical review of the work:

> We see gothic domes, processions, stately figures in the choirstalls. Everything comes to a climax in the artful figuration up to the enharmonically-placed solo entry of all the wind in B major – the trombones to the fore like three pious prelates giving the sign of blessing, whereon the organ tones again fade into a distant E♭ minor.[21]

The musical identity of the latter image at least can be confirmed by reference to other of Schumann's works. The closing bars of the third part of the *Scenes from Goethe's Faust* (1844–53), 'Scene in the Cathedral', feature just such echoing minor chords on the brass, suggesting a fading into the distant recesses of the building. But though an ecclesiastical mood is certainly evoked in the stately neo-Baroque idiom of the symphony movement, enhanced by the ecclesiastical association of trombones, the form of the main part of the movement does not as much suggest the drama of a service as the metaphor of a building: its developing sections and overtly contrapuntal working seem to suggest the creation of the successive levels and spans of a great physical structure. Since the construction of Cologne Cathedral was still incomplete in 1850 and was even then one

19. 'Nicht wohl'. Robert Schumann, *Tagebücher*, vol. III, *Haushaltbücher*, 1847–1856, ed. Gerd Nauhaus (Leipzig, 1982), p. 544. This is pointed out by Linda Roesner, who also notes that the day of the Schumanns' visit, 29 September, was an important feast day and that the service would have included much splendour and was the possible stimulus to the fourth movement's conception. This would accord with Wasielewski's assertion. See L. Roesner, ed., Schumann, Symphony No 3 in E♭ (Mainz: Eulenburg, 1986), preface, p. iv.
20. See 'Bericht über die Feier der Überreichung des Cardinalsbiretts' in *Deutsche Volkshalle* (Zugabe Nr. 22), November, 1850. Schumann read the reports of the enthronement in the press. I acknowledge with thanks the provision of a copy of this report by Dr Kracht of the Historisches Archiv des Erzbistums Köln.   21. See Kapp, *Schumann, Sinfonie Nr. 3*, p. 189.

Example 4.1 'Rhenish' Symphony, fourth movement

of the marvels of European architecture, such a metaphor is certainly not inappropriate.

The neo-Baroque idiom so effectively elaborated by Schumann resides in a sequence of rising fourths in imitation over a moving bass with quasi-imitation in the second voice (Ex. 4.1). The stylistic origins of the passage have been proposed by several writers. Gál,[22] stressing the religious association, notes the affinity with the 'cross' motive used in such Baroque passages as the opening of the *Stabat Mater* by Pergolesi and the chorus 'Laß ihn kreuzigen' from Bach's *St Matthew Passion*, as well as preludes in E♭ major and B minor from Book 1 of Bach's *Das Wohltemperierte Clavier*. Todd suggests rather the C♯ minor fugue of Book 1 (Ex. 4.2).[23] Most examples draw the parallel with the changing-note figure contained within the Schumann theme, with the semitone below the tonic and minor third above making an upward leap of the diminished fourth, then returning stepwise to the tonic. In terms of overall shape, however, it is the themes associated with E♭ major in Bach which are closer. The notable example of the organ fugue in E♭ (the so-called 'St Anne'), may well have offered a structural precedent for Schumann's movement in its use of a sectional form which includes the reintroduction of an augmented version of the fugue subject in counterpoint with the theme of the second section. But it is actually in the E♭ work with no religious associations that a more precise thematic and textural precedent is found: the imitative passage beginning at b. 10 of the Prelude in E♭ major from Book 1 of *Das Wohltemperierte Clavier*. It seems significant that Schumann employs the key of E♭ major for the

22. Hans Gál, *Schumann Orchestral Music*, (London: BBC, 1979), p. 27. Abraham also draws attention to the connection with 'Crucifixus themes'. Gerald Abraham, ed., *Schumann: A Symposium* (Oxford University Press, 1952), p. 236.

23. R. Larry Todd, ed., *Schumann and his World* (Princeton University Press, 1994), p. 99.

Example 4.2
(i) Pergolesi, *Stabat Mater*
(ii) Bach, *St Matthew Passion*, 'Laß ihn kreuzigen'
(iii) Bach, *Das Wohltemperierte Clavier* Book 1, Prelude in B minor
(iv) Bach, *Das Wohltemperierte Clavier* Book 1, Fugue in C♯ minor

Credo of his setting of the Latin Mass, written two years later in 1852, which clearly parallels the symphonic material as it reappears in its transformed version in the Finale at b. 45. This, with the fact that the key signature of the symphonic movement is E♭ major, suggests that Schumann may have thought of its minor-mode material as an inflection of a major-key archetype (Ex. 4.3).

However, Schumann's movement is not systematically imitative in this manner. Its essentially continuo-style idiom actually lies much closer to passages such as the slow section of Corelli's Concerto Grosso in C minor (and to a lesser extent, that in G minor), and, even more precisely, to the opening slow section of the Sonata in G minor in Muffat's *Harmonico Tributo* (from b. 5) (Ex. 4.4). Yet there is no evidence that

Example 4.3

(i) Bach, *Das Wohltemperierte Clavier* Book 1, Prelude in E♭ major

(ii) Bach, organ fugue in E♭ major ('St Anne')

(iii) Schumann, Mass, Credo

(i)

bb. 10–12

(ii)

(iii)

Example 4.4

(i) Corelli, Concerto Grosso in C minor, grave

(ii) Georg Muffat, *Harmonico Tributo*, Sonata in G minor

(i)

(ii)

b. 5

Example 4.5   Schumann, Trio in D minor, first theme (simplified)

Schumann knew the Muffat piece,[24] although sources for the Corelli
would have been more common. Rather than one model, it seems that
several sources or stylistic archetypes may have influenced the conception. Indeed, in keeping the question of creative stimulus in perspective, it
is clearly to a work of Schumann's own, rather than to any existing models
that the symphonic passage most closely relates: the opening subject of
Schumann's Piano Trio in D minor anticipates the harmonic/thematic
model, and also includes the distinctive figure ('x' in Ex. 4.5) of the orchestral passage at b. 5 at a parallel pre-cadential point. It seems no coincidence that this piece is recorded as having been played in the Schumann
household during the period of the composition of the symphony.[25]
Written in 1847, three years before the symphony, the Trio might well be
seen as the focus of a two-stage process, first drawing on Baroque archetypes transformed into modern chamber idiom, then revealing its deeper
source under the stimulus of the cathedral and of reports of the enthronement ceremony (Ex. 4.5).

The Baroque continuo aspect of this movement may also provide the
clue to the source of the character of the first part of the opening subject of
the finale which succeeds it, which is unique in Schumann's instrumental
and orchestral works. The textural idiom with which the movement
begins can be seen as drawing on the same stylistic source as the theme of
the fourth movement itself, and thus as suggesting that these passages, or
ones like them, provided a background for the relationship of the main
themes of the Schumann movements. If one turns again to the Corelli
Concerti, the 'vivo' and 'allegro' sections which succeed the respective
quoted slow passages of the C minor and G minor works reveal a similar
character, hardly diminished by the minor key signature, since they so

24. There is no evidence of these works in Boetticher's comprehensive listing of
    Schumann's library. See Wolfgang Boetticher, *Robert Schumann: Einführung
    in Persönlichkeit und Werk* (Berlin, 1941). I am also indebted to Dr Gerd
    Nauhaus of the Robert Schumann Haus, Zwickau, for confirming this point
    in respect of the Zwickau holdings.
25. On 28 October 1850 at home. See Litzmann, *Clara Schumann*, p. 229.

Example 4.6
(i) Corelli, Concerto Grosso in G minor, Allegro
(ii) Schumann, 'Rhenish' Symphony, finale

(i)

bb. 1–2   bb. 4–5

(ii)

Lebhaft

quickly move through the major (most strikingly in the G minor work).
Schumann thus creates a strongly animated yet stylistically unified
sequel which has been seen by many commentators as a metaphor for the
movement from the dark interior of the cathedral, as represented by the
heavy minor chords with which the fourth movement ends, into the
bright light of day (Ex. 4.6).

If Schumann's ideal of a 'national' character in the work is particularly apparent in the musical edifice he builds in the fourth movement and
its animated sequel, a comparably picturesque quality emerges in the second movement as well. The title 'Scherzo' is functional rather than stylistic: it represents the dance-equivalent movement in a four-movement
scheme. The steadily-moving idea in 3/4 in regular eight-bar phrasing is,
however, far removed from that associated with the term 'Scherzo' in the
period or in Schumann's other works. Gál characterises it as a 'sturdy,
slowish minuet or *ländler*',[26] also stressing its relation to German folk-
song in its simple diatonic style, both as manifest in the works of the
Viennese classics and elsewhere in Schumann's own music, such as
Kinderszenen or the *Album für die Jugend*. Schauffler locates its character
within Schumann's work more precisely in stating that 'it manages to
sound like . . . "The Happy Farmer" ["Der fröhliche Landmann" from

26. Gál, *Orchestral Music*, p. 25.

Example 4.7
(i) Schumann, 'The Happy Farmer' ('Der fröhliche Landmann')
(ii) Berlioz, *Harold in Italy*, Serenade

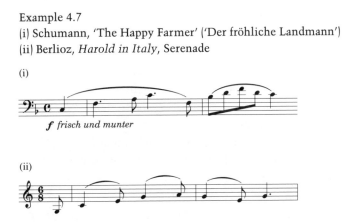

Clavierstücke für die Jugend] all dressed up in gala attire and sedately cel-
ebrating'.[27] But the influence of a popular style is not restricted to German
music. Another obvious stylistic link with the movement's open-air and
picturesque character is found in a work Schumann would have known
well by this time, Berlioz's *Harold in Italy*, the 'Serenade' of which has a
strikingly similar opening shape, although the rhythmic disposition
within the metre is different (Ex. 4.7).

    As well as in its shape, Berlioz's movement could also have provided
Schumann with a distinctive precedent for a picturesque movement
within a modern symphonic context. A more precise connection with
Schumann's avowed subject matter occurs early in the reception history,
where the idiom of the movement is associated with the river Rhine itself.
The early analytical account mentioned above describes the movement as
representing 'a comfortable life in the Rhineland: one thinks of beautiful
journeys on the water, between vine-green hills and friendly vintage-
festivals'.[28] After the first performance, Richard Pohl confirmed such an
interpretation of the movement – 'the second movement: Rhine journey',[29] while in later years Philipp Spitta credited the movement with 'the
romance . . . which hovers round the Rhine and its multitude of songs and
legends'.[30] The image of a river-journey is not prompted merely by the
even rhythm and steady movement of the parts, but also by the sectional

27. Robert H. Schauffler, *Florestan: The Life and Work of Robert Schumann*
(New York: Dover, 1963), p. 412.
28. See Kapp, *Schumann, Sinfonie Nr. 3*, p. 189.
29. See Boetticher, *Schumann*, p. 335.
30. Philipp Spitta, article 'Schumann' in *Grove's Dictionary of Music and
Musicians*, 2nd edn, ed. J. A.Fuller-Maitland (London: Macmillan), vol. iv,
p. 376.

structure, which has the capacity to effect the disclosure of new musical vistas, just as does the winding river, either through harmonic and rhythmic changes, or through striking instrumental imagery – as at the entry of the brass at b. 32, which immediately attracts the listener's attention to itself against the structural norms. In this respect, the movement bears comparison with Smetana's 'Vltava' from *Ma Vlast*, perhaps the classic depiction in music of the course of a river.

The character of the third movement lends itself less readily to picturesque images. The most compact and intimate of the five, it represents the still centre of the work. The early designation 'Intermezzo', though never included in the autograph or the published score, has clear connections with other Schumann works. Like the 'Intermezzo' of the Piano Concerto, it possess a story-telling quality which arises through the repetition of an intimate semiquaver figure which is common to both. Indeed the use of a similar figure, if in a somewhat quicker tempo, in the *Märchenerzählungen* (Fairytales), Op. 132 for piano trio seems to validate this interpretation (Ex. 4.8).[31]

Example 4.8
(i) 'Rhenish' Symphony, fourth movement
(ii) Piano Concerto, second movement
(iii) *Märchenerzählungen* No. 1

Of all the movements, the first is the least obviously 'popular' or picturesque in character. Rightly noted by Arnold Whittall as 'Schumann's finest single contribution to the genre',[32] this energetic and buoyant E♭ movement in 3/4 time generates a greater sense of span and growth than any of Schumann's other symphonic first movements, transcending their generally short-breathed patterns of rhythmic repetition and clear antecedent–consequent relationship, even that of the powerfully directed Fourth Symphony. By comparison, the single span of the first fourteen-bar

31. Carner implies a similar view in linking the 'intimate symphonic miniature', which he, quite independently, terms 'an intermezzo', to the 'Romanza' of the Fourth Symphony (Gerald Abraham, *Schumann: A Symposium* (London: Oxford University Press, 1952), p. 235) and echoes Schauffler in also relating it to to the world of *Kinderszenen* (Schauffler, *Florestan*, p. 412).

32. Arnold Whittall, *Romantic Music: A Concise History* (London: Thames and Hudson, 1987), p. 41.

theme (the 'extra' two bars arise from a retransition back to the main idea), prompts a second theme which is merely an aside, part of an ongoing momentum, rather than a separate self-contained idea, as is the case in the parallel symphonic movements. Despite its scope, therefore, the movement still communicates, like the other movements, the sense of a single state, or even 'scene'.[33] The momentum almost turns the driving 3/4 bars into double bars of 6/4 at times, especially when a hemiola effect is created by syncopation in the supporting chords, as at the recapitulation at bb. 411–16.

But if the movement is not 'popular' in the picturesque sense, its 'national' character within the tradition of the symphony can be seen in its obvious relation to one of its greatest examples – the first movement of Beethoven's 'Eroica' Symphony. The coincidence of key (E♭ major), triadically based theme, triple metre – unusual for a symphonic first movement – and the striking rhythmic features which emerge from this, to which can be added the very direct opening with no introduction (a feature strikingly independent of the other Schumann symphonic first movements which preceded it) – point to the 'Eroica' as the model. Indeed, the fact that Schumann's earliest symphonic effort was in E♭ and displayed rhythmic features already clearly reflecting an acquaintance with Beethoven's striking use of syncopation, confirms the lineage. But the links can be traced beyond the many stylistic features learned from Beethoven into direct structural parallels.

A comparison of the development sections of both works reveals an apparently conscious effort on Schumann's part to use the 'Eroica' movement to provide the weight and variety lacking in the largely sequential developments of the other symphonies. (It might even be argued that Schumann's working towards the recapitulation is almost overdone in its clear emulation of Beethovenian procedures.) The opening bars of the development section, bb. 185–97, clearly establish the figure which will permeate the texture until the new texture of the second subject takes over at b. 247, to which the figure serves as a countersubject at b. 239. The first part of the development of the 'Eroica' Symphony from bb. 167 to 179 is a built on a similar figure which recurs at b. 225 within successive stages of contrapuntal working, whereas Schumann's section extends the same ideas (Ex. 4.9).

33. When commending the *Rheinweinlied* to his publisher on 22 April 1853, Schumann draws attention to its 'broad character', observing further 'I think . . . it will be welcomed on the Rhine', a comment of possible relevance to his intention with the character of the symphonic movement. See Erler, *Robert Schumanns Leben*, vol. II, p. 191.

Example 4.9
(i) Schumann 'Rhenish' Symphony, first movement
(ii) Beethoven, 'Eroica' Symphony, first movement

(i)

b. 193

(ii)

b. 167

Although Beethoven is intent on a much more varied structure than is Schumann, the scope of his preparation for the recapitulation is a major feature emulated in the parallel Schumann passage. Beethoven establishes the preparatory dominant at b. 338, elaborating it through changes of mode and sequential harmony which lead to the tonicisation of C♭ major (b. 366) that functions as the lowered-sixth preparation for the stepwise movement to the dominant. This preparation, however, constantly alternates between major and minor forms of the implied 6/4 chord, before the famous 'dissonant' entry of the first theme on solo horn heralds the reprise at b. 398. Schumann employs a similarly long-term preparation, with the cadential 6/4 first established at b. 367 against the first subject, though this harmony is retained essentially intact until the recapitulation proper restates theme and harmony at b. 411, again prepared by the lower sixth in the bass. Schumann additionally exploits the lowered sixth as a tonal area in itself, notated as B major, though prior to the first preparatory 6/4 (b. 281, resolving to B♭, b. 303). In bringing the first subject back so powerfully over 6/4 harmony he turns Beethoven's principle to a use ideally suited to his own material (Ex. 4.10). No other model could have stimulated Schumann to such a structurally adventurous passage. And since the composer in question was also a native of Bonn, a Rhineland city, closely situated to Cologne, the possibility of an extra-musical stimulus on this movement cannot also be excluded from Schumann's general attribution of regional association.

III

The character of the first movement signals and determines the clearly defined structural contour of the work as a whole. Had Schumann wished to 'mirror pieces of life' through a sequence of evocative or descriptive scenes of the kind exemplified by the inner three movements, he would have produced a work of a very different type. Following such an expansive first movement, the inner movements inevitably bring an expecta-

Example 4.10
(i) Beethoven, 'Eroica' Symphony, first movement
(ii) Schumann, 'Rhenish' Symphony, first movement

(i)

(ii)

tion of a comparably powerful last movement, a finale as summation and
resolution. In fact, in the scope of the finale, Schumann goes beyond providing mere balance. This close-knit and cumulative movement, certainly
the most ingeniously planned of any of his symphonic finales, offers an
ideal structural resolution, yet as part of a very different and more individual 'plot'. The unique large-scale structure of the work thus reveals two
areas for examination in symphonic terms. First, the outer contour and
balance of the movements, particularly in relation to symphonic tradition, including the works of Schumann himself. Secondly, the inner structural processes, especially the role of motive: the work displays a
remarkable degree of motivic integration, which provides a background
from which the composer can effect the contrast of tension or relaxation
in the unfolding of the structure. While the unusual five-movement
design makes evaluation of the structure in relation to symphonic tradition problematic, herein also lies its fascination. Any structural analysis
must centre on the role of the fourth movement, which can be seen from
two different standpoints: either simply as an additional movement, linking to one or more of its flanking movements in a four-movement scheme,
or as an additional movement whose specific formal character determines
for it an equal role among the movements, and thus defines the unique formal character of the work as a whole.

The first view sees the fourth movement as a transition between the
slow, third, movement and finale. In a work which already contains a
Scherzo movement placed second, it therefore appears as the first part of
a composite paired unit, with preparation and resolution. The 'Pastoral'

Symphony offers the direct parallel in having an additional movement, 'The Storm', placed fourth. Yet although distinct in character and title, it is connected to the third and fifth movements and functions as an addition, an enlargement of the four-movement norm. Chronologically 'The Storm' extends the physical connection established in the Fifth Symphony between the pizzicato recapitulation of the Scherzo and the Finale, which gradually emerges as the goal of the cumulative transition into which it leads. Though the characters of the movements of the 'Pastoral' Symphony and their sequence are, as required by its programme, quite different from those of the 'Rhenish' Symphony, the explosions of 'The Storm' and their resolution in a peaceful 'Hymn of Thanksgiving' reveal the same principle of preparation and resolution through transition between movements. The resolution of Schumann's own Fourth Symphony follows closely the model of the transition in Beethoven's Fifth, achieving a connection from the quiet reprise of the second trio with the finale which is strikingly close in figuration as well as in principle. This, in turn, is the result of thematic similarities between the two Beethoven movements and Schumann's finale. Schumann's sensitivity to this point of symphonic structure is also apparent in the First and Second Symphonies; in the former he uses a harmonic transition, while in the latter the beginning of the finale theme is designed so as to effect a harmonic transition from the third to the fourth movement. By contrast, the fourth movement of the 'Rhenish' Symphony is a separate movement, but has an analogous function. The finale releases the constraints of the preceding movement's variation form, an effect intensified by its coda of the fourth movement, whose harmonic ambivalence (between the tonic and its enharmonic submediant B major, at the entry of the fanfare) hints at a transitional function. It is also feasible to interpret the 'March' of the 'Fantastic Symphony' as transitional. Though it is self-contained, its character anticipates the Finale and offers a distinct contrast with the third movement, which clearly emulates the 'Pastoral' Symphony.

The view of Schumann's fourth movement as transition and preparation ignores, however, its formal dimension. Unlike the 'Pastoral' or indeed the Berlioz March which either suspend or blur formal division, it has a clear formal structure: Theme (bb. 1–8, including codetta); Variation 1 (bb. 8–23); Variation 2 (bb. 23–44); Variation 3 (shortened recapitulation of Variation 1, bb. 44–52); Coda (bb. 52–67). The variation form of the fourth movement has no precedent among the symphonic works Schumann would have known, since variation structure had been traditionally associated either with slow movements, or, less frequently, with finales. Variation form was clearly inappropriate in a movement designed

to anticipate the Finale and provide a contrast with the Third. It finds its
larger context through the way the Scherzo is designed, also with a variation dimension. Together with the fourth movement, the Scherzo frames
the central 'Intermezzo' to create a middle section for the entire structure,
outlining a broad A B A Coda scheme in which the variation at the point of
reprise serves a double function. The scheme of the Scherzo is as follows:
Theme (in two equal parts), bb. 1–16 (with second-half repeat); Variation 1,
bb. 16–32 (likewise); Variation 2, bb. 32–48 (both halves repeated);
Variation 3, bb. 49–79 (modulating development of main theme);
Variation 4, bb. 79–115 (varied reprise of main theme); Coda, bb. 115–33.
This symmetry of form, to which can be added the fact that both movements end more freely than the preceding main parts, provides an additional element of balance for the work.

The formal shaping of the symphony comes into much clearer focus
once its motivic working is revealed. The principle of motivic recurrence
to be found in many Schumann works is deployed with a new directness
and thoroughness in this work. In structural function it even bids to
exceed that of the Fourth Symphony, the work traditionally regarded as
most extensively based on a single motive. In the 'Rhenish' Symphony an
even more elemental shape – in essence simply a triad – permits more per-
vasive links between the movements while also achieving the 'popular'
character Schumann wanted. The motive has often been noted in the literature in general triadic terms. Yet in the most thoroughgoing account of
its manifestations in the work, David Epstein designates it 'a 6/4 tonic
triad variously ornamented',[34] a description which permits him to show
a distinction between what he terms the notion of 'triad as norm versus
triad as a unique concept': the latter function pervades the Symphony
as its *Grundgestalt* (Ex. 4.11).

Example 4.11   'Rhenish' Symphony, first movement: Epstein's notation
of the first subject

Although Epstein's designation naturally implies a harmonic setting, the motive appears in a 6/4 harmonic context only in the development section of the first movement, where Epstein shows its large-scale
unfolding in a 'melodic overline' to demonstrate its *Grundgestalt* func-

34. David Epstein, *Beyond Orpheus: Studies in Musical Structure* (Cambridge,
    Mass.: MIT Press, 1979), p. 149.

tion. This example, and others adduced by Epstein, serves to demonstrate the profoundly organic nature of the work. But although the *Grundgestalt* function validates the work's symphonic credentials, it is another aspect of its motivic organisation that I wish to explore here: the role of the motive as a constant in varied contexts, rather than its familiar role as a transformed element in developing variation. Though typically concerning only the first presentation of the main themes of the work rather than entire movements, the maintenance of a constant constitutes an original compositional feature, and has an unmistakable aural identity (not necessarily a *Grundgestalt* property).

The identification of the motivic structure takes on a new perspective when the motivic kernel of the main theme of the fourth movement is examined. Since Wasielewski implies that the fourth movement had a primary role in the compositional process,[35] it may therefore constitute the motivic source of the work. If we assume this to be the case, a sharper picture of motivic function emerges, one which emphasises both the connection of the fourth movement and Finale and the function of the fourth as a transition. A distinctive sequence of motivic generation then emerges in two stages: (1) from fourth movement into the Finale, and from the fourth back to the first, with the Scherzo and the third drawn from the first; (2) from the Finale to first, the first movement recalled and reintegrated into the finale's coda to complete the work as a closed structure. In the fourth movement, the interval of the fourth can be seen as constituting the source of the main theme, built on a progression of three fourths, repeated in sequence to reach a high E♭ which falls back to the lower tonic to complete the theme. Alternatively, the theme can be seen as drawn from two three-note motives with the intervals of the fourth and the semitone, differently arranged, treated similarly. Harmonically, the theme emerges as a decoration of the tonic triad in minor with auxiliary notes to the tonic and the third (Ex. 4.12).

35. Wasielewski, *Schumann*, p. 173. The autograph sketch evidence gives little clue to the priority of the generation of ideas. Although the *Haushaltbuch* notes the days on which Schumann worked on the various movements, and when he completed them, the surviving sketches (Paris, Bibliothèque Nationale MS 329, MS334) are all in fairly neat continuity sketches which show significant working only in the complex counterpoint of the fourth movement, and suggest that the ideas were already well established in his mind. Since Schumann's first experience of the cathedral was as early as the end of September, and the composition is not recorded as beginning until November, this leaves a period of at least a month in which Schumann could have registered his musical impressions in preliminary sketch form or in his imagination. He noted on 1 December 'still brooding over the Adagio of the Symphony', and on 4 December 'reasonably finished with the Symphony'.

Example 4.12 Fourth movement: motivic content of theme, bb. 1–2

Of the distinctive shapes to emerge from the fourth-movement material, the most directly related appears in the exposition of the Finale, where the interval of rising fourth is reintroduced in four clearly defined stages at regular structural points, until the material of the fourth movement is more extensively incorporated into the coda: (1) the first theme, built on the filled-in rising fourth, which then falls back; (2) the syncopated figure (b. 46) at the beginning of the transition to the dominant B♭, which outlines the main theme of the fourth movement more overtly by giving it a distinctive rhythmic profile; (3) the diminished versions of the fourth movement motive (b. 6, reworked at b. 23), here woven into the 'development' of the Finale (bb. 99–125) and powerfully contributing to its cumulative sense prior to the recapitulation; (4) the recapitulation (b. 153), heralded by a fanfare figure (b. 149) which echoes the fanfare at b. 129, the latter in turn seeming to extend the fanfare of the fourth movement (bb. 52–8), a link intensified by their shared B♭ major chord. While the details of the resolution to the 6/4 and tonic E♭ are different – the finale passage reaches its resolution indirectly – the goal is the same. In the Finale the fanfare is capped by a climactic minim figure crucial to the generation of the concluding coda theme, though it also refers back to one of the fourth movement's three-note motives, which is especially emphasised at the end of that movement (bb. 60–3: Fig. 'y' in Ex. 4.13).

At the end of the (slightly truncated) recapitulation, this motive now forms part of the chorale-like sequence, the 'fermatas' of which are reinforced by orchestral articulation to produce a great sense of structural climax. A reprise of the fourth-movement motive in superimposition and sequence over a prolonged 6/4 chord is crowned with another fanfare (b. 394) which appears to adapt the preceding fanfare to the shape of the first subject of the work, with its distinctive stress on the pitch C. The remaining bars of peroration continue to weave in the rising-fourth figure of the fourth movement and closely parallel the affirmative mood of the first-movement conclusion (Ex. 4.14).

This movement is notable for its formal unfolding, in which the expositional and developmental sections have constrained roles, there being no second subject in a contrasting key nor significant modulation. Their purpose is rather to provide a context for the gradual reintegration of earlier material, the emphasis shifted rather to the latter part of the move-

Example 4.13   Finale

ment to create a recapitulation and coda for the entire work. Thus the symphony is analogous to the Piano Quintet in E♭, whose finale recalls the first subject of the work, and to the finale of the Second Symphony. Newcomb's comment that the latter 'starts as one thing and becomes another, and this formal transformation is part of its meaning'[36] is equally appropriate to the 'Rhenish' Symphony: the transformation of the norm (rondo or sonata movement) for a specific formal purpose produces what might be characterised as modified sonata form.

The link back to the first movement of the 'Rhenish' (bb. 294–9) may perhaps disclose the origin of its first subject in the compositional process, though equally the theme could have arisen through the independent juxtaposition of fourth intervals. Either way, movements 1–3 stand apart

36. Anthony Newcomb, '"Between Absolute and Program Music": Schumann's Second Symphony', *19th-Century Music*, 7/3 (1984), 240. Newcomb discusses 'plot archetypes' in Schumann more generally, p. 234.

Example 4.14   Finale

Example 4.15
(i) First movement, bb. 1–5
(ii) Second movement (transposed), bb. 1–2
(iii) Third movement, bb. 1–4

from movements 4–5 in essential motivic contour. The second movement theme draws directly on the contour of the first, though rising through the initial fourth rather than falling. The third movement abstracts the rising sixth as well as the outlining octave from the first theme to further emphasise the triad, and also exploits the function of the neighbour note already present in the themes of the first movement and Scherzo (Ex. 4.15). Motivically, therefore, there exists a three-stage process, in which the first two movements are clearly related, and the third more distantly. This yields in the fourth movement to a pattern more overtly dependent on the interval of a fourth, which is then dominant until the circle of the work is closed with the reintroduction of the essential contour of its opening theme in the Finale.

Were the individual movements of the 'Rhenish' Symphony merely
united by a common thematic shape and its derivatives, the work would
not necessarily achieve its teleological formal character, especially its
sense of directed resolution secured through the structural role of the
motive. Schumann treats its harmonic setting, in particular the harmonic
context of the distinctive sixth above the bass, variously according to its
structural purpose, to create tension requiring resolution thus generating
musical space, and, consequently, relaxation inviting contrast or variation. The three stages of the motivic shaping are naturally complemented
by this harmonic dimension, and throw new light on it. In the first movement the first subject presents the auxiliary sixth, C, as a strong dissonance against the tonic chord, a feature emphasised rhythmically, so
that the sixth requires prolongation through seven bars to achieve its
satisfactory resolution in the perfect cadence at bb. 13–14 (Ex. 4.16).

Example 4.16   First movement, bb. 1–14

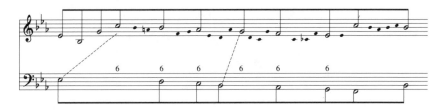

This version recurs only once in the movement (b. 57, fig. A) at the
commencement of the transition to the second theme, where its effect is
reinforced by scoring and register (and also in its course by added counterpoints). Elsewhere the effect of the dissonant C of the theme is mollified.
The most prominent example is its appearance over a 6/4 chord in a cadential context, most strikingly at the preparation for, and at the point of,
recapitulation (though this is anticipated in the exposition bb. 21–2)
(Ex. 4.17). In these passages, though a dissonance still exists between the
B♭ in the bass and the C of the upper part, the stepwise resolution of the
latter to the octave rather than the fifth of the first presentation permits a
more direct resolution in a V–I cadence, minimising its force and thus
maximising the striking effect of the extensive prolongation of this structural moment (b. 411; see above). In other places the omnipresent opening
motive of the first subject is more completely accommodated to the
harmony in the course of the movement. As early as b. 23, the rising

Example 4.17   First movement, bb. 371–7

Example 4.18   First movement

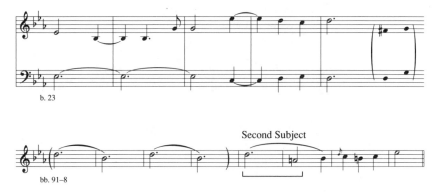

sixth is transformed into an octave and creates consonant harmony in the modulatory passage passage towards G major which paraphrases the first subject group; the falling fourth finds a very neutral place within the singing second theme (it is signalled in the preparation from b. 91) (Ex. 4.18).

In the Scherzo and third movements, the harmonic accommodation of dissonance occurs predominantly in the main themes. The opening theme of the second movement presents the sixth above the bass, A in C major (C in E♭, transposed in Ex. 4.18) as a brief neighbouring note to the fifth degree. This remains elaborative rather than structural since the strict repetition of the rhythm of the theme attached the neighbouring note to a variety of pitches (Ex. 4.19). Although strong harmonic tension is later created by the placing of the variant figure at bb. 32–47 against a sustained tonic bass, the general impression through the movement is one of a stable and contained treatment of the basic motive as it dominates the main theme. This impression is even stronger in the third movement, where the first three bars of the theme lie entirely on tonic harmony, with double neighbouring notes to the third and fifth of the triad. The analogous point of dissonance is now even less stressed, a point of interest since the harmonic progression of the theme is very similar despite its more

144 · Michael Musgrave

Example 4.19   Second movement, bb. 1–2

etc.

bb. 1–2

Example 4.20
(i) Third movement (transposed), bb. 1–5
(ii) Third movement, bb. 48–54

(i)

bb. 1–2

(ii)

b. 48

b. 52

mobile upper voice to that of the first subject of the first movement: it
almost might be seen as a recomposition. So tranquil is the conclusion of
the movement that the subtle introduction of a higher level of dissonance
associated with the rising-fourth figure against pedal harmony (b. 48) is
hardly noticed. Stated again prior to the restoration of the final tonic, this
provides a subtle aural link to the movement to follow (Ex. 4.20).

The different disposition of the interval of the fourth in the theme of
the fourth movement gives it a different role. Rather than being presented
over tonic harmony, the theme is harmonised by a walking bass, which
accommodates the fourths, a feature naturally retained through the variations. Moreover, the fact that this disposition of fourths tends to reinforce
the triad by emphasising the third and fifth rather than creating a dissonance against the tonic means that it can be accommodated to that triad
if the harmony is frozen, as occurs at the close of the movement (bb. 61–3)

Example 4.21   Fourth movement

bb. 1–4

bb. 61–4

Example 4.22   Fourth movement, b. 52

(Ex. 4.21). Thus a greater point of motivic interest occurs at b. 52 (Fig. D) where the tonality switches to B major for a brass and wind fanfare on a stark chord in which the rising fourth to tonic is consonant: F♯ to B as part of the arpeggio D♯ to D♯, resolving to the E♭ minor chord in 6/4 position by step (Ex. 4.22).

The first function of the main theme of the finale is to reintegrate the still insufficiently stable E♭, on which the top line concludes, as the unambiguous tonic of E♭ major. This is done, for the first time in the themes of the work, by exploiting the upper tetrachord B♭–E♭. The walking bass which counterpoints this rising stepwise progression is consonant harmonically, and so is the more overt presentation of the interval of the fourth at b. 48 and its subsequent incorporation into the elaboration (Ex. 4.23). The diminished version of the motive of the fourth movement (b. 99) is reintroduced in the course of a modulation. But with the appearance of the arpeggio fanfare figure (b. 133) which heralds the climax of the development section, an important cadence is inaugurated which presents this figure first on a 6/4 in B♭, then in the tonic, E♭,

Example 4.23   Finale, bb. 1–2

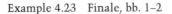

Example 4.24   Finale, bb. 153, 156

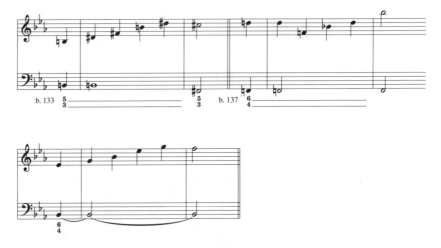

to usher in the recapitulation, so that it has the effect of making the antecedent of the first subject (bb. 153–61) appear to take the role of its consequent, until the function of the latter becomes clear (Ex. 4.24). The final stage of motivic reincorporation occurs at the beginning of the coda (b. 244) where the 'chorale' progression is given with orchestral reinforcement of each phrase firmly within the tonic. The prolonged 6/4 which supports the superimposed fourths of the fourth movement returns to give the strongest reference so far to that movement. The 6/4 leads to the transformed fanfare (bb. 294–8) recalling the first movement, though it now resolves for the first time to the dominant seventh on Bb via clinching diminished progressions, and thus to the concluding (*schneller*) passage which reinforces the tonic and incorporates final references to the rising fourth figure of the fourth movement (Ex. 4.25).

IV

The 'Rhenish' Symphony is a remarkable achievement. Schumann creates five quite distinctive, often picturesque movements, communicating an

Example 4.25   Finale, bb. 294–8

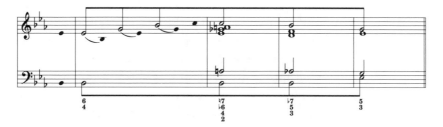

expressiveness which has easily lent itself to the provision of titles,[37] yet
so disposed and related as to create a large-scale structure which is effective in purely structural terms. Only a composer with Schumann's gift for
combining short movements according to a narrative principle (in his
groups of songs or piano pieces), and also for experiment with classical
instrumental forms, could have achieved such a unity between a sequence
of static scenes, or *Seelenzustände*, and the dynamics of a large-scale
structure. Such a very personal work could have no natural successor.
The 'second age of the symphony' was to keep to four-movement
schemes. Whatever the extent of their secret references, in outer form
at least the symphonies of Bruckner, Brahms and Dvořák keep to
Beethovenian and Schubertian models and achieve their expression
through the intensification of musical processes and characteristics rather
than through a broadened concept of the genre. And when the next generation again sought more openly to expand the generic boundaries of the
symphony and reintegrate vocal and dramatic aspects, especially in the
works of Zemlinsky and Mahler, the scale had widened vastly beyond the
scope of Schumann's still quite intimately scaled work, which he
described to his publisher as no longer than a four-movement symphony.
Where the influence of Schumann's symphonic thought on later composers has been cited, it is invariably in connection with the D minor
Symphony, whose intricate thematic transformation serves the highly
individual formal structure first designated as 'symphonic fantasy'.

But if the 'Rhenish' Symphony is of its time, it possessed one important structural feature which anticipates the future within the field of
purely instrumental music: the principle of return. Unlike the plot arche-

37. For a recent survey of responses to the extra-musical dimension of the work
see Todd, ed., *Schumann and his World*. For discussion of the visual and
picturesque associations of the work see Leon Botstein, 'History, Rhetoric
and the Self: Robert Schumann and Music-Making in German-Speaking
Europe, 1800–1860', in Todd, ed., *Schumann and his World*, pp. 35–9.

types of the D minor symphony, which links Beethoven's Fifth to Brahms's First (and even Mahler's Second), often designated 'per ardua ad astra', Schumann invokes the principle of intervallic retention and eventual motivic return which had clear consequences for Brahms. The Third Symphony and the *Requiem* both create highly individual forms by recalling opening material variously transformed, and the effect relies on a subtle process of motivic retention and variation, the achievement of contrast and the re-establishment of connection. It was to be a powerful principle in the works of Brahms's successors, perhaps most notably Schoenberg. In surveying the place of the 'Rhenish' Symphony within the tradition of the nineteenth-century symphony, therefore, it can be seen not merely as reflecting upon issues of the past, but, in its very individual way, anticipating those of the future.

5

The poetry of Debussy's *En blanc et noir*

Jonathan Dunsby

I want to preface discussing Debussy's thought by discussing a certain history, briefly, if only to indicate why this essay will be doggedly inconclusive, although it is dedicated to the spirit of discovery.[1]

Carl Dahlhaus opened up by grand statement the idea of a space between Romanticism and Modernism.[2] Obviously, there is a real attraction here, in the comfort of seeing some music as specially in transition,[3] as if music were not always so. I sense it is no accident how neatly, between those two commanding volumes *Romantic Music*[4] and *Music Since the First World War*,[5] Arnold Whittall circumscribes the works of Debussy, though he is mentioned in both books. Debussy is a composer who has always decisively resisted analytical flattery, but it is frustrating, nevertheless, not to be able to point to a critico-analytical literature which shows how what Debussy did stands head and shoulders above the compositional crowd.[6] One gets the impression from David Lewin, for example, that Debussy can be sucked in to theory debate along with

1. Much of the initial historical and literary research for this chapter was completed in 1992 when I was fortunate to hold a visiting fellowship in Oxford, and I am most grateful to the Warden and Fellows of New College for the opportunity. I am also grateful to Marie Rolf of Eastman School of Music for reading a version of this material at the 1993 American Musicological Society Annual Meeting that I was unable to attend; it resulted in some helpful, corrective feedback from various expert quarters.
2. *Between Romanticism and Modernism: Four Studies in the Music of the Later Nineteenth Century*, trans. Mary Whittall (Berkeley: University of California Press, 1980).
3. Jim Samson, *Music in Transition: A Study of Tonal Expansion and Atonality* (London: J. M. Dent, 1977).
4. Arnold Whittall, *Romantic Music: A Concise History from Schubert to Sibelius* (London: Thames and Hudson, 1987).
5. Arnold Whittall, *Music Since the First World War* (London: J. M. Dent, 1977).
6. Any reader who may be jolted by the idea of analysis as a test of artistic worth is referred to Victor Zuckerkandl's *Man the Musician: Sound and Symbol* (Princeton University Press, 1973), vol. II, pp. 206–14, where the author takes Edmund Gurney to task for showing only theoretical similarities between good and bad melodies, although proper analysis, it appears,

Dallapiccola, Stockhausen and Webern as if he were a card-carrying modernist.[7] Most critics take Debussy as some sort of modernist starting point, and thus he is colonised in historiography, 'just as in 'pure' analysis (voice-leading, semiological, octatonic, golden section, and so on). Well, let us begin to put this straight. After half a predicted lifetime of playing and pondering Debussy's musical notes, which better analysts and historians than I have failed to sew up in prose (Whittall, like the best of the others, knows just what he is doing, or rather not doing), I turn, in tribute, to a little of Debussy's verbal legacy, safe in the knowledge that this work demands to be attempted unless we are to ignore matters about which the composer cared very deeply.

The poetry in Debussy's soul is no poor hare to hunt. I do not call this music singular with the customary rhetorical pathos by which analysts covet the listener's sympathy. I am not trying to persuade you that *En blanc et noir* is artistically unique, and unquestionably worth close attention. On the contrary, to claim that would be to fly in the face of the reception-history of Debussy studies, in which this piece has been essentially ignored, and of compositional and theoretical studies of early twentieth-century music, in which to my knowledge it has been virtually written out of history. One might see this rectified if someone took it into their head to write a history of music for two pianos, from Brahms and Chabrier to Boulez, Ligeti and beyond – which I don't think has been done.[8] Even so, there has been a very long critical silence since 1915, and I commend Roger Nichols for daring to call *En blanc et noir* a 'masterpiece'.[9] If it is truly a masterpiece, it is one of the most taken-for-granted masterpieces of post-Romantic music.

The great tangle of poietic information in the case of Debussy seems to me to have inhibited rather than nourished research on his music. Jarocinski's *Debussy: Impressionism and Symbolism*[10] is ironic

can reveal sharp aesthetic differences! It must be a matter for regret, however, that Zuckerkandl was so imperious in his purview of the repertoire. Debussy, who wrote when hearing that Japan was thinking of joining in the First World War 'why not the Martians while we're about it?', would have called this purview just another case of xenophobia.

7. See 'A Transformational Basis for Form and Prolongation in Debussy's "Feux d'artifice"' in David Lewin, *Musical Form and Transformation: 4 Analytic Essays* (New Haven: Yale University Press, 1993), pp. 97–159.
8. Hans Moldenhauer's interesting *Duo-Pianism: A Dissertation* (Chicago: Chicago Musical College Press, 1950) is a descriptive catalogue.
9. Roger Nichols, 'Debussy', in *The New Grove Twentieth-Century French Masters*, ed. J.-M. Nectoux (London: Macmillan, 1986), p. 99.
10. Trans. R. Myers (London: Eulenburg Books, 1976).

testimony, for it claims just this about the first fifty years of work on
Debussy, then proceeds to add enough well-intentioned entanglement to
see us safely if uneasily into the next century. As evidence for the pro-
posal, one need only turn to the utterly threatening opinion of William
Austin, 'utterly' because Austin was, if one historian could be, the definitive mid-century chronicler of early twentieth-century music, and
threatening because of the ideal agenda it sets for any conscientious
researcher:

> Debussy is one of the few composers whose whole work is relevant
> to the appreciation of each single piece. Late works illuminate the
> early ones, and early ones, in turn, when understood more thor-
> oughly than before, point to meanings in the late ones that we have
> missed when considering them separately.[11]

As if Austin's appeal to an essential musical intertextuality were not
enough, there is Debussy the man of opinion to contend with. Modern
books on nineteenth-century music would feel flawed, even alien without
their sentences that begin approximately 'Debussy believed that . . .' on all
sorts of key issues, not only Wagnerian (this is an of itself insignificant but
historiographically pertinent feature of both Plantinga's[12] and Whittall's
books on Romantic music). And to see what Debussy did and thought as
inevitable props in the act of writing the history of subsequent music is
simple enough, in fact a welcome, culturally reassuring mark of his pre-
eminent influences (so that, for example, no eyebrow need be raised when
Debussy first appears on stage in *Music Since the First World War* rather
casually, as a source of Bartók's style, alongside Liszt and Strauss, who
also need no introduction[13]).

I am struck most of all, however, by the gaps. Debussy falls into
the gap between Romantic music and music since the First World War.
He also falls into the gap between theory and history, colonised to some
extent as I have said, but also rather feared and neglected by both, out
of tune with ideologies then and since, very hard to 'place'. He is not
understood partly because he is a poet (thus no opus numbers). We can
read the poetry at work in a deliciously chiselled letter to Stravinsky:

11. *Music in the 20th Century: From Debussy through Stravinsky* (London:
    Dent, 1966), p. 6.
12. Leon Plantinga, *Romantic Music* (New York: Norton, 1984).
13. p. 31.

> You're surprised at my calling it *Jeux* and prefer 'Le Parc'! Please
> believe me, *Jeux* is better. For one thing it's shorter; and for another
> it's a convenient way of expressing the 'horrors' that take place
> between the three participants.[14]

And thus another, little 'gap' appears by analogy: what, in fact, does the
title 'En blanc et noir' mean? Léon Vallas says it is a 'rather vague' one.[15] Is
'Jeux' vague? Was it acceptable for Debussy to attach the word 'sketches'
to *La Mer*? Goodness knows what we are to make of the *Prelude to the
'Afternoon of a Faun'*. Titles are not only to play with, but to play at, for
instance by putting them at the end of each *Prélude*. Titles for Debussy
(and in this too he may as well be called the 'father' of musical modernism) are part of the poetry of creation. Unlike Stravinsky, and a little
unlike Schoenberg, he moved so easily between word and sound that we
can easily miss what he is up to. The resonances of 'En blanc et noir' are
vast, and probably, like all poetry, simply not finite. A number of these
resonances are now outlined.

In English, we say 'black and white'. One exception I have found is in
the idiom of and around chess – the struggle between the white queen and
the black queen, the white knight and the black, and in general we think
of the struggle between good and evil, not evil and good. My first proposi-
tion, then, is that (as we know in any case) *En blanc et noir* is a war piece,
and this is embodied in its title. For in French, too, the normal idiom is
'black and white', 'noir et blanc' or, sometimes, 'noir sur blanc'. In a letter
deploring Debussy's latest, quasi 'cubist' compositional monstrosities,
Saint-Saëns's memory fooled him into the actual inscription of the wraith
title *Noir et blanc*.[16] As will be revealed, the very words 'in white and
black' are Debussy's signal of struggle, and resignation.

Secondly, the piano keyboard is also an exception, to some extent: it
seems that the linguistic competence of most speakers would tip them
towards saying 'the white and black keys of the piano' rather than vice
versa. Is there anything 'white and black keys'ish about *En blanc et noir*?
Certainly: the octatonic scale, more specifically C major and F$\sharp$ major triads together, even more specifically *Petrushka*. Debussy adored this bal-
let, and told Stravinsky so:

14. *Debussy Letters*, ed. Francois Lesure and Roger Nichols, trans. Roger Nichols
    (London: Faber, 1987), p. 265.
15. *Claude Debussy: His Life and Works* (New York: Dover, 1973 [1933]), p. 255.
16. See *Oeuvres Complètes de Claude Debussy*, Série 1, vol. VIII, ed. Noël Lee,
    (Paris: Durand-Costallat, 1986), p. xx.

> Saturday 13 April 1912
>
> Cher ami
>
> Thanks to you I've spent a lovely Easter holiday in the company of Petrushka, the terrible Moor and the delightful ballerina. I imagine you too must have spent some incomparable moments with these three puppets.

> 5 November 1912
>
> But the good news is that here your name is mentioned once a day – at least – and your friend Chouchou [Debussy's daughter, then aged seven] has composed a fantasy on *Petrushka* which is enough to make a tiger roar . . . For all the punishments I threaten her with, she still goes on claiming 'you'd find it excellent'.

He also told Diaghilev some two years after *En blanc et noir* was composed:

> 26 May 1917
>
> *Petrushka* is definitely a masterpiece. They haven't anything of the sort in Germany and never will have.[17]

Is *En blanc et noir* a fantasy in white and black notes on *Petrushka*? There is certainly an exposition of the C plus F♯ major triad octatonic subset right from the first non-diatonic swerve of *En blanc et noir* (see Ex. 5. 1a), and much more specific resonance can be found (cf. Ex. 5.1b and 5.1c).

Thirdly, white and black may suggest *chiaroscuro*, and Debussy let out this secret twice in letters to Durand and Godet:

> 14 July 1915
>
> I must confess I've made a slight change in the colour of the second of the *Caprices* (Ballade de Villon contre les ennemis de la France); it was too profoundly black and almost as tragic as a 'Caprice' by Goya!

> Friday 4 February 1916
>
> Bring your brain to bear on *En blanc et noir* . . . These pieces draw their colour, their emotion, simply from the piano, like the 'greys' of Velázquez, if I may so suggest? Anyway all the orchestral musicians are at the front and those who are left behind – by whatever piece of administrative providence – are hard to put up with because they

17. *Letters*, ed. Lesure and Nichols, pp. 256, 265 and 327 respectively.

Example 5.1
(a) *En blanc et noir*, I, bb. 1–6
(b) Stravinsky, *Trois Mouvements de Pétrouchka*, No. II, 'Chez Pétrouchka',
bb. 1–12
(c) *En blanc et noir*, II, bb. 1–8

(a)

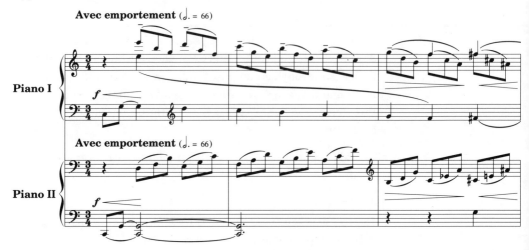

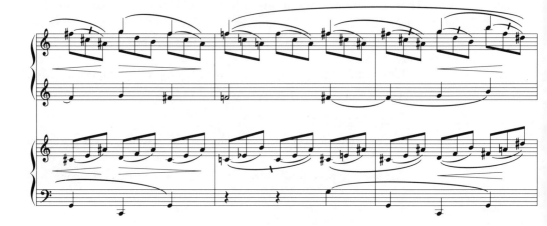

(b)

(c)

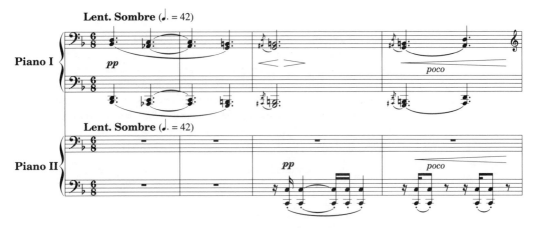

can't console themselves by comfortably hamming it through 'The Ride of Valkyries' as usual.[18]

Again the poetry of war speaks – his music can only be in white and black, that is, as piano music, because the Germans are killing the best orchestral players – and through it speaks the torture of this 'musicien français' par excellence.

The epigraph at the head of No. III is '*Yver, vous n'este qu'un vil[l]ain* (Charles d'Orléans)'. Those who infer ('*Yver*' meaning 'winter') a seasonal evocation will find plenty of snow-white and pitch-black music here, in the ethereal opening (which is, however, marked *Scherzando*), in the soft chromaticism of the *Poco meno mosso* beginning as in Ex. 5.2b,[19] and in virtually the entire final 'development' from where the reprise beginning at b. 84 is cut in to, thirteen bars later. The closing pages of *En blanc et noir* are stark indeed. Yet there is more poetry in the air here, for Debussy had already set the whole poem in the third of the *Trois Chansons de Charles d'Orléans* for four unaccompanied mixed voices, first performed in 1909:

18. *Ibid.*, pp. 297 and 314 respectively. I am indebted to Craig Ayrey for pointing out, among many other of his insights, the possible connection between 'En blanc et noir' and *chiaroscuro*, which is in French 'le clair-obscur'. Doubtless Debussy had seen reproductions of Goya's war-caprice drawings, which are indeed tragic in a way that he would have found teutonic and repulsive. The authoritative H. G. Schenk, in *The Mind of the European Romantics: An Essay in Cultural History* (London: Constable, 1966), confirms this interpretation:

> Goya concentrated so much on the portrayal of the most painful aspects of life that almost the whole œuvre of those last thirty-five years might be interpreted as the pictorial illustration to Schopenhauer's jeremiad in *Die Welt als Wille und Vorstellung* published nine years before Goya's death . . . It may be that his mind somehow anticipated the accentuated horrors of the twentieth century. One of the plates of the 'Desastres de la Guerra' shows us an amorphous group of starving and emasculated victims, old and young alike, all clad in rags, and on the other side of the picture two well-fed gentlemen, elegantly dressed, without the slightest touch of compassion on their faces. The caption reads: '¿Si son de otro linage?' (Do they belong to another race?). Another sinister plate conveys something of the horrific atmosphere of Buchenwald. (p. 62)

19. In *Oeuvres*, p. xx Noël Lee compares the theme in the second piano to the great closing theme of Stravinsky's *L'Oiseau de feu*, and Ex. 5.2c will show what a compelling derivation this appears to be; however, as I indicate in Ex. 5.2a and 5.2b, this firebird is blown by a chill wind.

Winter, you are no better than a rascal; Summer is pleasant and kind, as May and April can testify, accompanying it evening and morning.

Summer covers the fields, woods, and flowers with his verdant livery, and many other colo[u]rs too, according to nature.

But you, Winter, are too full of snow, wind, rain and hail. You ought to be exiled. [Not flattering you at all, I speak frankly.] Winter, you are no better than a rascal.[20]

Further to note 19, I suspect that Debussy has re-assembled an old narrative in *En blanc et noir*. Charles d'Orléans's 'wind' is here part of the exposition of Winter rather than its return, 'Le vent sur la plaine' absorbed into the first secondary musical image of '*Yver*' (cf. Ex. 5.2a and 5.2b).[21] On the other hand, it is explained poetically how 'Summer' can appear, festive, I would say, in Ex. 5.2d, and as an ambivalent impression in Ex. 5.2e, and in Ex. 5.2f, the bars cut off by the reprise. If Debussy is ready to quote a

20. This translation is taken from *The Poetic Debussy: A Collection of His Song Texts and Selected Letters*, ed. Margaret C. Cobb (Boston: Northeastern University Press, 1982), p. 145. Cobb notes that 'the penultimate line is omitted', but this is not nowadays true: 'Sans point flater je parle plein' appears in the varied reprise in all parts in bb. 48–53, and I have added my translation of it in square brackets. I have not been able to examine the source materials from which Cobb may have been working. The scansion of the last two lines is precisely the same, and it may be that Debussy originally used the last line for the entire reprise. This would make sense musically, with the E minor opening section and reprise occupied only with the first and last lines that are the same – the *En blanc et noir* epigraph. Poetically, however, there is much to be said for a reprise that points up the 'Sans point flater' clause first. The author's strategy was to transform into Summer at the first piquant opportunity in the first verse, then exclude it absolutely, crushingly from the third. The composer takes what is probably the only musical option by putting everything about Summer and the dramatic return to Winter into a second 'verse', the middle section, which moves from a 'pleasant' tonic major through unstable harmonies (vocal accents, vocal staccatos, *forte crescendo*) to a sinister secondary dominant that gives way to the dominant minor of the reprise (brought to the tonic minor by fugal answer). Obviously, there is no question of Debussy committing poetic 'disrespect', any more than we can speak of it in Schumann's reorganisations of the technically transcendent Heine in *Dichterliebe*. Any uncertainty there may be about what Debussy did with the penultimate line of the poem is irrelevant to all my comments in the main part of this text.

21. Subsequently to becoming convinced of this correlation, I discovered that it was mentioned in general by G. M. Gatti in 'The Piano Works of Claude Debussy', *The Musical Quarterly*, 7 (1921), 418–60 (see p. 450). Gatti claims that the products of Debussy's last three years, with the exception 'perhaps' of the *Etudes*, are 'weak' (p. 448).

Example 5.2

(a) *Le vent sur la plaine*, bb. 1–3

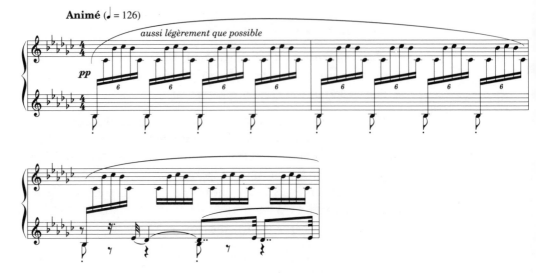

chorale and Stravinsky and who will ever know what else in *En blanc et noir*, why should he not be self-reflexive too? Not only is 'Le vent . . .' alluded to, but the third *Chanson* itself. I have scoured deeply for some 'analytical' correspondence that would pin down '*Yver*' for good and all. In the end, however, it is an artistic matter, a question of whether you believe that Ex. 5.3a and 5.3b are particularly linked or not. After all, how many dozens or hundreds of times in his masterpieces did Debussy 'feature' the ascending minor third? And in any case, tenors highlight a major third, and sopranos top it with the descending semitone that basses also reinforce. I nevertheless find a striking image here.

Why did Debussy fix upon Charles d'Orléans? Although it is impossible to say unless further evidence comes to light, there must be a strong presumption that it resulted from his renewed poetic engagement, in composing the second caprice, with François Villon (born probably in 1431, last known to have been alive in 1463), d'Orléans's approximate mid-fifteenth-century contemporary, unknowing wordsmith for Debussy's *Trois Ballades de François Villon* of 1910. Specialists argue, but Villon has been called France's greatest lyric poet, and has been a major engager of fine minds in his 'time' of some five hundred years:

> In the history of French literary criticism, Villon's is the longest
> unbroken record, his predecessors having been largely forgotten
> until the revival of interest in the medieval period owed to the

Example 5.2
(b) *En blanc et noir*, III, bb. 23–8

(c) Stravinsky, *Firebird*, F♯ major theme ex. *OCCD*

Example 5.2
(d) *En blanc et noir*, III, bb. 35–8

Romantic movement. Only the seventeenth century saw no new edition of Villon's poetry.[22]

In a letter in July 1903 to his friend Pierre Louÿs, Debussy writes, in receipt of a gift from Louÿs's personal library, 'Say what you like, a volume of Villon is more use than a walking stick!';[23] and a *mémoire* published in 1937 mentions that there were relatively few books in Debussy's study near the Bois de Boulogne, 'only authors that Debussy had chosen as his

22. John Fox, *Villon: Poems* (London: Grant and Cutler, 1984), p. 99.
23. *Letters*, ed. Lesure and Nichols, p. 136.

Example 5.2
(e) *En blanc et noir*, III, bb. 49–54

particular favourites – Rossetti, Maeterlinck, François Villon in an old edition, Mallarmé'.[24]

The epigraph to the second caprice is the last stanza, the 'envoi',
from the *Ballade contre les ennemis de la France* by Villon:[25]

24. E. Robert Schmitz, 'A Plea for the Real Debussy', reprinted in *Debussy Remembered*, ed. Roger Nichols (London: Faber, 1992), p. 168.
25. This *Ballade* is of doubtful authorship. See J. Rychner and A. Henry, *Les Lais de Villon et les poèmes variés*, vol. II, *Commentaire* (Geneva: Droz, 1977), p. 96.

162 · Jonathan Dunsby

Example 5.2
(f) *En blanc et noir*, III, bb. 76–83

Prince, porté soit des serfs Eolus
En la forest ou domine Glaucus.
Ou privé soit de paix et d'espérance
Car digne n'est de posséder vertus
Qui mal vouldroit au royaume de France

'Prince' means nothing more than a convention (the poetry-master of the medieval ballade is named at the 'envoi'), 'les serfs Eolus' means the

Example 5.3

(a) *Trois Chansons . . .*, 'Yver', bb. 34⁴–6

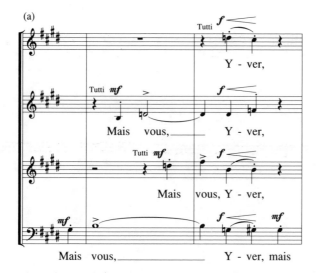

wind, and the next line is more or less agreed to refer to the sea. Finally, among the many calamities that may be visited upon the enemy of France, forget all peace and hope.[26] As an epigraph, Debussy's quotation from Villon is rather plain. Like 'To be, or not to be . . .', for the English speaker, it is an endless puzzle that nevertheless refers clearly. Whatever else it conveys, the Villon epigraph is addressed to Frenchmen (may I be permitted the gendered term authentistically?) in time of war. It also leaves, I believe, a trace of the title of this music. Every educated French person will have been confronted with Villon's famous Ballade about the self, 'Debate with My Heart'. 'Le débat du cuer et du corps de Villon' is the traditional French title, and there, in lines 15–16, is a find: 'Rien ne cognois. – Si fais. – Quoy? – Mouche en let; L'ung et blanc, l'autre est noir, c'est la distance.'[27] Fly in the milk: the milk was white; the black fly stains it.

Thus Villon finds a double resonance in *En blanc et noir*. Overtly, his epigraph signals a programme for the second caprice, where a 'pre-

26. *Ibid.*

27. Fox (see above, note 22) translates this as 'Fly in milk. One's white, the other black, that's distance', p. 93. The first line of the *Ballade*: '*Je connais bien mouches en lait*', 'I know about flies in milk', of which Villon offers no further explanation, suggests that this image must have been taken for granted, long ago. See *Villon: Poésies* (Paris: Hachette, 1979).

Example 5.3
(b) *En blanc et noir*, III, bb. 13–16

Marseillaise'[28] melody triumphs over the Lutheran chorale tune 'Ein' feste Burg' and disperses its 'noxious gases',[29] the Germans being unworthy of any virtue in view of their assault on the Kingdom of France (not that France was any longer a kingdom). We might find some Symbolist representation here were it not for the dire and direct dedication 'for Lieutenant Jacques Charlot [Durand's nephew], killed by the enemy in 1915, March

28. *Lettres de Claude Debussy à son Editeur* (Paris: Durand, 1927), p. 138. It is not at all clear precisely which bit of musical material here may be deemed *Marseillaise*-like. I had always assumed it to be around b. 140, but Mark DeVoto noted at the AMS (see above, note 1), to general agreement, that it is actually not to be found.   29. *Ibid.*, p. 143.

3ʳᵈ'. Actually, the epigraph and dedication taken together in order seem to me to make another bit of poetry, for the past participles move from alliterative attention, 'porté' ('carried')/'privé' ('deprived of') (Villon), to pathos, 'tué' ('killed') (Debussy). However that may be, Villon has been given his literal voice by Debussy, who translates 'Qui' at the beginning of Villon's last line ('whoever', any enemy of France) into the battle between a cultural anthem, the first two phrases of *the* German chorale, and a Marseillaise-like melodic fragment.

Had the Martians joined in the war (see above, note 6), we might well have heard transcribed in *En blanc et noir* the first real music from other planets. We may forget all too easily, be it poring over Debussy's letters, or in contemplating Schoenberg (String Quartet No. 2 of 1907–8, Finale, with its celebrated first line of text by Stefan George, 'ich fühle luft von anderen planeten', 'I feel the air of another planet') or, for instance, Holst's mighty orchestral suite *The Planets* (1915), how vividly the solar system figured in people's imaginations in the early 1900s. The world was under incessant contraction, through flight and other mechanised travel, telephones, recorded sound, and, most pertinently here, film; expansion beyond the earth might be but a step away. Although it is entrancing now to look at what Debussy thought was going on around him, it is also apparent that he had little idea of it and was perhaps more a creature of his past and of Symbolist art. He was, however, seized by film, and we may assume that what he saw here was a new field of constructive techniques never before available to the human imagination, and finely matched to the habits of Symbolism. That is more or less what he himself wrote in a magazine article in November 1913, under two years before *En blanc et noir*:

> There remains but one way of reviving the taste for symphonic music among our contemporaries: to apply to pure music the techniques of cinematography. It is the film – the Ariadne's thread – that will show us the way out of this disquieting labyrinth.[30]

Anyone who cares to make an analysis of *En blanc et noir* by analogy with film-cutting techniques in the emergence of black and white cinema can have a field day. It is entirely plausible that Debussy took his conception of programme music – and programme music the second caprice certainly is in some degree – to be a cinematographic scene captured in music. Perhaps here the familiar instruction 'lointain', as the quasi-folksong is heard for the last time before the battles (bb. 47–52), actually carries some

30. *Debussy on Music*, ed. Richard Langham Smith (London: Secker and Warburg, 1977), p. 298.

visual inspiration: and the scene-changing musical contrasts at bb. 53, 73, 89, 98 and 107, each in quicker tempo,[31] might derive from the then relatively fresh experience of the 'cut', a new mode of expression endemic to cinematography after its invention in 1895, scattering promiscuously what only artists had before been able to effect. That is supposition, but I am wedded to the idea that Debussy knew precisely what he was doing with his title, which is for the whole piece, and which plays a little with the language. Black and white film may be a resonance among resonances, especially in play in the second caprice, but here the 'real' secret lies, as I have said, in Villon.

I have worked backwards through the epigraphs, and now come to the first, for what seems to me the good reason that we can conclude with what is most musically concrete:

Qui reste à sa place
Et ne danse pas
De quelque disgrâce
Fait l'aveu tout bas

This verse means, roughly, that there is something very wrong with whoever will not dance. It is taken from the libretto of Gounod's opera *Roméo et Juliette*, by Barbier and Carré. The source, in the fifth scene of Shakespeare's play, is most obviously 'Ah ha! my mistresses, which of you all / Will now deny to dance? she that makes dainty, she, / I'll swear, hath corns' (I, v, 22–4), and those familiar with *Romeo and Juliet* will recall that Capulet, after his boisterous encouragement of the maskers, is feeling his age: 'Nay, sit, nay, sit, good cousin Capulet, / For you and I are past our dancing days' (34–5). One commentator after another on *En blanc et noir* has made the perfectly valid point that the literary image of not dancing, and thus revealing some physical defect, is an allusion to Debussy's situa-

---

31. It must remain a matter of opinion whether there is a last tempo change. The section designations here are *Sourdement tumultueux* (b. 53), *Poco più, Sempre animato, Alerte (Sempre animato)* and *Molto tumultuoso* (b. 107) respectively. If there is any narrative to be gleaned here from the interplay between French and Italian (that is, foreign terms), it escapes me. However, the designation *Joyeux* of the French victory that begins at bar 129 is replete with more than technical meaning for the performers: one can speak of a 'Joyeux' section, but hardly, expressively, of a 'Poco più' section – where the noxious chorale marches forward. The two indications Debussy offers to each pianist in shaping, first one 'stanza' of the chorale theme in two phrases, then just the first phrase which the French music interrupts for the first time, are 'lourd' and 'rude', 'heavy' or, more likely, 'ponderous', and 'uncouth' or, more likely if the pianist is asked to convey a people, 'primitive'.

tion in the war, and his lamentation about this situation is well documented in the correspondence. It seems to me, however, that it is not just Gounod's relatively tame librettists who have been plundered by Debussy; this would appear to be unlikely in any case, from a composer of Debussy's calibre of literary sensibility – he would have quoted from Shakespeare himself had he cared to. Rather, I believe he is quoting from Gounod's actual music (Ex. 5.4). Perhaps on its own this generic or 'family' resemblance would be thought tenuous beyond credibility (though you only have to play the two extracts in the same key and at the same speed on the piano to experience their strong affinity); the epigraph, however, firmly points to it. Why Gounod? I think it is because Gounod was Debussy's musical symbol for the anti-German. Shortly before the

Example 5.4
(a) Gounod, *Roméo et Juliette*, Capulet aria, vocal score p. 28, bb. 1–5
(b) *En blanc et noir*, bb. 1–3^1 reduced

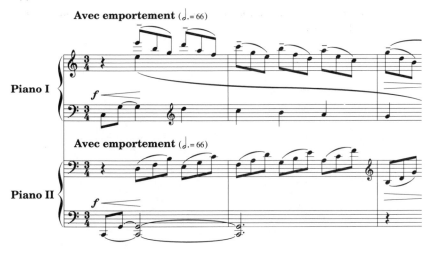

onset of the war Debussy had been assembling essays from 1901–5 which were published in 1921, posthumously, as *Monsieur Croche Antidilettante*. This included an article explaining why the Opera was right to continue to stage Gounod's *Faust*, the chief reason being 'that Gounod's art represents a phase of French aesthetic development'. Gounod, writes Debussy, 'deserves our praise for having evaded the domination of the genius of Wagner' and 'with all his faults, is needed . . . let us, without being over dogmatic, take the opportunity of rendering our homage to him'.[32] Despite Debussy's ambivalence towards Gounod (who was guilty, after all, of bringing Goethe into the heart of French culture), the very first musical impulse of *En blanc et noir* has the old man (Capulet–Gounod–Debussy) waving the *tricolore* defiantly.

When Boulez composed for two pianos, decades later but in the aftermath of further Franco-German carnage, he was adamant that all in the past had been swept away, and without doubt his title *Structures* was beautifully conceived for its time of disengaged optimism. In *En blanc et noir*, Debussy the *musicien français* reached back, as we have seen, into a deep cultural past in a way and to an extent that has not been fully appreciated; nor, for sure, have I unearthed it all. There is an important lesson in this, one that reflects the central concerns of contemporary musical discourse. No degree of analysis of the purely musical structures of *En blanc et noir* can possibly reveal its historical moment, and thus it completely resists formalism. Without the poetry, it is a denuded score. It is not, however, 'programme' music overall, not a 'depiction', but a work of high Symbolism in which the poetic and the musical intertwine in a way to which there is no 'solution' beyond the profound lure of interpretation.

32. *Three Classics in the Aesthetic of Music* (New York: Dover Publications, Inc., 1962), pp. 65–7.

6

Poem as non-verbal text: Elliott Carter's Concerto for Orchestra and Saint-John Perse's *Winds*

Jonathan W. Bernard

I

Other than his well-known penchant for writing music of an unusual and particular density, complexity and difficulty, what sets Elliott Carter apart from most other composers of the twentieth century is the sustained intensity of his interest in artistic activity outside the realm of music. There is hardly an article by or published interview with Carter that does not bear ample testimony to the depth and breadth of his response to the nonmusical arts, especially literature.[1] It is not surprising to learn that Carter's disposition in this regard was evidently formed early in his education.[2] Music was not even among his major subjects for the bachelor's degree he earned at Harvard in 1930; instead, he studied English, philoso-

1. See especially *The Writings of Elliott Carter* (hereafter *Writings*), ed. Else Stone and Kurt Stone (Bloomington: Indiana University Press, 1977), passim; Allen Edwards, *Flawed Words and Stubborn Sounds: A Conversation with Elliott Carter* (New York: Norton, 1971); Jonathan W. Bernard, 'An Interview with Elliott Carter', *Perspectives of New Music*, 28/2 (Summer, 1990), 180–214; and *Elliott Carter: In Conversation with Enzo Restagno for Settembre Musica 1989*, trans. Katherine S. Wolfthal (Brooklyn: Institute for Studies in American Music, 1991). Carter's abiding interest in a wide range of artistic endeavour has also shaped in significant ways the kind of critical attention his music has received. David Schiff's study, *The Music of Elliott Carter* (London: Eulenburg, 1983), draws many parallels between Carter's aesthetic and techniques and those of writers, painters, filmmakers and choreographers. Noteworthy as well is Lawrence Kramer's sensitive analysis of John Ashbery's poem 'Syringa' and Carter's work by the same title in *Music and Poetry: The Nineteenth Century and After* (Berkeley: University of California Press, 1984), pp. 203–21.
2. Arnold Whittall has even speculated that this 'special openness to the form and content of non-musical works of art', reflected in 'his capacity for associating musical with non-musical stimuli, may have made the finding of musical focus and direction particularly difficult for Carter' – hence explaining the notably long evolution that his compositional style underwent (Arnold Whittall, 'Elliott Carter', in *First American Music Conference: Keele University, England, April 18–21, 1975*, pp. 82–98).

169

phy, mathematics and classics. Although intensive and exclusively musical studies began immediately thereafter, it is probably not irrelevant to Carter's future development that three of his principal undergraduate subjects involved the study of texts. Certainly, the graceful prose that Carter began publishing in 1937 as a music critic attests to a sensitivity to language that was by then well developed.

Carter's catalogue of compositions, beginning in 1928 with the earliest piece he now acknowledges, also reflects the strength of his attraction to texts, though not as straightforwardly as one might expect. Until 1938, every work included the voice in its scoring, and vocal music continued to dominate his output until 1945.[3] This pattern was disrupted by the appearance in 1946 of the Piano Sonata, now generally recognised as the great watershed of Carter's early career – a major work that presaged the initiation of a long, new line of development in which matters of pitch and rhythm underwent radical changes in compositional treatment. After *Emblems* of 1947, Carter wrote no vocal works for almost thirty years – until *A Mirror on Which to Dwell* (1975).

What does this dramatic shift signify? Not, in fact, that Carter had suddenly lost interest in the expression of text through music. Rather, his natural inclinations in this direction had been displaced by other developments. His recourse to purely instrumental media from the late 1940s on was born of necessity, for the compositional technique that came to fruition around then demanded a level of virtuosity in performance that stood little chance of realisation except through instrumental means. At that time, even the best of solo vocal artists who were serious about contemporary music would probably have found Carter's new style almost impossible to sing in; and choruses, with their customarily far more limited technical prowess, would simply have been out of the question.[4] It is interesting to note that recently, when Carter has returned to writing for the voice, he has treated it in a basically instrumental way, one which demands a level of accomplishment that few singers, at least at present, have. As late as 1968, in fact, Carter effectively declared that he would never again approach the problem of text setting as he had earlier in his life. Responding in an interview to the question, 'How do you feel about the idea of dealing musically with a

3. Throughout his career, Carter has exhibited rather catholic tastes in his choices of texts, ranging from Sophocles to Allen Tate. Especially attractive to him, though – especially after 1940 – seem to be American poets, including Hart Crane, Robert Frost, Emily Dickinson, Walt Whitman, Elizabeth Bishop, Robert Lowell and John Ashbery.

4. See Bernard, 'An Interview with Elliott Carter', pp. 184–5.

literary text which already presents a dramatic structure of its own?',
he said:

> It is difficult to find a text that I would like to set to music. Let me
> say that I have the offer of a rather large and expansive commission
> for which I could finally do the thing I've thought about for a good
> part of my life, which is to make an oratorio out of Hart Crane's mag-
> nificent poem *The Bridge*. But now I'm not sure I want to do it,
> because I find that the speed of presentation in words is very differ-
> ent from the speed of presentation in my music. Also I don't under-
> stand words very well when they're sung, which is a troublesome
> problem. It seems to me that vocal music in general has to be
> rethought completely and that I don't have the time or the
> patience to do that single-handedly.[5]

With the benefit of hindsight, almost thirty years later, it now seems
clear that something happened during those nearly three decades of writing
nothing but instrumental works which eventually impelled him to do just
that: to rethink the problem of vocal composition. Driven underground,
as it were, by the exigencies of his evolution as a composer, his involvement
with texts had taken a new form – but it was none the less intense for that.
For some of his largest works of this period, certain texts had been very
much on his mind during the compositional process. Carter himself has
spoken of those which played a role in his work on the Double Concerto of
1961 (Lucretius's *De rerum natura* and Pope's *Dunciad*), the Concerto for
Orchestra of 1969 (Saint-John Perse's *Winds*) and *A Symphony of Three
Orchestras* of 1976 (Crane's *The Bridge*).[6] What has not been clear up to now,
however, is the nature of the relationship between these texts and these
pieces: the aspects of the text that are engaged – ranging from the larger
formal considerations to the details of use of language – and the form that
an appropriate musical response might assume.

This essay is devoted to one of Carter's instrumental 'texted' works,
the Concerto for Orchestra, and its debt to Perse's epic poem. This
investigation reveals a connection between the two that is far more
intimate, far richer and more interesting than even Carter's attribution

5. Edwards, *Flawed Words*, p. 106.
6. See Carter, 'The Orchestral Composer's Point of View' (1970), in *Writings*, pp.
282–300; Carter, 'Music and the Time Screen' (1976), in *Writings*, pp. 343–65;
Carter, 'A Symphony of Three Orchestras' (1977), in *Writings*, pp. 366–7;
Carter, Foreword to Concerto for Orchestra, score (New York: Associated
Music Publishers, 1972), pp. iii–v; Schiff, *Elliott Carter*, pp. 208–26, 243–53,
295–8.

of significance to certain specific parts of the poem might have led one to believe. There can be little doubt, once the evidence is examined, that *Winds* had a crucial impact upon Carter's aesthetic consciousness at the time when his piece was beginning to take shape, and that the Concerto for Orchestra could not have come out the way it did without the prior existence of *Winds* as a model.

Invoking the idea of a literary model for a musical work requires some care in defining one's terms. Specifically, to call *Winds* a model for the Concerto for Orchestra is not to claim that the latter simply enacts or recapitulates the former in musically equivalent form, whatever that might be. Most musicians are suspicious of such claims – and rightly so, for they are redolent of programme music, that conceit dear to the nineteenth century which, owing to the modernist rebellion against it in the early twentieth, has by now largely fallen out of favour, despite various recent attempts to rehabilitate it.[7] The judgement as 'false and banal' lodged by Schoenberg against 'the assumption that a piece of music must summon up images of one sort or another, and that if these are absent the piece of music has not been understood or is worthless' arouses a sympathetic response in the educated listener.[8] So do Irving Babbitt's comments in *The New Laokoon* – a book well known to Carter – to the effect that in the presence of a programme, 'music comes to be less interested in its own proper harmonies than in working miracles of suggestiveness' and that 'In general, primary emphasis on suggestiveness plunges one into an abyss of subjectivity.'[9] The idea of text as *model*, though, suggests on the one hand a considerable flexibility of interpretation in musical terms, so that there is no question of the piece slavishly following the dictates of the text; and on the other, that the resulting piece can be heard quite independently of

7. See, in particular, Peter Kivy's *Sound and Semblance: Reflections on Musical Representation* (Princeton University Press, 1984). The term 'programme music' is invoked here in the narrow, or 'proper' sense ascribed to it by Roger Scruton, which follows Liszt's definition in requiring an attempt at representation, as opposed to expression, of a (pre-existent) programme that is usually, though not always, narrative in nature, and of which listeners must be cognisant if they are not to misunderstand the musical work (*The New Grove*, s.v. 'Programme Music').

8. Arnold Schoenberg, 'The Relationship to the Text' (1912), in *Style and Idea: Selected Writings of Arnold Schoenberg*, ed. Leonard Stein (London: Faber, 1975), p. 141.

9. Irving Babbitt, *The New Laokoon: An Essay on the Confusion of the Arts* (Boston: Houghton Mifflin, 1910), pp. 162–3, 169. See 'Programme Music', pp. 159–72.

the text, so that there is no question of *needing* the text to understand the piece, in the musical sense.

Actually, the issues that arise in the Concerto are not so very different from those in works that *are* literal text settings. Schoenberg's assertion that the words of a Schubert song not only have no bearing whatever on understanding its musical content but in fact *hinder* real musical understanding may seem rather extreme; but surely one does not have to understand sung German or read the words while listening to grasp the musical meaning of the song.[10] Explicitly or implicitly texted, a piece of music has its own logic. But to say this is not to deny that this logic might take, as its point of departure or as a part of its strength, something not exclusively musical, or perhaps something not even musical at all. For this reason, it is worth while to attempt retracing a composer's relationship to a text and the uses to which he has put it, looking beyond the simplistic critical views implied by ideas of mechanical correspondence, on the one hand, or mere atmospheric evocation on the other.

There is every reason to think it likely that Carter's ambitions in approaching a text would tend to develop the kind of intricate and sophisticated relationship between it and the resulting composition that would lend the modelling real artistic significance. Consider, for instance, the published score of *Voyage* (1945), a song set to a Hart Crane text, which is prefaced by a commentary of several hundred words explaining the meaning of the poem as Carter perceived it.[11] Carter does not go into technical detail about how his interpretation of Crane has shaped *Voyage*, but the composer's line-by-line exegesis clearly implies that a close investigation of such shaping would not be irrelevant to understanding the piece better.

II

Carter's Concerto for Orchestra is conceived on a grand scale and continues a trend established in the composition of his previous several works, each of which had taken at least two and sometimes as many as four years to complete. In his Second String Quartet (1959), Carter had sought to project 'simultaneously interacting heterogeneous character-continuities' by assigning each of the four instruments its own repertoire of musical elements, gestures and typical 'behaviours'.[12] He continued to develop his

10. Schoenberg, 'The Relationship to the Text', p. 144.
11. Carter, *Voyage*, score (South Hadley, Mass.: Valley Music Press, 1945), p. 1; reprinted in Schiff, *Elliott Carter*, pp. 326–7. The text is the third of the six poems collectively entitled 'Voyages' and first published by Crane in *White Buildings* (1926).   12. Edwards, *Flawed Words*, p. 101.

ideas along these lines in his next two works, the Double Concerto (1961) and the Piano Concerto (1965), particularly with regard to the solo parts. Approaching the composition of the Concerto for Orchestra, by his own account, he sought to treat practically every instrument in the orchestra as a soloist.[13] His compositional plan for the piece is his most elaborate to that time. Ex. 6.1 reproduces Carter's summary of the materials of the Concerto.[14] The work is in four movements plus introduction and coda, all played without pause; each of the four movements has its own repertoire of intervals and harmonies, the latter comprising three-, four-, five- and seven-note chords to be used horizontally as well as vertically. Carter elects to apportion the eleven intervals, twelve trichords, twenty-nine tetrachords, thirty-eight pentachords and thirty-eight heptachords available in the chromatic pitch system as equally as possible among the four movements.[15] He further particularises the collective voice of each movement by assigning it a reigning collection of instruments (including unpitched percussion) distinct from each of the other three and by designing each movement according to a unique overall rhythmic/durational plan. On all of these fronts, the idea is to exhaust all possibilities available by giving each component of the repertoire in question a specific place in the scheme. In the case of the rhythmic/durational plans, there are obviously infinitely many others that could have been adopted, but within the limits imposed by balance, relative simplicity and symmetry, the four chosen are a complete and universal set.[16]

The idea of *symmetry* in the plan of the work is clearly important

13. Carter, Foreword to Concerto for Orchestra, score, p. iii.
14. Carter, Concerto for Orchestra, outline of materials used in each of the four movements, reprinted in facsimile in *Elliott Carter: Sketches and Scores in Manuscript* (New York: New York Public Library, 1973), pp. 54–5; also in Schiff, *Elliott Carter*, pp. 244–5.
15. The available resources of the chromatic or twelve-note 'universe' have been charted and classified by Allen Forte in *The Structure of Atonal Music* (New Haven: Yale University Press, 1973) in a form that is now widely accepted by music theorists. Carter recognises essentially the same resources as do Forte and others, with some significant differences, as will be shown below.
16. Carter's summary chart requires a word of explanation. It is not, properly speaking, a sketch, since it was apparently drawn up after the Concerto was finished. Each movement occupies one quadrant of the chart. The intervals and chords 'assigned' to each movement are given here in 'characteristic' spacings and pitch locations. In the actual piece, intervals and chords alike appear in many different forms, related to their aspects in the chart by transposition and inversion. (Some of the inversions are given explicitly, in those cases where two chords are linked by a horizontal bracket.) Furthermore, in the Concerto the chords' spacings are varied extensively, especially those of

and plays much more of a role in the formal design than it did in either of the previous concertos.[17] This formal symmetry can readily be traced back to the structure of *Winds*, which is in four sections (each with its own distinct character, drawn in ways to be discussed), the first and last of which consist of seven cantos each, the second and third six each. The resemblance with respect to form apparently does not extend beyond these larger matters, for there are no divisions within Carter's movements that can be said to correspond to Perse's cantos. As a kind of substitute, perhaps, the rhythmic/durational plans are arranged in a symmetry of their own: the first and third movements form one pair, the second and fourth another.[18] Interestingly, the second and fourth movements also have the larger repertoires of chords: eight each of the tetrachords, ten each of both the pentachords and the heptachords, while the first and third movements are allotted only seven and six tetrachords respectively, and only nine each of the pentachords and heptachords.[19]

The distinctive voices provided by harmony, rhythm, duration, instrumentation and register make feasible another principal feature of the Concerto: the literal instrusion of material from each of the movements into each of the other three. Such occasions are in fact quite numerous, though not to the extent that the identity of the dominant movement is ever in question (see Ex. 6.1). At such points in the piece, the intruding material may proceed for a time in parallel with what is 'native' to the movement, or it may eclipse the native material for as much as several measures. Both situations have fairly radical musical implications, but

the pentachords and heptachords. The chords are numbered according to a system of Carter's own devising; trichord numbers appear in triangles, tetrachord numbers in squares. (For a summary of Carter's numbering system, see Schiff, *Elliott Carter*, pp. 324–5.) Heptachords are given by implication: in all cases except for the first such chord of the first movement, they consist of the seven notes (out of the twelve of the total chromatic) omitted from each pentachord. Other features of this chart are discussed later.

17. Symmetry is, however, an important governing factor in other respects in these two pieces.

18. One might make a case for the first and second, third and fourth being paired instead, since *ritard.* and *accel.*, respectively, are employed in the two. This seems less defensible than the pairing given above, however, since the rhythmic procedure of the first movement really involves slowing *and* speeding up in a mutually dependent, complementary relationship, while the third movement does the same, but in inverse.

19. There are two mistakes in Carter's chart in the counts of these larger sets. His caption for the first movement reads '10 × five & seven note chords most characteristic'; his caption for the fourth movement reads '9 × 5 & 7 note chords'. These should be 9 × and 10 × instead, respectively.

Example 6.1 Concerto for Orchestra: Carter's summary chart

they represent a logical extension of ideas that Carter had implemented in his works of the previous decade. The notion of 'simultaneous streams of different things going on together' had occurred to him as early as the mid-1940s; by the time of the Double Concerto, he had at last developed the technical means to realise it fully.[20] Never before the Concerto for Orchestra, however, had Carter 'intercut' different sections of a piece, foreshadowing and recalling materials whose primary locations in the work are elsewhere. In a way, each of the four movements is really in progress from the beginning to the end of the piece; thus Carter's term 'movement' cannot be taken exclusively in its usual or conventional sense.[21] This new application of simultaneity, though, seems appropriate to the basic concept of a concerto for orchestra, in which there are not just two competing forces (as in a 'traditional' concerto, and as in Carter's previous two concertos) but many, all vying for attention. It is very much in line with Carter's tendency to anthropomorphise his musical forces and resources (as in the Second Quartet) that in the present Concerto the bands of instruments, in their particular harmonies, rhythms and registers, should make their presences felt outside their nominal spheres of influence – for the most part only ephemerally, but in some instances taking complete charge.

As the elements of the four movements intertwine and interact, they also realise a cyclical, wavelike design that runs essentially unbroken throughout the entire work. Carter implemented this design as an application of immensely larger scale of the structural idea that controls the Coda of the Double Concerto, where a pattern of waves is set violently in motion and gradually disperses. The general nature of such a design, as well as the specific imagery it might evoke, has implications for the relationship to Perse's text, as will become clear a little further on.[22]

It may be counted as particularly fortunate that Carter came upon

20. See Jonathan W. Bernard, 'The Evolution of Elliott Carter's Rhythmic Practice', *Perspectives of New Music*, 26/2 (Summer, 1988), 164–203.

21. I am grateful to Michael Golden for this insight. In his 'Toward a Humanistic Music Theory' D.M.A. dissertation, University of Washington, 1992, Golden discusses some aspects of the Concerto for Orchestra in interesting detail.

22. Schiff, *Elliott Carter*, pp. 256–7, discusses this 'structural polyrhythm' and its effects but does not explain how it is articulated in the music, or why some of the points of convergence or near-convergence of the wave patterns correspond to points of division between movements but others do not. That Carter did intend some sort of wavelike design in the Concerto is evident from certain of the sketch materials (now housed at the Paul Sacher Stiftung in Basel); the actual manifestation of the scheme in the piece, however, remains somewhat obscure.

Winds at an early stage in his work on the Concerto – for, poised as he was in 1965 to write a piece with the kinds of features that the Concerto turned out to display, he could only have been encouraged to proceed with its realisation by what he found in the poem. *Winds* lends itself beautifully to a plan in which the individual expressions of the various instruments of the orchestra were to be disposed in richly complex arrangements: some successive, some simultaneous in presentation. *Winds* has a clearly linear plot, but this is not its most important feature; the poem is multi-levelled, with many of its themes and motifs projected simultaneously, overlapped and combined – now standing out brilliantly, now thrust into the shadow thrown by other themes and motifs being brought to the fore. Furthermore, the sweeping, universal character of the poem, despite the overtones of Whitman that Carter found not quite sympathetic,[23] resonates very well with the global nature of the compositional plans that Carter had realised in his previous few works, and it seems to have struck him as a framework of sufficient strength to support a global conception of even greater complexity and incorporating even more variegated elements than anything he had done up until then.

III

From the time of its publication in 1946, *Winds* was acclaimed as a masterpiece, perhaps the greatest work to that date from a poet whose renown was already well established. Its epic length (over sixty pages in the now standard edition) and its highly original use of language and form have attracted considerable attention from literary critics over the past fifty years. One has noted that *Winds* is not 'a narrative in any ordinary sense, fixed in time and moving in space', but rather is characterised by 'that clear free movement of the stream of the present which is one of Perse's most significant contributions to poetry . . .'[24] Another finds in it 'no less than a reinvention of the universe'.[25] The overall form of *Winds*

23. In his Foreword to the published score, Carter notes that this aspect of the poem could not accurately be portrayed in the format he had chosen for the piece. Somewhat later, in an interview with Charles Rosen, Carter recalls that the 'bombastic' qualities and the 'false primitiveness' of *Winds* created difficulties for him – remarks which, however, cannot be taken to repudiate the close connection between his work and Perse's that he had previously outlined. See Charles Rosen, *The Musical Languages of Elliott Carter* (Washington: Library of Congress, 1984), p. 42.
24. Katherine Garrison Chapin, 'Saint-John Perse: Notes on a French Poet and an Epic Poem', *Sewanee Review*, 66 (1958), 40–1.
25. Alain Bosquet, *Saint-John Perse* (Paris: Seghers, 1953), p. 61. Unless otherwise noted, all translations are by the author.

is calculated to emphasise this cosmic character: the symmetry of division into cantos, 'reinforced by echoing verses and parallel images, underlines its circular structure and emphasises the cyclical nature of the fundamental theme . . .'. Indeed, thanks to the overall conception, which resides mainly in the imagery associated with the winds and their power both to destroy and sweep away the vestiges of the past and to bring in the new, 'Winds appears as a complex structure made up of multiple superimposed and related levels.'[26] Katherine Chapin sees the philosophy embodied in the poem as relating to 'the ancient cult of Shiva, the belief that the moment of most complete destruction and dis-integration is the moment of rebirth. Life moves in cycles, like great waves, and the depth of each wave marks the movement of its rise again to the crest of another.'[27] In that it is wavelike and cyclical, this struc-ture has much in common with the form of Carter's Concerto. And the fact that it is *winds* which serve as the generating force of the poem has given it a character that makes it especially susceptible to analogous musical treatment. Alain Bosquet identifies 'perpetual movement' as its underlying principle, and points out that the essence of wind lies both in what it stirs up and what creates it: it is at once its origin, itself, and its end.[28]

Within the overarching, unifying structure, the four sections of roughly equal length are each lent a distinct character through the fre-quent recurrence of certain specific images and themes. In Ex. 6.2 are listed the principal distinguishing features of each section of *Winds*. These lists, however, should not be taken to identify *exclusive* locations of these elements in the text of the poem. Just as the winds themselves blow on many levels throughout the poem, and penetrate every corner of it, so does every theme and image find its foreshadowings and recollec-tions outside of its 'home' section. Roger Caillois, in his valuable study of Perse's poetic technique, identifies the use of 'landmarks' (*repères*) as important to Perse's style in general and also notes that the longer the poem, the more numerous and distinct these landmarks are. *Winds*, the second longest of all of Perse's works, has them in abundance. Among Caillois's examples of inter-sectional reference are the phrases 'With this porous taste of the soul, on the tongue, like that of a clay piastre', which first appears in Canto II,5 (p. 285) and recurs nearly verbatim in IV,6 (p. 355), and 'And you had so little time to be born to this instant!' from

26. René Galand, *St.-John Perse* (New York: Twayne Publishers, Inc., 1972), pp. 104–5.   27. Chapin, 'Saint-John Perse', pp. 39–40.
28. Bosquet, *Saint-John Perse*, pp. 74, 62–3.

Example 6.2 *Winds*: summary of principal images and themes

Section I	Section II
rustling (straw)	newness, freshness
rattling and clicking	flood waters: waves, rivers
(stone, bone, shells)	flocks of birds
death and rebirth	swarms of insects
(metamorphosis)	winter (cold)
dust, powder	*tabula rasa* (man stripped to essentials)
dissolution, crumbling	
winds' force and violence	quest for revelation
Poet's first appearance	South: decay, stagnation
'all things scaling off	West: ascent to heights
toward nothingness'	

Section III	Section IV
confronting the wind	return
(explorers, immigrants)	reunion with humanity
discovery (epiphany)	'the causeway of men'
subterranean images:	triumph of living over dead
death, closed space	refuse of past swept away
man's instinct/man's reason	
'grand organs'	
thunder, lightning	
the Black Sun from below	
Poet's exhortations	

III,6 (p. 315) and IV,5 (p. 351).[29] Reading any particular section of the poem,
one is always both being reminded of lines that have occurred earlier and,
at the same time, being provided with premonitions of material that will
emerge fully in due course, or which will itself be recollected subsequently.

Beyond these literal or near-literal landmarks, there is a vast net-

29. Roger Caillois, *Poétique de Saint-John Perse* (Paris: Gallimard, 1954), p. 50.
    The phrases to which Caillois refers occur in Saint-John Perse, *Winds*, trans.
    Hugh Chisholm, in *Saint-John Perse: Collected Poems – Complete Edition*
    (Princeton University Press, 1983), pp. 285, 355, 315 and 351 respectively. All
    quotations from *Winds* in this article are from this edition, and henceforth
    will be referred to with page numbers in parentheses. All ellipses (. . .) are
    part of Perse's actual text except for those set apart from the text, which
    represent the author's abridgements.

work of allusion in the more general sense. Sometimes this device serves almost a normal narrative function, as in Canto IV,4: 'One autumn evening we shall return, on the last rumblings of the storm, when the dense trias of the gulfs opens its pits of blue tar to the Sun of the dead . . .' (p. 335). Here in the context of return occurs an allusion to the black sun, the depths (trias) and the noise of the storm of Section III. A little later in the same canto, the text 'One autumn evening we shall return, with the taste of ivy on our lips; with this taste of mangrove swamps and grass-lands and silt beyond the estuaries' (p. 337) embeds an allusion to another part of the poem, this time the South of Section II.

Other uses of allusion are more fragmentary, such as the invocation 'O you whom the storm refreshes . . . freshness and promise of freshness', which first appears at the beginning of Canto I,2 (p. 229) and is repeated exactly in I,6 (p. 251) but seems at these points to foreshadow its true locus in the second section of the poem, in the words 'And there is a fresh-ness of free waters' (II,1, p. 263) and in other uses. Finally, it is recalled in the fourth section, 'O freshness, O freshness rediscovered among the sources of language!' (IV,5, p. 351).[30] Less literal, but no less powerful, is the invocation of Eâ, god of the abyss, in I,5 and again in I,7; this and the city struck thrice by lightning in I,6 clearly prefigure these images in their principal location, Section III. Section III, in turn, reaches into IV, exerting its power in the personage of the mysterious scar-faced stranger who, as Galand puts it, 'recalls those men "transfixed by lightning" or put by lightning in "the path of veracious dreams" who bring salvation to other men, "in wisdom and vehemence" (I,6; III,5)'.[31] Not incidentally, the sudden appearance of this disfigured man is accompanied by a bolt of lightning.

It must be emphasised that this sort of cross-reference is absolutely endemic to the poem; applications of the technique are evident on every page. In this way, as in numerous others, *Winds* is a worthy realisation of Perse's poetic ideals: not to be 'a mere feast of music'[32] – that is, in a poet's terms, sound for its own sake – but to be based in 'a free play, extremely allusive and mysterious, of hidden analogies or correspondences, and even of multiple associations, on the extreme verges of what consciousness can grasp', proceeding 'by means of analogical and symbolic thinking, by

30. All but the last of these are enumerated in Yves-Alain Favre, *Saint-John Perse: Le langage et le sacré* (Paris: José Corti, 1977), p. 39.
31. Galand, *Saint-John Perse*, p. 101.
32. Perse, 'On Poetry' (speech on occasion of receiving the Nobel Prize, 1960), trans. W. H. Auden, in *Saint-John Perse: Two Addresses* (New York: Pantheon, 1966), p. 12.

means of the far-reaching light of the mediating image and its play of correspondences, by way of a thousand chains of reactions and unusual associations'.[33]

IV

In his notes on the genesis of the Concerto, Carter has acknowledged,
to varying degrees, his response to the cross-cutting, mutually inter-
penetrative nature of *Winds*.[34] In attempting to describe more precisely
the nature of that response, however, one discovers that his attribution of
the importance of Perse's poem to his own work has not always taken the
same form. In the Foreword to the published score, Carter quotes excerpts
from the four sections of the poem in strict serial correspondence to the
four movements of the Concerto, with Sections I and IV providing the text
for the Introduction and Coda respectively (see Ex. 6.3a). By contrast, in
his summary chart of the materials used in the four movements of the
Concerto (shown in Ex. 6.1), Carter does not quote specific lines of text as
in the Foreword but instead cites cantos by number alone, intermingling
parts of the poem in the process (Ex. 6.3b).

Example 6.3 Comparison of Carter's citations of *Winds*

	(a) from Foreword to published score (1972)	(b) from analytical chart (ca. 1970)
Intro.	Canto I,1	I,1
Mvt 1	I,1	I,1; III,2,3
Mvt 2	II,1,4	II,1,2,4
Mvt 3	III,4,5	III,5; I,2
Mvt 4	IV,2,4,6	IV,5,6,7
Coda	IV,6	(IV,5,6,7)

These discrepancies have a significance, surely, beyond their indicating that Carter's recollection changed over time as to how exactly the
poem served as model for his piece. Two conclusions seem warranted:
first, that these *textes choisis* are intended by the composer only to give
a general idea of what the poem has meant to him; secondly, that for
Carter, Perse's poem lent itself so readily to ideas of simultaneous

33. Perse (1956), quoted in Arthur Knodel, *Saint-John Perse: A Study of His
    Poetry* (Edinburgh University Press, 1966), p. 95; Perse, 'On Poetry', p. 11.
34. Carter, Foreword to Concerto for Orchestra, p. iv; Carter, programme note for
    the premiere of the Concerto for Orchestra, reprinted in Edward Downes, *The
    New York Philharmonic Guide to the Symphony* (New York: Walker and Co.,
    1976), pp. 246–7.

presentation of different thematic strands and their development that part of Section III's text could actually be transplanted, conceptually, into the first movement, and part of Section I's text into the third. Carter, in other words, would seem to have made literal what in the poem is only implicit. Do the actual contents of the transplanted text support this assertion?

Canto III,2 takes as its principal subject the search for a new order to replace the one lost through the winds' action (p. 301):

> For our quest is no longer for copper or virgin gold, no longer for coal or naphtha, but like the germ itself beneath its vault in the crypts of life, and like the bell itself beneath the lightning in the caverns of the Seer, we seek, in the kernel and the ovule and the core of new species, at the hearth of force, the very spark of its cry! . . .

The words 'From the pigsties of night, the torches of a singular destiny will flare' that follow soon thereafter (p. 301) evoke, as Arthur Knodel explains, the light of a new age that will rise out of 'the swill and garbage of a declining age, steeped in the bloody filth of war'.[35] This resonates particularly strongly with the images of death and rebirth presented in Section I, and there is as well a specific linking image: the pigsties, or buildings that were as 'low as pigsties' in I,3 (p. 235), among the many objects scattered and destroyed by the winds.

Canto III,3 dwells more specifically upon the forces waiting to be unleashed from within – and, of course, from *below* as well. Man now holds 'the seal of his power . . . like a great golden marigold', which may be intended to evoke yet contrast with the golden grass of I,6; the difference lies between the wish (in I,6) that 'some very powerful movement carry us to our limits, and beyond our limits' (p. 255) and the fulfilment of that wish, alluded to throughout Section III, in man's acquisition of the means to destroy himself.[36]

In the third movement, by contrast, Carter's text reference casts a glance backwards to Canto I,2. This is the section of the poem in which the Poet, a shamanistic figure, first makes his appearance. This shaman 'has eaten the rice of the dead', but 'his word is for the living, his hands for the fountains of the future'. He is the one 'whom the storm refreshes' as he 'mounts the ramparts in the freshness of ruins and rubble' (pp. 229, 231). He is the facilitator in the world's passage from the violent destruction of its past to its rebirth – hence the prevalence of both kinds of

---

35. Knodel, *Saint-John Perse*, p. 118.   36. Galand, *Saint-John Perse*, p. 98.

images here.[37] It is interesting that this excerpt from the text evokes, from a different angle, what in the first movement was evoked from Section III; the two movements are thereby placed in a kind of complementary relationship.

Just as the themes and images of *Winds* develop a network of interconnection on many levels, so do Carter's materials, as enumerated in his precompositional plan, not only lend themselves to interconnection – they develop it more or less inevitably. This interconnection is very much dependent on the concept of set class. At about the same time that theorists such as Milton Babbitt, Allen Forte and David Lewin were formally developing the idea of the set class, Carter was arriving at it independently. In his hands, it took on a slightly yet crucially different character. While Carter's definition recognised the same criteria for classification and distinction – the sorting into cardinalities and the non-derivability of one from any other by transposition, inversion or their combination – it was aimed already at the time of its complete formulation at certain specific compositional problems. That is, from the start, Carter's definition of set class was coloured by distinctions based on interval as opposed to interval class. Although the equivalences under interval class are obviously integral to the concept of set class – under Carter's definition as well as the 'classical' definition – Carter refused to recognise such equivalences for every musical purpose. His plan for the Concerto, like those of his previous three pieces, distinguishes intervals on the basis of their actual size rather than their membership in an interval class. Thus, for instance, the minor sixth in the first movement, eight semitones in breadth, is considered different from the major third in the second movement, four semitones in breadth.[38] Distinctions made among inter-

37. Throughout *Winds*, the Poet is a kind of Janus-faced figure, a role that contributes considerably to the reader's perception of simultaneous presentation. The epithets of II,6 especially affirm this: 'Texts received in clear language! versions given on two sides! . . . You, yourself, a stele and a corner-stone! . . . And for new bewilderments, I summon you in litigation on your dihedral chair, / O Poet, O bilingual one, amidst all things two-pronged . . .!' (pp. 289, 291).

38. The only interval with a place in more than one movement is the minor seventh, found in both the second and the third movements. Carter seems to have allowed this exception for the sake of providing each movement with three intervals, out of a total stock of eleven. In the dimension of register the two uses of the minor seventh are kept maximally distinct, since the characteristic registral location of the materials in the second movement is the highest in the work, that of the materials in the third movement the lowest.

vals on this basis have implications for the way the chords of Carter's plan are deployed: notice that the 'most characteristic' spacings of the trichords, tetrachords and pentachords shown in the chart for each movement (Ex. 6.1) are constructed almost exclusively, as far as vertical adjacencies are concerned, from the component intervals listed for that movement. In practice, these chordal spacings are not used in a way that even approaches exclusivity, but they do function, as Carter says, in tandem with the other distinguishing features to give each movement a characteristic sound. Put another way, the intervals [8], [9] and [11] might be called the 'sonic facts' of the first movement.[39]

It becomes clear, however, from an examination of these characteristic spacings, that they include elements other than the sonic facts. For instance, trichord no. 8 in the second movement is displayed in vertical spacing [4][6]. The [6], or tritone, is a characteristic interval, not of the second, but of the fourth movement. Another example is trichord no. 12 in the third movement, shown in [3][10] spacing. The [3], or minor third, is also characteristic of the fourth movement. Built into this scheme, then, are potential links between the components of the different movements, which can assume varying levels of importance depending on similarity or contrast produced in other distinguishing dimensions (register, orchestration, rhythm). In Ex. 6.4 (bb. 306–9), the native material of III exposes the interval [3], which is then picked up in the violas to form trichord no. 2; this event serves as the onset of an intrusion of fourth-movement material at this point.[40] For chords of more than three notes, there is correspondingly more potential for such links to develop – especially since the larger the number of notes in the chord, the less the likelihood that it will even appear in a characteristic spacing.[41]

Carter employs other methods as well of blurring distinctions between materials that properly belong to different movements. For example, in bb. 253–7 (second movement), harmonies intrude from the fourth movement (see Ex. 6.5). However, the characteristic even rhythm

39. Numbers in square brackets denote sizes of intervals in semitones. In more traditional terminology, [8] would be called a minor sixth (or augmented fifth), [9] a major sixth (or diminished seventh) and so on.
40. In Ex. 6.4, the roman numerals refer to the movements of Carter's work.
41. In his article 'Pitch Structure in Elliott Carter's String Quartet No. 3', *Perspectives of New Music*, 22/1–2 (1983–4), 31–60, Andrew Mead offers a clear exposition of the effect that intervals shared between sets have upon structure in this work. See also Jonathan W. Bernard, 'Spatial Sets in Recent Music of Elliott Carter', *Music Analysis*, 2 (1983), 5–34, for a discussion of shared intervals in Carter's Piano Concerto.

Example 6.4   Concerto for Orchestra, bb. 306–9, strings

of that movement has been replaced with the jagged accelerative pattern of the third movement.[42] The instrumentation of this passage actually mediates between the groups that are central to each of these movements: trombones from the third movement, trumpets and horns from the fourth. Thus two kinds (levels) of simultaneity are expressed at once. This sort of technique finds its literary analogue in the statement of themes transplanted from elsewhere in the poem *in terms of* those that are truly native to the actual section – this as opposed to the technique of juxtaposing different materials in sharp contrast.

At least as important to the structure of the Concerto for Orchestra is the rhythmic/durational dimension – in keeping with Carter's contemporaneous statement that in his music in general he considers this aspect 'just as intrinsic as pitch'.[43] Its power in the Concerto to character-

42. The numbers below the horizontal brackets in Ex. 6.5 denote beats' duration. The numbers in triangles and pentagons and with the prefix 'hept.' refer to chord types by number of elements and according to Carter's numbering system. (For the meaning of the square brackets, see note 39.) Interestingly, Carter himself identifies these measures as an intrusion from movement 3 only; rhythm seems to take precedence over harmony, at least here.

43. Benjamin Boretz, 'Conversation with Elliott Carter' (1968), *Perspectives of New Music*, 8/2 (Spring–Summer 1970), 1–22.

Example 6.5   Concerto for Orchestra, bb. 253–7, brass

ise and differentiate, in conjunction with the instrumental and registral choices, results in some fascinating parallels with the modelling text, which are worth discussing movement by movement.

The formal layout of the Concerto, in that it includes an Introduction (bb. 1–23) and a Coda (bb. 533–600), does not exactly parallel that of *Winds*. However, in choosing to depart in this way from the explicit form of the poem, Carter has succeeded in expressing something about it which would have been harder, if not impossible, to do had he stuck rigidly and exclusively with a one-to-one correspondence of section to movement. As composed, the Introduction depicts strikingly the rising of the winds and their omnipotent nature, blowing eventually 'throughout the entire world of things' (I,1; p. 227). As listeners, we receive a powerful impression of that irresistible force in the cataclysmic accumulation of the initial measures of the piece, as all four groups enter in their characteristic registers and instrumentations.

Of all the movements, the first bears the most strikingly onomatopoeic resemblance to its corresponding section of the poem. The struck and plucked instruments of definite pitch – piano, harp, marimba, pizz. and sul pont. cellos – and the rattled, scratched, clicking and buzzing percussion certainly evoke very well the 'men of straw in the year of straw', the 'great tree shuddering in its rattles of dead wood and its corollas of baked clay', and the 'lingerie of wings in their sheaths and sheafs of new wings in the quiver' (I,1; I,3). The particular rhythmic scheme of this movement expresses uncannily well the rising power of the wind: 'all things scaling off into nothingness' (p. 241) as each gust blows itself out in ritardando, but each successive gust in turn begins at an even faster rate, to correspond to the winds' 'increasing and whistling', and to the Poet/shaman's 'counsel with the new conspiracies in the bed of the wind / And once again it is counsel of force and of violence' (I,3; I,5). Some writers have identified the halting or gasping rhythm of this first section of the poem as originating in the violence of the wind.[44] The winds also leave the men of straw 'in their wake' (I,1) – a process to which Carter's rhythmic design well conforms. The gusts of wind continuously overlap in the music, so that the listener hardly ever has a clear sense of where exactly one has begun or has left off; this too is to be found in the winds' characterisation, in the opening lines of the poem, as having 'neither eyrie nor resting-place' (I,1). This perpetual movement, mentioned earlier, must

---

44. See, for instance, Jean Bollack, 'En l'an de paille', in *Honneur à Saint-John Perse: Hommages et témoignages littéraires* (Paris: Gallimard, 1965), pp. 473–9.

especially have attracted Carter, a composer who has chided his fellow
composers (and analysts of their music) on occasion for paying attention
only to 'this or that peculiar local rhythmic combination or sound-texture
or novel harmony' and not to the fact that 'the really interesting thing
about music is the time of it – the way it all goes along'.[45] His attitude
seems perfectly matched to Perse's general feeling that 'poetry is, above all
else, movement – in its inception as well as in its development and final
elaboration . . . The metric of poetry, which is usually considered a purely
rhetorical matter, strives only for movement and contact with movement
– with movement in all its living, most unpredictable forms.'[46] One is jus-
tified also in ascribing to certain other special features of the poem a parallel treatment in the music. For example, the three different voices that
speak in succession in I,6 – the one calling for new leaders, the Babouvist
philosopher and the Poet himself – seem personified by the successive
soloistic disposition of the first movement in general: harp, cellos, piano
and marimba are all distinctive (and by and large separated, if overlapping,
voices).[47]

The parallels in the second movement are less direct but also
more complexly related to the poem's content. The general velocity,
scherzando, of this movement certainly corresponds to the now untram-
melled ranging of the winds over the entire world, having reached this
pitch in the first movement. What, then, are we to make of the gradual
slowing of this velocity as the second movement of Carter's piece pro-
gresses? Two possibilities spring to mind, by no means mutually exclusive: (1) the turn to the South in the Poet's journey, and the attendant
stagnation and decay (II,3); (2) the arduous ascent to the heights of the
West, so tremendously evident in the later cantos of this section (especially in II,5). Here it is clear that these way-stations in the poem are not
successively delineated in the Concerto, but in Carter's hands become a
more general characterisation of the journey of the Poet that accompanies
the winds' inducement of metamorphosis in the landscape.

The velocity of this movement expresses something else as well:
namely, the freshness brought by the winds. In the first section of the
poem, Perse dwells mainly on the destructive character of the winds and
only secondarily on what they might promise for the future; here the

---

45. Edwards, *Flawed Words*, p. 90.
46. Perse, quoted in Knodel, *Saint-John Perse*, pp. 91–2.
47. Galand, in *Saint-John Perse*, identifies these voices and comments that they
    are distinct but also related, in that each welcomes the winds' destruction
    (pp. 92–4).

opposite seems true, as life-giving images predominate. The swarms of insects and flocks of birds are additional signs of life; they also enrich and strengthen the sense of velocity.[48] Further, the winds' motion is linked to 'the relentless flow of rivers' and their power to carry away the 'dead works of this century' (II,3) and give birth to a new song 'amid the corpses of the dead works'.[49] Inextricably entwined with the freshness, though, is coldness and remoteness, of which the reader receives an unmistakable impression in the wintry images of II,2 and the remote high reaches of II,5,6. Helping considerably in creating a parallel impression in the music are the brilliant timbres of the violins in their upper registers and the high woodwinds, along with the shimmering sounds of metallic percussion (cymbals, triangle, tam-tam).

In the third movement, low sounds assume the principal, characteristic role, straightforwardly reflecting the images of depth and of the subterranean found throughout the third section of the poem. Onomatopoeia is also in evidence in the timpani and the flashes of brass (as thunder and lightning). Less obvious is the relationship to the voice of the Poet in this movement (aside from the fact that he is obviously speaking to us from the depths too); much more than anywhere else in the poem, his voice takes on a rhetorical, exhortatory character. Again, rhythm plays a crucial role: this is the movement of irregularly accelerating phrases which overall exhibit a tendency to start at progressively slower speeds. The accelerandos are thereby lent an ever more dramatic character as the movement goes on. Carter's choice of rhythmic profile plausibly conveys the rhythm of a spoken exhortation, one in which the words come ever faster and more exaggeratedly accented.[50] This profile also allows the composer to parallel the end of the third section of the poem, where the speech rhythms become halt-

48. That the swarms of living creatures bear a real relation to the swirling of the winds could not be more evident than it is in II,4, where Perse speaks of 'Those flights of insects going off in clouds to lose themselves at sea . . . like tatters of errant prophecies' (p. 279). This echo of 'all things scaling off toward nothingness' is included, tellingly, in Carter's excerpt from the poem for his second movement (Foreword, p. iv).
49. Galand, *Saint-John Perse*, p. 95.
50. Schiff, *Elliott Carter*, p. 252, has speculated that Carter intended a kind of parody of the 'overblown Whitmanesque gestures' of this section of the poem in his choice of the tubas and basses as the central instrumental voices in this movement. This is possible (as a kind of private joke), but as a public statement the voice of the third movement seems less an embodiment of 'grotesque irony', in Schiff's words, than like the voice of an Old Testament prophet.

ing and fragmented, as an urgency born of fear and foreboding infuses the text (p. 319):

> And still the Poet is with us . . . This hour perhaps the last, this minute even, this instant! . . . And we have so little time to be born to this instant!
>
> '. . . And at this extreme point of expectation, where promise itself becomes a breath,
>
> You yourselves would do better to hold your breath . . . And will the Seer not have his chance? the Listener his answer? . . .'
>
> Poet still amongst us . . . This hour perhaps the last . . . this minute even! . . . this instant! . . .
>
> – 'The cry! the piercing cry of the god upon us!'

The fourth movement, even more than the second, seems relatively loosely tied to the conception of the poem. It is tempting to speculate that here Carter in his interpretation of Perse has sacrificed close correspondence for the sake of working out a global scheme of his own in which the final pieces fall into place here at the end. Most noticeable of all the discrepancies is the lack of an analogue to the wrenching reversal of the Poet's course in IV,3, at the hands of the mysterious, scar-faced stranger in the passage previously discussed. Carter concentrates instead, it would seem, wholly upon the imagery of return in Cantos IV,4–7.

As a result, however, another kind of resemblance between the two works becomes evident: the fourth movement of the Concerto, like the fourth section of the poem, differs expressively from all that has preceded it. One clue to this difference is the core instrumental group, which is unique among the four of this work in having neither an extreme registral position, as do those of the second and third movements, nor a highly distinct timbral profile like that of the first. These are decidedly middle-range instruments with no extraordinarily distinctive collective sound: trumpets, clarinets, violas, horns, snare drum. But this medium character is precisely right for the fourth movement: it is human territory, between the extremes of hot and cold, high and low. And as the Poet rejoins humankind and the winds finish their task, this is the material that dominates the texture.[51] Bosquet suggests that Section IV celebrates the allying of man and wind: the wind has become humanised, man has found in the wind the expression of all existence.[52] This affirmation of human qualities

---

51. As Schiff has pointed out, wryly, 'it is a rare orchestral work where the violas triumph over the violins'. *Elliott Carter*, p. 253.
52. Bosquet, *Saint-John Perse*, p. 72.

– that man must be the instrument of his own salvation – finds a useful parallel in the general concept of Carter's Concerto, in which the individual voices that contribute to the whole are meant to be expressive of human character. The constant (eventually dizzying) acceleration of the fourth movement, then, actually represents, not a disregard of the winds' dying away in the poem, but an imparting of the Poet with ever greater speed as he returns from the edge of oblivion. One of the most frequently recurring themes of this section actually emphasises the idea of (increasing) speed: 'the causeway of men'. Moreover, although Carter does not explicitly mention it, the winds do die out near the very end of the Concerto – in the final bars of the Coda, starting around b. 560. And the idea evident in the poem that men are not simply acted upon by the wind but have learned how to *confront* it (III,1), and even how to turn its force to their benefit, sweeping away the last vestiges of the refuse of the past (IV,5), means that the thoroughgoing acceleration of the fourth movement is not at all out of keeping with the spirit of the poem. As the Poet rejoins the human, 'the Winds must ever serve as a reminder, an irritant, a goad', 'lest life . . . with its calm and redundancy . . . engulf [him]'.[53]

Finally, the Coda, which in Carter's accounting is focused upon IV,5,6,7, consists of a rapid alternation and simultaneous treatment of material from all four movements, with the fourth dominating. In this respect, it assumes some resemblance to the tone of the last cantos in the poem, which offer a highly condensed summary of what has gone before. The difference between the technique at work here and the general echoing and foreshadowing that has gone on throughout the poem resides in a greater prevalence of literal restatement and its deployment in the manner of a summary. For example, at the head of Canto IV,6 we find the words 'These were very great winds . . .' – the precise words that open the poem. In this canto we also find 'The porous taste of the soul on his tongue, like a clay piastre' (one of Caillois's 'landmarks' cited earlier) and 'O you whom the storm refreshes', found verbatim in I,2 though more substantially evocative of II in general. Canto IV,6 also contains a remarkable figure, much commented upon in the literature on this poem, in which the swimmer who after extended movement and rolling about, seeking, 'on each side, a new vision of the sky', suddenly feels the immobile sands beneath his feet. 'And the movement still dwells within him and drives him on – a movement which remains only memory . . .' But he remains 'a long time out of breath – a man still in the memory of the wind, a man still enam-

---

53. Erika Ostrovsky, *Under the Sign of Ambiguity: Saint-John Perse/Alexis Léger* (New York University Press, 1985), p. 171.

ored of the wind . . .' (pp. 353–5). The swimmer's experience is simultaneously what he remembers and what he feels at this moment; the two are
effectively fused. This usage is expressive of a new, more intense role for
the device of simultaneity: echoes which serve not simply to remind of
what has gone before, but which have been absorbed, effectively, into
consciousness. The summary nature of the Coda is prefigured in the
fourth movement; we notice that for the first time in bb. 490–504 material
from all three other movements appears simultaneously with the native
material.[54] This happens again briefly in b. 530; then, in the Coda, a mas-
sive climax is brought about from b. 544 to b. 558, again with the music
of all four movements in full cry at once.

Besides these general characteristics, the modelling influence of
Winds upon the Concerto works at more specific levels. This influence is
traceable through prosodic devices that are characteristic of the poem.
Although it is not possible to go beyond a certain degree of specificity in
drawing correspondences between musical and verbal syntax, there are
some fascinating parallels that deserve to be pointed out.

One particularly important feature of Perse's style, especially in his
later work (of which *Winds* is a part), has been identified as *énumération*:
a process of drawing 'from the entire universe . . . a vast inventory of
beings and things whose origins are in very different epochs and places'. It
allows the poet simultaneously 'to apprehend . . . the entire universe [and]
to grasp each thing [within it] in its individual and eternal existence'.[55] For
example, in a passage near the beginning of *Winds*: 'Scenting out the purple, the haircloth, scenting out the ivory and the potsherd, scenting out
the entire world of things . . .' (I,1; p. 227) and so forth; the canto goes on to
describe many other things the winds do. The reader is made aware of the
enumeration through the employment of anaphora and other related techniques that emphasise the repetition of words or phrases. Here at the
opening of the poem, the device obviously has a special relation to the
'incessant blowing of the winds',[56] but it is used as well in many other
contexts, such as the lines addressed by the Poet to Winter (II,2; p. 271):

54. The first time, that is, aside from the fragmentary presentations in the
    Introduction.
55. Anne Churchman, 'L'Enumération chez Saint-John Perse: A Propos d'une
    page de *Vents*', in *Studies in Modern French Literature: Presented to
    P. Mansell Jones by Pupils, Colleagues, and Friends*, ed. L. J. Austin et al.
    (Manchester University Press, 1981), pp. 61–70.
56. Ruth N. Horry, *Paul Claudel and Saint-John Perse: Parallels and Contrasts*
    (Chapel Hill: University of North Carolina Press, 1971), p. 94. Horry has
    noted the thoroughgoing use of repetition in *Winds*.

'Winter curly as a bison, Winter crinkled as white horsehair moss,
Winter with wells of red arsenic, with pockets of oil and bitumen,
Winter with the taste of skunk, of carabid beetle and smoke of
    hickory wood,
Winter with prisms and crystals at the black diamond crossroads . . .'

This idea of a repertoire of disparate elements which nevertheless contribute to a profound unity, guaranteed by Perse's technique of creating 'a rich network of relationships and correspondences',[57] does indeed have a parallel of a sort in Carter's piece, in the repertoires of chords and intervals that generate each movement. But the two techniques can hardly be regarded as exactly analogous. For one thing, the scale of the enumerated units is not the same in both works. Carter's intervals, at least, might be thought of more as phonemes than words, since they rarely appear as discrete units. More to the point is that Carter's repertoires are used *absolutely* globally, with all resources available at every moment, while Perse's patterns make use of discernible repetition of just a few elements, which then gives way to repetition of other elements, and so on. Still, the 'through-composed' sound of Carter's textures is also a feature at least some of the time in *Winds*; as Yves-Alain Favre has attested concerning Section I, 'no canto . . . can be separated from the others' because of the manifold connections between them.[58]

Repetition on levels other than that of the chordal and intervallic repertoires, though, does appear to have a special importance in the Concerto; as such, it may well be a response to specific prosodic features of Perse's work. Bars 29–43 in the first movement serve as an apt example (see Ex. 6.6). Here the syntactic units may be identified as shown in the key. The 'main argument' is carried, of course, by the 'A' elements (first movement music), and their periodically interjected statements each in the characteristic decelerating rhythm of the first movement form a clearly repetitive structure. As the numerical suffixes indicate, however, there is a certain amount of variety within this pattern – in fact even more than the schematic shows, for the tuttis in the cellos can be either unison or divisi, and in bb. 41–2 they are reduced to an accompanimental role against the solo piano. Besides this level of diversity within unity, there is the variable feature of the brief intrusions of material from the other three movements. There is no particular regularity in their arrangement, but second movement material is heard the most often and seems to lead to the extended intrusion of bb. 43ff., which eclipses the first movement

57. Churchman, 'L'Enumération', p. 66.
58. Favre, *Saint-John Perse*, p. 39 and chart, p. 43.

Example 6.6   Concerto for Orchestra, bb. 28–43. Key: **A**, cellos; **A1**, piano solo or with harp and/or marimba: **B**, momentary intrusion of second movement; **C**, momentary intrusion of third movement; **D**, momentary intrusion of fourth movement

Example 6.6 (cont.)

Example 6.6   (cont.)

Example 6.6 (*cont.*)

Example 6.6   (cont.)

Example 6.6   (*cont.*)

B (extended intrusion)

material for several measures. It is probably wisest not to read any parallel
to the actual sense of the poem into this sequence of musical events, but
certainly the repetitions of I,1 ('very great winds', 'very great tree') give
way in I,2 to 'O you whom the storm refreshes', clearly drawn from
Section II. Even if this is no more than a coincidence, still it is not difficult
to hear the rhetorical configurations of Perse's lines conveyed in a general
way throughout this movement and the third – though perhaps less so in
the second and fourth, where the rhythmic movement is more continuous, less given over to the kind of gestural repetition to which the phrase-
by-phrase rhythmic organisation of the first and third lends itself.

V

There is certainly no particular reason to *expect* to find correspondences
of the sort discussed above between the works of Carter and Perse, whose
cultural background, aesthetic predilections and psychological character
are in general quite markedly dissimilar. All the more interesting, then,
that certain of Perse's remarks about modern French poetry and certain of
Carter's about twentieth-century American music have a kind of common
ground, which seems to have been arrived at from entirely different angles
of approach. Here is an excerpt from one of Perse's letters:

> It is very important not to make any mistake, where French poetry
> is concerned, about the basic impulse that leads to the expansive-
> ness of inclusive poems like *Vents* or *Amers*. It would be erroneous
> to see verbal amplification or oratorical self-indulgence in them
> when, in fact, such elaborations, strictly imposed by the theme
> itself, are still a vast linking together of ellipses, shortcuts, contrac-
> tions, and even, on occasion, of simple flashes devoid of all transi-
> tional material.[59]

Now Carter, in his article 'Expressionism and American Music':

> a sense of inner cohesion is closely allied with the general tendency
> among Expressionists toward 'reduction' in technique, to finding the
> basic material of any given work . . . As in literature, much concern
> and invention was lavished on new methods of fragmentary
> presentation, such as starting *in medias res* or ending with an
> uncompleted phrase. Closely allied with this was the tendency
> toward very short, concentrated totalities . . . not only this type of

---

59. Perse, letter to Mrs Francis Biddle (Katherine Garrison Chapin), 12 December
  1955, in *Letters*, trans. and ed. Arthur J. Knodel (Princeton University Press,
  1979), p. 422.

fragmentation was common among Expressionists but also the fragmentation of the materials of the work.[60]

Though Carter himself cannot be classified as an Expressionist, the composers discussed in his article include Ives, Cowell, Ruggles and Varèse – all of whose influence Carter has identified at one time or another as particularly significant to his own development. Thus it is not surprising to find fragmented, elliptical and extremely condensed types of expression in his music, even though the pieces themselves are rarely short; nor is it surprising to find that Carter, too, has adopted methods that originate in literature.

The natural interest of Perse's work for Carter extends even beyond this general mode of communication, however. For Perse has also said of modern French poetry that: 'Going far beyond any mimetic action, it finally *is* the thing itself, in that thing's own movement and duration. It lives the thing and "animates" it totally and most scrupulously, and with infinite variation submits to the thing's own measure and rhythm.'[61] We remember, in this connection, that moment in Canto I,1, after the description of the rustling, rattling tree, in which the Poet says: 'And does not my whole page itself already rustle, / Like that great magical tree in its winter squalor . . .' (p. 229).

Perhaps what attracted Carter to the poem in the first place was just this self-referential feature, a quality which would suggest a close kinship to 'absolute music' in general and to Carter's vigorously individualistic, contextually-based compositional method in particular. *Winds*'s resemblance to music in this respect is also a powerful argument against interpreting Carter's piece as mere programme music – since how, after all, could a poem that is not itself primarily narrative in nature control the sequential events of a piece of music as if it *were* a narrative? Even more convincing than this observation, however, is the evidence of the Concerto itself. For to call *Winds* a model for the Concerto is also to identify the musical work as a response to the literary one – in this case, a response that assumes the stature of a reading, an interpretation, of the poem at the same time as it achieves self-sufficiency as a work of art. Under these circumstances – quite different from those of programme music, in which the programme arbitrarily dictates the avenues along which the music may be understood and thus effectively subjugates the music to its will – Carter's music enters into a kind of reciprocal relation-

60. Carter, 'Expressionism and American Music' (1965/72), in *Writings*, p. 240.
61. Perse, quoted in Knodel, *Saint-John Perse*, p. 90.

ship with Perse's text, such that as much may be grasped of *Winds* through the Concerto as the reverse. Making it worth our while to read as well as listen more closely – in this as in other works – is one of Carter's most significant accomplishments as a composer.

Rhetorics

7

Birtwistle's secret theatres

Jonathan Cross

Birtwistle's creative output has been punctuated by the regular production
of major works for the stage: *Punch and Judy* (1967), music for *The
Oresteia* at the National Theatre (1981), *The Mask of Orpheus* (1973–83,
first performed 1986), *Yan Tan Tethera* (1986), *Gawain* (1991) and, most
recently, *The Second Mrs Kong* (1994). In these, as in all his theatrical projects, he has worked closely and directly with his librettists, directors and
actors: music and drama are so intimately linked in Birtwistle's imagination that it is impossible to conceive of one without the other.
Furthermore, ideas about theatre and drama have provided the impetus for
many of his non-stage compositions. Nearly all his music can be described
as 'dramatic' in some sense, in that conflicts or contradictions are worked
out in a ritualistic manner and are contained within highly formalised
frames.

The dramatic sources of Birtwistle's ideas are many and varied:
examples include Baroque opera and the Passions of Bach (*Punch and
Judy*), Japanese theatre (*Bow Down*, 1977), the pastoral and traditional
English Mummers' Play (*Down by the Greenwood Side*, 1968–9) and even
cinema (*The Second Mrs Kong*). It is not primarily the subject-matter in
these heterogeneous kinds of theatre that attracts the composer, though
their themes and characters, from Father Christmas to King Kong,
inevitably find their way into his works. Rather, it is the stylised, ritualised structures of the drama that fascinate him, that provide him with
situations within which he can operate as a composer. Such formality is
an on-going obsession, as evinced even by the titles of his works from the
early *Refrains and Choruses* (1959) to the recent *Antiphonies* (1992), and
this is something which, uncharacteristically, he has often discussed in
public: 'There are certain things you don't have to justify in an opera, and
one of these is its formality . . . I am interested in exploring a different
order of formality, a different ritual situation – possibly something to do
with oriental theatre.'[1]

---

1. Birtwistle, in a talk on *The Mask of Orpheus* to the Friends of English
   National Opera, 21 April 1986.

207

The one source which has been of enduring fascination to Birtwistle, however, is that of Attic theatre. His works are peopled with characters from Greek tragedy and mythology – Orpheus and Eurydice (on many occasions – including, most recently, the Head of Orpheus and his lost lover in *The Second Mrs Kong*), the Watchman from Aeschylus' *Agamemnon*, and even the Choregos figure. But, with the notable exception of the National Theatre *Oresteia* project with Peter Hall, he has never simply 'set' a Greek play to music. What interests Birtwistle is the *idea* of Greek tragedy, an abstract, generalised notion of the formality of the plays, of their ritualised presentation of passionate emotions, of the roles characters play rather than the characters themselves – just as in his most recent opera, it is not King Kong as represented in the 1933 film who is of interest, but the *idea* that Kong stands for. Thus, even when the subject-matter for an opera is drawn directly from Greek mythology, as is the case with *The Mask of Orpheus*, where the story of the love of Orpheus and Eurydice and their violent deaths is retold, its representation is far from simple. In this work, each of the principal characters has three roles, and the 'Orphic inheritance', as the librettist describes it[2] – the 'idea' of Orpheus, if you like – is represented in multiple versions. Orpheus dies many deaths during the course of the work: he hangs himself, Zeus kills him with a thunderbolt, he is torn apart by the Maenads. This stage work, like all of Birtwistle's music, is not primarily concerned with narrative continuity. As in Wagner (certainly a valid comparison in the case of the multi-dimensional *Orpheus*, a modern-day *Gesamtkunstwerk*), it is the telling rather than the tale which is the principal focus. Indeed, not only is *The Mask of Orpheus* a distillation of the many versions of the Orpheus myth, it also contains within itself six tales of Dionysus and Apollo, taken from Ovid and told in mime, which interrupt the main unfolding of the work: these are known as the 'Passing Clouds of Abandon' and the 'Allegorical Flowers of Reason' and while self-contained and ostensibly unrelated to the principal drama, their themes nevertheless broaden its context. In typically paradoxical manner, the composer has commented, 'They seem to be external to the narrative, but at the same time they're not.'[3]

It is not only the stage works that have drawn on Attic drama. Some concert pieces, such as *Nenia: the Death of Orpheus* (a 'dramatic scene',

---

2. Peter Zinovieff, libretto to *The Mask of Orpheus* (London: Universal Edition, 1986), p. 2.
3. Birtwistle in conversation with Michael Hall, in the English National Opera Programme for *The Mask of Orpheus*, ed. Nicholas John (1986).

1970), also take aspects of Greek mythology for their subject-matter. But perhaps the most intriguing category of works derived from Ancient Greek material is that of instrumental pieces where the drama is not at all explicit in terms of any particular narrative. One highly significant work in this regard is *Tragoedia* (1965) where, again, Greek tragedy has provided the dramatic context for the music – though not, in this case, any specific play but a generalised notion of the formal structure of Greek tragedy, an abstract drama intended, in the composer's words, to 'bridge the gap between "absolute music" and theatre music'.[4] Each formal section of *Tragoedia* takes its title from the constituent elements of tragedy as defined by Aristotle:

> The prologue is the whole part of a tragedy that precedes the parode, or first entry of the Chorus. An episode is the whole of that part of the tragedy that comes between complete choral songs. The exode is the whole of that part of the tragedy which is followed by a song of the Chorus, and a stasimon is a choral song without anapaests or trochees.[5]

The work, according to Meirion Bowen, is a study 'in bilateral symmetry, wherein the formal layout and scoring lend force to each other'.[6] The scoring is quite boldly confrontational, both of solo instruments (the 'odd men out', as Birtwistle describes them, the cello and horn, who 'act as individual opponents within the conflict'[7]), and of instrumental groups (wind quintet and string quartet with the harp in between – the latter's recurrent cadential figure (Ex. 7.1) serving an important function in punctuating the progress of the music/drama). The formal layout is given in Fig. 7.1, where the work's controlling symmetry – of concentric layers 'grouped outwards from a central static pillar'[8] – is able to contain the music's essential oppositions.

In many ways, *Tragoedia* encapsulates Birtwistle's continuing musical preoccupations. Ancient Attic tragedy, containing, as it does, extremely passionate and confrontational subject matter within a highly stylised formal framework, has proved to be an enduring model for Birtwistle. The Greek plays are concerned less with narrative continuity

---

4. The composer's note on the work, quoted in Michael Hall, *Harrison Birtwistle* (London: Robson Books, 1984), p. 173.
5. Aristotle, *On the Art of Poetry*, in *Classical Literary Criticism*, trans. T. S. Dorsch (Harmondsworth: Penguin, 1965), p. 47.
6. Meirion Bowen in *British Music Now*, ed. Lewis Foreman (London: Elik, 1975), p. 67.
7. Hall, *Harrison Birtwistle*, p. 174.   8. *Ibid.*

Example 7.1

and development than with exploring certain recurring, volatile situations: 'tragedy is a representation, not of men, but of action and life'.[9] Birtwistle's music, too, is not so much concerned with development as with a creative response to deep, often unconscious, issues of ritual and formality. *Tragoedia* is able to explore them in one way, *Punch and Judy* in another; in both cases, however, the composer's intentions would seem to be the same. 'I discovered a world in *Tragoedia*; then in *Punch and Judy* I exploited it.'[10]

The 'latent' theatre of *Tragoedia* is also realised in *Verses for Ensembles* (1969) where the instrumentalists move about the concert platform according to the changing musical roles they play. Precedent for such a practice can be found in Berio's *Circles* (1960) which requires the movement of the singer (who, like the wind players in *Tragoedia*, also takes up claves to play), but Berio's theatre is of a very different order from Birtwistle's, as is made clear by some of the early *Sequenzas* (particularly Nos. III and V) which date from around the same time. The overall structure of *Verses for Ensembles* in terms of its sectional organisation, however, is remarkably close to that of *Tragoedia* (see Fig. 7.1). The opening section (from the beginning to Fig. 6) is the Prologue: [11] here the block-like treatment of instrumental groups is established and the future independent roles of the horn and two trumpets are precipitated. As in *Tragoedia*, this section stands outside the main argument of the work. A slow, static section follows the low woodwind ensemble, punctuated by a brass ritornello; appropriately, the entire woodwind ensemble plays here – the entry song of the Chorus or Parados. A renewed dynamism is set up at Fig. 13 with a horn cadenza which anticipates the first Episodion (Figs.

---

9. Aristotle, *On the Art of Poetry*, p. 39.
10. Birtwistle in interview in Paul Griffiths, *New Sounds, New Personalities: British Composers of the 1980s* (London: Faber, 1985), p. 190.
11. The use of terms from Greek tragedy is mine, not the composer's.

Figure 7.1 Comparison of formal layouts of *Tragoedia*, *Verses for Ensembles* and *Punch and Judy*

a) *Tragoedia*

Prologue				
	Parados			
		Episodion: Strophe I		
			Antistrophe I	
				Stasimon
		Episodion: Strophe II		
			Antistrophe II	
	Exodus			

b) *Verses for Ensembles*

Prologue				
	Parados			
		Episodion: I		
				Stasimon
		Episodion: II		
	Exodus			

c) *Punch and Judy*

Prologue					
		Melodrama I	Passion Chorale I	Quest I	
		Melodrama II	Passion Chorale II	Quest II	
		Melodrama III			
					Nightmare
				Quest III	
			Passion Chorale III		
		Melodrama IV			
	Punch Triumphans				
Epilogue					

18–30). This consists principally of bold antiphony between instrumental blocks, but with the two trumpets musically and physically liberated in a manner reminiscent of the dialogue between horn and cello in the central Anapaest of *Tragoedia*'s Episodion I. The entire section is repeated exactly as Episodion II (Figs. 58–70). These two episodes are separated by a section which is itself built from a series of verses and refrains, i.e. solos for each of the high woodwinds plus horn, separated by brass ritornelli, thus linking it with the earlier, more static Parados (its nearest Greek equivalent is the Stasimon). A final section (Figs. 70ff.) brings together most of the work's ideas and is thus the Exodos which sums up the salient features of the 'play'. The parallels are also striking between this abstract piece of theatre and the overt theatrical statement which preceded it, *Punch and Judy*. Like *Verses for Ensembles*, it consists of a ritual cycle of verse–refrain patterns organised around the central Nightmare section, i.e. the moment, found in all Classical tragedies, of *peripeteia* or reversal (defined by Aristotle as 'a change from one state of affairs to its opposite, one which conforms . . . to probability or necessity').[12]

In what ways, then, is the drama of *Verses for Ensembles* 'enacted', and how is its musico-dramatic structure articulated? Firstly, a carefully specified arrangement of the players on the concert platform represents, in spatial terms, the divisions between groups of instruments within the music. The woodwind, seated at the front of the stage, use one block of seating on the left when they are playing as a high-pitched ensemble, and another block on the right when they play as a low ensemble. Hence, when the bassoonist takes up the contrabassoon, for instance, she has to move from the left to the right of the stage. A change in the instrument's role is thus articulated musically by the change in the instrument's range and timbre and physically by the change in the player's position within the performing space. Seated behind the woodwind is the brass quintet, and behind this are two further levels, one for the untuned percussion and one for the tuned. The two different types of percussion are played by the same players so that movement between the two levels becomes necessary; however, each distinct group always plays as an ensemble (tuned and untuned are never mixed) so again their movements articulate timbral changes. The brass play as a full ensemble less frequently. The horn has an important solo role whilst the two trumpets demonstrate a tendency to break away and continue an independent musical 'conversation'. This too is represented theatrically as each soloist moves to a new position at one of four solo platforms around the stage, two at the back and two at the

12. Aristotle, *On the Art of Poetry*, p. 46.

front. The trombones never take on the roles of soloists so remain permanently seated in their ensemble positions.

Such movements bring to mind another kind of drama being enacted on the platform, one where the stage becomes a church. Here, the rows of players make up the choir, while 'lessons' are read from lecterns and musicians call to one another from the galleries. Hall even goes so far as to identify two kinds of chant from the Christian liturgy in the work: antiphonal (the alternation of choirs) and responsorial (the alternation of soloists and a single choir).[13] In Peter Brook's categorisation of theatrical types, the 'holy theatre' is one where ritual movement, repetition and stylised role-playing are of deeper significance than narrative: 'A holy theatre not only presents the invisible but also offers conditions that make its perception possible.'[14] In *Verses for Ensembles*, this ritual becomes the principal focus of attention and it is the formality of the musical structure which provides a context within which the work's 'invisible' subject-matter (its 'secret theatre') can be made meaningful.

The formal layout of *Verses for Ensembles*, with its dependence on verse–refrain patterns, has already been discussed in outline. This stylised structure is articulated by a number of artificial means, most notably the repetition of material, on both the small and large scale. The arch shape to the five main sections is quite clearly achieved by repetition to create symmetries about the central section. This is made to stand apart from the rest of the work, being surrounded by two large-scale *literal* repetitions (relatively unusual in Birtwistle), i.e. Episodion I is repeated *note for note*. It is the work's 'still' centre, the point of turning or reversal. The three central sections are also contained within two outer sections which are defined by the varied repetition of the same material. Thus, the work takes on the overall symmetrical shape of Prologue A B C B A'.

Repetition within these blocks is also of significance and this is most apparent in the central section, whose solo–ritornello patterns are a microcosm of the verse–refrain structures of the piece as a whole. Each of the high woodwind instruments has, in turn, a virtuosic solo obbligato over a ground-like idea in the horn, almost a passacaglia. Little attempt is made at development or transition either within or between sections, emphasising the independent nature of each block; the adoption of such techniques confirms that, as so often in Birtwistle, particularly in works of the 1960s, this music is concerned with exploring the changing relationship between repeated ideas rather than with any continuous narra-

13. Hall, *Harrison Birtwistle*, p. 52.
14. Peter Brook, *The Empty Space* (London: Pelican, 1968), p. 63.

tive. By their spatial distribution and simple movements about the platform, the players present to the audience a highly stylised drama whose
plot is not explicit but where the physical relationships between individuals and groups is always changing – an abstract drama like *Tragoedia*, but
one in which the visual theatre now mirrors the processes at work inside
the music.

Birtwistle's original title for *Verses for Ensembles* was to have been
'Signals' and this is evident in the way in which the main sections of this
work are articulated or signalled, musically and physically. In particular,
the horn and the trumpet are important in marking the beginnings and
endings of blocks of material. With the exception of the central
horn/woodwind dialogues, it is only the horn and trumpets who move to
occupy the solo platforms and it is often from these positions, detached
from the rest of the players, that they announce new sections or bring others to a close. Like the Greek Chorus, they stand outside the main action,
both to comment on past events and to announce the arrival of new characters (as well as, at other times, being absorbed back into the main body
of events). At these major moments of articulation, the physically remote
soloists present musical material which is quite distinct and which only
occurs in the same form at the beginnings or ends of sections. Indeed, in a
brief but highly perceptive article, Michael Nyman has commented that
'the formation of a new and entirely convincing cadential "language" is
one of the most original features of the score'.[15]

It is generally the horn which signals the start of each main section
with a musical object characterised by interval class 5 (Ex. 7.2). We have
already seen the horn playing the role of protagonist in *Tragoedia*, and
even as far back as *Refrains and Choruses* the horn is, in places, set apart
from the rest of the quintet.[16] There is, in particular, a striking similarity
between the animated horn line (marked *fff possibile!*) at the centre of
Refrains and Choruses (bb. 73–89), which is made up of overlapping forms
of pitch-class set 3–5 [100011] (see Ex. 7.3), and Ex. 7.2 from *Verses for
Ensembles*, comprising overlapping forms of pc sets 3–5 and 3–4 [100110],
i.e. holding ic1 and ic5 invariant. Ex. 7.2 always occurs at moments of
structural opening: at the very beginning of the work ('Prologue'); at Figs.
13 and 14 (a pre-echo of section B); Fig. 18 (the beginning of section B
proper); a more extended appearance in a varied form throughout the cen-

15. Michael Nyman, 'Two New Works by Birtwistle', *Tempo*, 88 (Spring 1969),
    p. 50.
16. However, I cannot go along with Michael Hall (*Harrison Birtwistle*,
    pp. 10–15) in identifying a *consistent* role of protagonist for the horn in this
    work.

Example 7.2

Example 7.3

Example 7.4

tral C section, Figs. 34–53; see below); and at Fig. 57 (the start of the repeat of section B).

If the role of the horn, as protagonist, is one of opening, the role of the trumpets is one of closure; like the horn, they repeat certain striking musical ideas at moments of structural importance. They have two quite distinct musical ideas associated with different structural blocks (and, hence, different parts of the platform), although they are related in terms of their antiphonal writing. The first idea is built around a perfect fourth (E–A, Ex. 7.4) and brings both the Prologue (Figs. 4–6) and the entire work (Figs. 75ff.) to a conclusion. On both these occasions, like masters-of-ceremonies, the trumpeters step forward to the solo desks at the front of the stage and announce the beginning and end of the 'drama', in just the same way as Choregos opens and concludes *Punch and Judy*. (In the Prologue to the opera, Choregos sings, 'Let's trumpets sound'; the fanfare figurations which follow, with their reiterations of a single note, are similar in effect to the trumpet figures in *Verses for Ensembles*.) The appearance of this music at Figs. 4ff. is anticipated at Figs. 2–3 by the horn and oboe, who reiterate a tritone Ab–D, from *within* the ensemble; the true cadential nature of the more stable perfect fourths in the trumpets is confirmed by their movement to the front of the stage at Fig. 3 (almost implying a *Hauptstimme*, as if the players' movements were somehow 'analysing' the articulatory function of the intervals they play). As Nyman has observed, the conflict set up at the beginning between these pairs of dyads (Ab–D, E–A) is resolved at the end of the work into an A–E–D chord;[17] the horn is integrated into the final cadential progression with a chromatic scale rising to an A.

The second group of trumpet ideas is always associated with the two central Episodes (sections B). The trumpets' first entry here is with the glockenspiels (Fig. 24), the only instruments in the entire section not to play homorhythmically. Eventually, the trumpets assert an even greater independence, first by taking up antiphonal ideas from the glockenspiels (Fig. 27), and then by escaping entirely the metrical hegemony of the main ensemble (Fig. 28 – Ex. 7.5a). The musical isolation of the trumpets is echoed in theatrical terms by their occupying the two distant solo platforms whose stereophonic positioning also gives a spatial representation to the antiphony between the two instruments. However, at Fig. 29 (Ex. 7.5b) the trumpets rejoin the tempo of the main ensemble which, combined with the cadential character of Ex. 7.5b material on a perfect fifth, signals a role of closure. At this point the trumpets return to their positions within the ensemble – they have been musically and physically reintegrated.

Ex. 7.5a is also of interest in this context because it illustrates the close relationship between solo writing, limited indeterminacy and spatial separation. On each occasion that players are given choices of pitches or freedom of tempo, they are required to move to a new position away from the main body of players, symbolising their independence from the tyranny of the conductor (and composer) and realising, in visual terms, the verse-like nature of their music. Instances include such solo verses as the horn cadenza at Fig. 13, the high woodwind verses in the central section, and even the lyrical passages for the entire woodwinds at Figs. 6ff. when the players move to take up their low-pitched cousins. The only inde-

17. 'Two New Works by Birtwistle', p. 49.

Example 7.5

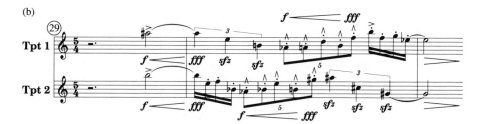

Example 7.6

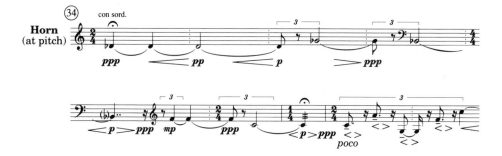

terminate sections for which players do not move are the brass ritornelli
(first heard at Fig. 16); in the central section, their *lack* of movement is significant in defining the role of the ritornelli as refrains to the horn and
woodwind verses. In fact, each appearance of the ritornello is prompted
by a presentation of material derived from Ex. 7.2 by the horn: the horn
cadenza at Fig. 13 springs from a statement of Ex. 7.2, and the ground over
which the winds play their verses is a variation on Ex. 7.2 (for example,
compare Ex. 7.6, which accompanies the bassoon verse, with Ex. 7.2).
Each horn/woodwind verse from the front of the stage is answered by
a brass refrain from among the ensemble.

Fifteen years separate *Verses for Ensembles* from the next instrumental
work by Birtwistle to require the movement of players about the concert
platform. *Secret Theatre* (1984) is an altogether more complex work,
whose title can be understood to refer both to the abstract nature of the
drama it presents and, unlike *Tragoedia* and *Verses for Ensembles*, to the
less overt 'rules' by which that drama is enacted. Its source is a poem of
the same name by Robert Graves,[18] quoted in part in the front of the score,
and which suggests a change in the tone of the drama away from the bold
conflicts of the works of the 1960s: as Arnold Whittall has proposed, it
'evokes the private celebrations of human love rather than the public rituals of epic drama'.[19] Nevertheless, the members of the ensemble still play
roles (Birtwistle even describes them as the 'dramatis personae') and they
are divided between two groups – the main ensemble, designated the
Continuum (seated), and the soloists or Cantus (standing behind the
Continuum). Certain players move from the Continuum to the Cantus,
though often the reasons for this movement are not clear-cut (as the
Graves poem puts it, 'we mount the stage as though at random'). It is 'an
unforeseen and fiery entertainment'; nonetheless the overt confrontation
of soloist and ensemble or verse and chorus is generally eschewed here in
favour of an apparently more continuous music whose ideas are heard to
flow between the two groups.

   A clear example of this is to be found at the very beginning of the
work (Ex. 7.7). The flute takes up the Cantus position ('a flute signals far

----

18. Robert Graves, 'Secret Theatre' in *Collected Poems 1975* (London: Cassell,
    1975), p. 402.

   When from your sleepy mind the day's burden
   Falls like a bushel sack on a barn floor,
   Be prepared for music, for natural mirages
   And for night's incomparable parade of colour.

   Neither of us daring to assume direction
   Of an unforeseen and fiery entertainment,
   We clutch hands in the seventh row of the stalls
   And watch together, quivering, astonished, silent.

   It is hours past midnight now; a flute signals
   Far off; we mount the stage as though at random,
   Boldly ring down the curtain, then dance out our love:
   Lost to the outraged, humming auditorium.

   The passages in italics are omitted by the composer from the front
   of the score.
19. Arnold Whittall, 'The Geometry of Comedy', *Musical Times*, 134
    (January 1993), 17.

Example 7.7   *Secret Theatre*, bb. 1–9

off . . .') and presents a near-continuous melody which takes E as its focus and moves freely round the eight pitch classes of two superimposed chromatic tetrachords (D–E♭–E–F; A♭–A–B♭–B). The Continuum appears to be more mechanistic with its regular presentation of an insistent D–F motif in the upper strings and cycling of sets of pitches in the lower strings (the cello, for example, rotates the pitches of a pair of chromatic trichords, C–C♯–D and G–G♯–A).[20] There *is* an opposition here (perhaps one of the starkest of the entire piece) between the evident linearity of the Cantus and the circularity of the Continuum, and this is dramatised by the players' physical separation, but the distinction is mitigated by the fact that both groups process not dissimilar pitch-class material in similar ways.

This subtle distinction between the repeating processes of horizontal Cantus and vertical Continuum forms a central concern of the work. In notes made prior to the work's composition, Birtwistle asks 'at what point does an ostinato cease to function as such, due to the number of notes present in it? or the amount of time for it to register as a repeat? . . . ostinato into melody perhaps'.[21] For the most part, it is the Cantus that is associated with continuous quasi-melodic ideas. A certain location is thus identified with a certain kind of musical material and a player 'mounts the stage' only when she has a narrative to deliver. Even when the Cantus consists of more than one player (which in fact, apart from the very opening, is almost always the case), it always speaks with a single voice: in unison or octaves, heterophonically, or in a complex kind of organum. However, as has already been suggested, this piece, unlike its progenitors from the 1960s, is not merely concerned with setting up a bold opposition between groups which is then maintained throughout the work. Rather, the musical drama enacted by the players' movements explores the changing relationships *between* the two ensembles – Whittall has written of an exchange of characteristics between groups 'that question[s] the logic of the basic Cantus/Continuum distinction at the same time as it is being reinforced'.[22] This manifests itself in various ways.

Take, for instance, the passage initiated by the flute's temporary return to the Continuum at the very moment the trumpet and horn begin to play with the Cantus (just after Fig. 6). When the flute starts to play from within the ensemble (Fig. 7) its rather hesitant falling dyads

---

20. For a fuller discussion, see Jonathan Cross, 'Lines and Circles: On Birtwistle's *Punch and Judy* and *Secret Theatre*', *Music Analysis*, 13 (1994), 203–25.
21. London Sinfonietta 'Response' Programme Book (1987), p. 19.
22. 'The Geometry of Comedy', p. 19.

('... quivering, astonished ...') stand apart from the rest of the ensemble's music, as they do not seem to belong. By Fig. 9, it is participating in organum-like writing with strings and vibraphone whose formation is highly reminiscent of the flute's melody from the beginning of the work; this is accompanied by contrabassoon, double bass and piano rotating pitches in a manner similar to the Continuum at the opening. It was noted above how these initially opposed ideas nevertheless shared certain characteristics (as kinds of ostinati): this is now confirmed by the flute's movement back into the Continuum. Meanwhile, the Cantus (oboe, clarinet, trumpet, horn) contributes another stratum to the texture – a unison melody with the important D–F dyad which had been a prominent component of the opening *Continuum* music. This exchange of ideas and roles is brought directly into the foreground when, at the change of tempo (b. 9 of Fig. 9), the Continuum suddenly suspends its motion with a sustained chord while the Cantus 'blurts out' a kind of compressed echo of the Continuum's material, only for the idea to return hurriedly to the Continuum. The flute initiated this change in relationship and it is the flute which now signals an explicit link between Cantus and Continuum (as implied by the poem ... 'signals far off'). At Fig. 12, still from within the Continuum, it plays a short 'refrain' figure (Ex. 7.8) while the other instruments pause. It occurs four times in close succession, each occur-

Example 7.8

(flute)

rence being varied. On the fourth occasion, the work's opening opposition is resumed (mechanistic Continuum, sustained Cantus), the flute's held F merges with the Cantus (Fig. 14), and finally the flute moves back to its solo position to play the refrain for the fifth and last time. Thus, though the musical context here is much more fluid than in *Verses for Ensembles*, the movements of the players serve a similar function in articulating physically the changing musical relationships between distinct groups of players.

There are many other moments in the work where Cantus-like ideas appear in the Continuum. Sometimes the reasons for this are relatively straightforward, such as the appearance of 'melodic' material in the vibraphone at Figs. 30–5 or the piano at Fig. 42 (these instruments cannot physically be moved to the soloists' platform); on other occasions, solo material from within the Continuum is signalled, as in *Verses for Ensembles*, by temporal freedom, e.g. the horn, Figs. 35–6, which plays 'slightly faster than tempo of conductor'. The bassoon, which never moves from the Continuum, often takes on the role of soloist, giving the impression of a kind of quirky spokesman/woman from out of the Chorus. At other moments, there seems little significant difference between Cantus and Continuum: for example, at Figs. 66–8, the two principal strata (i.e. sustained material derived from the D–F motif and rapid staccato passages built from chromatic segments) are shared equally between the two bodies. All this confirms the fact that this work is not just about confrontation but also about dialogue. After all, the Cantus is born out of the Continuum, and occasionally returns to it, so the work is concerned with the musical and physical shifts in the relationship between the two groups; its overall structure (which is, of course, more difficult to grasp than in *Tragoedia* or *Verses for Ensembles*) explores the changing degrees of relative distance or proximity between players and material (an idea that Birtwistle followed up in his wind quintet of 1993, *Five Distances for Five Instruments*).

It has already been mentioned that the D–F motif, usually in the same register (Ex. 7.9), seems to play an important role in the piece: indeed, this

Example 7.9

dyad is a significant recurring motif in many works which precede *Secret Theatre* (note how even Strophe I in *Tragoedia* begins in this way). The motif is obviously an important structural signal, though its function is not as precisely defined as, say, the cadential role of the fourths in *Verses for Ensembles*. The motif begins and ends *Secret Theatre* and also punctuates the journey – Birtwistle has often spoken of the same object being looked at from different perspectives. Of *Secret Theatre* he has said:

> I drew up a lot of pre-compositional ideas about how things could progress, how they could get from point to point; I constructed a whole map, as it were. But then in the process of composition, in the journey, I went in other ways, so these original journeys are still there.[23]

23. Griffiths, *New Sounds*, p. 188.

The D–F dyad is a kind of trace of those original journeys, signposts along
the way, to which the music keeps returning only to move off in a new
direction again.

Key moments in the work's structure are signalled by the dyad's
presence and thus, as in earlier works, relate directly to its drama. For
example, the momentary migration of the flute into the Continuum and
back to the Cantus, discussed above, is signalled by the D–F motif's
appearance in both the Cantus and the vibraphone (see b. 5 of Fig. 7). It is
also probably not without significance that the flute's first brief utterance
from the Continuum begins and ends with F and D (Ex. 7.10). Departure
and arrival can be marked by the motif, either by extension (e.g. D–F–E–C♯

Example 7.10

in vibraphone, Fig. 34; violin 1 and horn, bb. 4ff. of Fig. 47; oboe, Fig. 59; or
D–F–E♭–A, piano, Fig. 42, accompanied by an augmented version in the
double bass; etc.), by suggesting a return to the Continuum material of the
opening (e.g. violin 1, Fig. 33; xylophone, bb. 3ff. of Fig. 39 (plus G♭); etc.),
or, as happens increasingly towards the end of the work, by isolated
appearances (e.g. all voices, Figs. 66ff.; etc.).

If, unlike the earlier Birtwistle works modelled directly on forms
from Greek tragedy, the drama of *Secret Theatre* is covert, and its overall
form can only be discussed, as the composer has suggested, as a set of
rules, as a kind of journey whose direction is 'unforeseen', can we rely on
Graves's poem to provide a context or suggest strategies for interpretations of the music, even though much of the work had been written before
the composer encountered the poem? In a simple way, the poem sets up a
distinction between passive auditorium/Continuum (the poem's anony-
mous subjects, in the stanza Birtwistle omits, 'clutch hands in the seventh row of the stalls / And watch together . . .') and active stage/Cantus
('we mount the stage . . . Boldly ring down the curtain, then dance out our
love'). The final line of the poem, also omitted in the score, describes the
lovers as being 'Lost to the outraged, humming auditorium'. Lost in love,
lost in music – these are the private celebrations to which Whittall
referred – but also lost to the auditorium in that they now play according
to different rules on the other side of the proscenium. The auditorium is
'outraged' because the lovers have transgressed the conventions of the

theatre, offended too by the audacity, the frankness of the love dance. Yet the auditorium is also 'humming': does it hum with barely contained indignation or does its humming echo and accompany the lovers' actions? Birtwistle's *Secret Theatre* clearly answers that it is the latter; the last line of Graves's text is evidently dropped from the score in order to avoid the implication that the Continuum is in sharp opposition to the Cantus and that it acts as mere accompaniment. Early on, Birtwistle rejected such a straightforward opposition: 'MELODY/ACCOMPANIMENT ... bad analogy, suggesting one more important than the other ... explore notion – FORE-GROUND/BACKGROUND'.[24] In *Secret Theatre*, what is foreground and what is background is constantly shifting, a change of focus that is articulated by the movements of the players.

Central to *Secret Theatre*, as to Graves's poem, is the idea of dance which, through ritualised movements, expresses deep emotions. Many of Birtwistle's stage characters declare their feelings of or about love through or in the context of dance. Punch's Serenades, for instance, are accompanied by Pretty Polly dancing first a Gavotte, then an Allemande, to the sound of the flute. In *Gawain*, Lady de Hautdesert anticipates the seduction scene of Act II with her dance aria ('Now we shall learn ... [something of courtly love]'), again with a prominent flute obbligato. Inanna's mournful aria in Act II of *The Second Mrs Kong*, lamenting the love she never had, is counterpointed by a flute melody to a dancing accordion accompaniment. The confluence of song, dance and the flute on all these occasions is striking and seems, for Birtwistle, to symbolise the passions and rituals of love and courtship. In *Secret Theatre*, the singers have no actual words, but the significance of their song (the literal meaning of 'Cantus') is no less apparent. (That Birtwistle believes instruments can take on expressive 'sung' roles as effectively as the human voice is made abundantly clear by the tuba in *The Cry of Anubis* (1995).) In all of this, as the poem tells us and as has already been noted, the flute takes the lead. As for the dancing, once the Cantus has 'called the tune' ('a flute signals far off ...'), the Continuum responds almost immediately with a strange but alluring trochaic dance accompaniment. It is first heard at Fig. 1 and is thereafter predominantly associated with the piano (playing a kind of continuo role, like the accordion in *Mrs Kong*), punctuating the journey of the song through the piece (see, for instance, Figs. 41–2 and 59–65) and coinciding with the focal D–F dyad. The dance reaches its furious climax at

24. *Ibid.* The composer's use of 'foreground' and 'background' here refers to a sense of musical perspective; there is no evidence to support an understanding of the music in terms of Schenkerian levels.

Fig. 78 with Cantus and Continuum playing together, after which the players disperse, exhausted, to leave only the viola (Continuum) reiterating its lone D–F motif, a gentle echo of the dance of love humming in the auditorium.

It has often been commented that Birtwistle is a single-minded composer who, in some senses, writes the same piece over and over again: even he has admitted this in his comment that 'Pieces don't really start: they're part of a continuous process.'[25] Meirion Bowen's description of him, after Isaiah Berlin, as the hedgehog who 'knows one big thing'[26] seems to have stuck. What this 'one big thing' is, is perhaps harder to define, but it is probably true to say that the underlying conception of *every* one of his pieces has something to do with drama – be it the explicit kind of theatre of the stage works or the hidden drama of many of the concert pieces. Drama, for Birtwistle, is concerned primarily with conflict and confrontation, and his work attempts to find ways of containing such conflicts and even of generating situations in which reconciliations between opposed ideas might take place. Birtwistle is not particularly interested in narrative – certainly not a simple or single kind of story-telling; rather, he is fascinated by notions of role playing within formal, ritualised contexts. Hence, he is drawn, time and again, to certain kinds of theatre and theatrical situations in which he can explore these ideas. And for this reason he constantly returns to Ancient Greek tragedy which controls, in Nietzsche's opposition, the primordial impulses of Dionysus within the rational forms of Apollo.

Such thinking is well suited to Birtwistle's essentially non-developmental musical language in which 'objects' are placed in a formal musical landscape where they can collide or interact. This is the 'one big thing', the 'secret' of Birtwistle's theatre. And this might go some way in helping to explain the impact, not just of immense theatrical undertakings like *The Mask of Orpheus*, but also the more intimate rituals explored in *Tragoedia*, *Verses for Ensembles* and – especially – *Secret Theatre*. If *Secret Theatre*'s secret were a mere programme, a hidden story to give meaning to an otherwise inscrutable surface, then its impact would likely be diminished. Its secret is rather, as Peter Brook reminds us, its ability to offer conditions in which it becomes possible, as in the theatre, as in church, to glimpse the invisible.

25. Griffiths, *New Sounds*, p. 188.   26. *British Music Now*, p. 60.

8

The narrative impulse in the second *Nachtmusik* from Mahler's Seventh Symphony

Kofi Agawu

An orchestral serenade marked 'Andante amoroso', complete with mandolin and guitar, and intended as *Nachtmusik*, is not the most natural
place to search for traces of narrative. Unlike the purposeful first movement, in which the act of telling, with its promise to unveil thematic and
tonal secrets, is foregrounded, the fourth movement of Mahler's Seventh
develops a nonurgent temporal profile. Celebratory music for lovers is
time-killing music, perhaps ultimately anti-music, for its normative
social function is simply to be music – a profoundly tautological prescrip-
tion that threatens to deny music its 'nomadic ability to attach itself to,
and become a part of, social formations'.[1] But it is precisely because the
Nachtmusik invites the construction of an alternative temporality that
it is a good place to study narrative. Gestures of denial, we have come
to believe, are richer sites for the construction of meaning than gestures
of normative enactment.

Discontinuity

The most obvious signs of the *Nachtmusik*'s will-to-be, its refusal to
submit, puppet-fashion, to the dictates of an external musical order, are
embodied in moments of disjunction or discontinuity, moments in which
linear fulfilment is withheld. The nine-bar fragment quoted in Ex. 8.1 is
one of two main joins in this A B A' movement (bb. 1–186, 187–259 and
259–390), that between a contrasting central section featuring decidedly
low-style, 'street' music interspersed with sudden excursions into a high
style (B), and the more consistently elevated music of the first section (A),
which now returns as a formal and subtly varied reprise (A'). The seam is
most visible at bar 259, where a sense of disjunction is distributed across
the dimensions of texture, timbre and harmony (though not necessarily
voice leading, as we will see later). There are contrasts between three
sounding voices and a solo violin, between the sound of winds and strings,

1. Edward Said, *Musical Elaborations* (New York: Columbia University Press,
   1989), p. 70.

and between, on the one hand, a V/VI harmony, goal of an archaic phry-
gian cadence that neither leads to nor refers back to D minor, and, on the
other, a broad cadential progression in the principal key of F major:
VII°⁷/V–V7–I. Bar 259 thus indicates an abandoned process, a denied tendency, the suspension of one level of narration. But where does this shift
in gear take us? Back to the beginning of the movement, of course, to the
inaugural motive (now reharmonised with an A♭ to enhance its potency).
The motive's once-upon-a-time quality, which it acquired because it was
the first thing we heard and because it enacted a conventional attention-
calling gesture by rising an octave, holding on to the high note, and then
descending gradually, is here recalled, embellished, and at the same time
put in question.

The events around b. 259 are not merely special effects – the results,
perhaps, of rhetorical exaggeration – but structurally necessary. Unity in
Mahler's music, according to Adorno, 'is attained not in spite of disjunction, but only through it'.[2] In order to effect a satisfactory return to a previous musical thought, we must abandon or transform the current one. Yet,
however deliberate and elaborate the technical means of abandonment or
transformation are, the mere fact of return to what in the *Nachtmusik* is a
familiar, frequently stated thought undermines our perception of the con-
nective force of b. 259. Our hearing takes in more than what the ending of
Ex. 8.1a suggests, however, for the passage from its inception is billed as a
transition, using what Adorno calls 'invisible quotation marks'.[3] The network of signs operative here is – typically for Mahler – not free of internal
contradictions. Instead of leading to the F major reprise by means of a
sequence, linear intervallic pattern, or rising or falling bass line, the passage leads away from it. Mahler needed to find a new tonal vantage point
from which to launch the approach, a vantage point that would convince
the listener that the F major of bb. 259ff. is a different F major from that
which was concluded decisively in bb. 251–2. So Mahler wrote the 'wrong'
syntax for this transition while retaining the *sense* of transition. To speak
of this as an incongruity is not to endow the moment with poetry, and
thus to deny it well-formedness, but rather to speak of what is normative
or routine in Mahler.

The 'sense of transition', however, is complexly constructed, for, on
the one hand, and in flat contradiction of the assertion that b. 259 marks a
moment of disjunction, the onset of the reprise can be heard as part of a

2. Theodor W. Adorno, *Mahler: A Musical Physiognomy*, trans. Edmund
   Jephcott (University of Chicago Press, 1992), p. 33.
3. Adorno, *Mahler*, p. 32.

Example 8.1

(a) Mahler, Seventh Symphony, fourth movement, bb. 252–60

(b) Origins of bb. 257–64

rising bass motion A–B–C, a pattern of outer voice tenths showing no discontinuity. Ex. 8.1b suggests the origins of the passage: level a is the diatonic background of parallel tenths leading to a perfect cadence; level b fills in the missing chromatic spaces of level a; level c constructs a new, chromaticised background from the expanded resources of level b; and level d, Mahler's music, supplies the missing inner parts of level c. On the other hand, a sense of otherness is conveyed by the archaic cadential syntax, and this sense is reinforced by a textural differentiation between high, suspended strings and a tinkling harp figuration. There is an emptying out of discursive content here, a suggestion that we are about to return not to a specific beginning but to the idea of beginning.

The passage upon which we have been meditating is only one of several propositions for discontinuity in the *Nachtmusik*. Another is bb. 211–27, which comes from the B section (see Ex. 8.2). Here, two types of material are starkly juxtaposed, with no apparent attempt to reconcile them. If we call the first four bars X and the next four Y, then the design of the passage is X Y X Y X/Y, a simple alternation ending with a more complex gesture that is as much X as it is Y. The X material is dark and full of passionate expression; it carries to one extreme the muted outbursts of a more serious tone that characterised some earlier sections of B. The Y material, by contrast, is lighter, carrying on the serenade affect single-mindedly. It is in the nature of tonal and motivic syntax, however, in particular the semitone logic of later nineteenth-century harmony, that few configurations are differentiated enough to support claims of total discontinuity. For example, the motive played by bassoons and string bass at the beginning of X recalls that which announced the B section. And the

Example 8.2   Mahler, Seventh Symphony, fourth movement, bb. 211–27

Example 8.2   (*cont.*)

fact that the dotted figure played by cellos in b. 211 is immediately picked up by the horn in b. 215 suggests a level of continuity within the passage. It would be more accurate to describe the inner dynamic of Ex. 8.2 not in terms of a simple juxtaposition of two different kinds of material but in terms of an active interruption of Y by X (b. 218). I say that the serious style 'interrupts' the serenade style and not the other way round because the serenade grounds the movement affectively, articulating its primary field of discourse. When Y returns in b. 222, it is tonally and gesturally even further removed from X. Its squareness and four-bar length suggest an aloofness, a deafness perhaps to the interruption in b. 218. But the brilliant stroke in Ex. 8.2 is the way the X and Y materials are conflated in the last two bars (226–7). Although these bars begin like previous Xs (bb. 211–12 or 218–19), they contain a melodic echo of the last two bars of the most recent Y, ending melodically on E (compare bb. 225 and 227), thus providing two contrasting viewpoints of the same leading note.

The kinds of extreme contrasts identified here as disjunctions or discontinuities have a number of precedents, perhaps most notably in Beethoven and – despite the chronological reversal – in Stravinsky. The first movement of Beethoven's String Quartet, Op. 130, for example, although it exists on a much larger scale, provides a cogent parallel to Ex. 8.2, in that it proceeds with two distinct types of material presented in alternation and ultimately integrated. Similarly, the technique of stratification that Edward T. Cone has identified in Stravinsky's music (the *Symphonies of Wind Instruments* is a good representative) can be easily identified in Mahler too.[4] Mahler's procedures occupy a halfway stage between Beethoven and Stravinsky. The organic thrust of Beethoven's tonal thinking ensures that however extreme the contrasts are, they are usually rationalised by means of an integrative concluding gesture. By contrast, Stravinsky's blocks of material, although they sometimes lead to synthesis, are for the most part without life beyond themselves, without linear goals. Mahler extends the connectedness of Beethoven as far as it can go, far enough to challenge the evocation of facile analogies between polyphonic or compound melodies and stratification without ultimately negating their validity. That is why the metaphor of narration, undoubtedly appropriate for Beethoven and for Mahler, seems less appropriate for Stravinsky.

While the two passages discussed so far feature surface contrasts that have allowed us to speak in terms of discontinuities, discontinuity could just as easily come from the choice of an indirect tonal goal, a structurally

---

4. Edward T. Cone, 'Stravinsky: The Progress of a Method', *Perspectives of New Music*, 1 (1962), 18–26.

Example 8.3   Mahler, Seventh Symphony, fourth movement, bb. 299–304

parenthetical progression whose parentheses are erased. The passage summarised in chordal reduction in Ex. 8.3 is from the reprise (bb. 295–304). Beginning in F major, it slips into E♭ major before returning to F. The move to E♭ develops the profile of an interpolation or purple patch, a momentary intrusion of another 'voice,' a 'crack' in the tonal narrative. It is true that the key of E♭ major is easily explained as ♭VII or V/IV in the key of F, or as part of a deceptive cadence in G minor, V–VI. Yet, decoding the progression according to the constraints of a closed, abstract, and minimally historicised system of relations mutes the rhetorical – that is to say narrative – force of the moment.

A crack in the tonal narrative may or may not be underlined timbrally. The passage quoted in Ex. 8.4, played exclusively by strings, is the familiar opening motto of the movement. It ends on the downbeat of b. 4 with the solo violin playing a solitary F, the rest of the strings dropping out on the upbeat. Guitar and harp enter with the solo violin's F. The strings, in other words, relinquish their harmonic and timbral responsibility, leaving guitar and harp to close the motto at the same time as they begin exposing the accompaniment figures that define the next unit of the movement. A hastily constructed hierarchy that consigns timbral logic to a secondary role will miss the interplay between continuity and discontinuity in this passage, and with that a sense of the music's multiple voices.

Intertextuality

Just as the discontinuity principle highlights the music's narrative capabilities – when an on-going process is abandoned, we become more aware of its status as process – so intertextuality, by forcing an engagement with other texts (musical, literary, as well as critical), guarantees the perception of narrative features. It is well known that Mahler frequently refers to or quotes from other works (his own included). But it is not merely in this sense – of a work as 'a mosaic of citations'[5] – that his work is intertextual; it is rather in the sense in which individual works play with their enabling

---

5. Julia Kristeva, *Semeiotiké: Recherches pour une Sémanalyse* (Paris: Seuil, 1969), p. 146.

Example 8.4   Mahler, Seventh Symphony, fourth movement, bb. 1–4

codes and conventions, making knowledge of those codes and conventions indispensable to a proper understanding of the work. It is therefore
not merely in the fact that the opening of the last movement of Mahler's
Ninth, for example, recalls the 'Lebewohl' motif of Beethoven's 'Les
adieux' sonata, or that the first movement of the Fourth is in sonata form,
but also that the First takes over and transforms a major song source, the
Lieder eines fahrenden Gesellen. Mahler's intertextuality raises a host of
questions about what it means for Mahler to quote himself, what the relationship between a work and its 'sources' might be, and what kinds of conceptual boundaries are placed upon the notion of a 'symphony'. In what

follows, I do not engage in a full-scale exploration of intertextuality in Mahler; rather, referring to a handful of references, I ask how intertextual resonances interrupt and thus help to define narrativity in the *Nachtmusik*.

We may distinguish between two types of reference in this movement: references to specific composers and/or works; and references to common-place signs or symbols that are presumed by the composer to be in his listeners' competence. A number of writers have been struck by the resemblance between the opening of the *Nachtmusik* and Robert Schumann's 'Träumerei', the seventh of his *Kinderszenen* collection.[6] Both are in F, and both share a melodic gesture defined by an ascending octave leap (F–F) followed by a gradual and extended descent. More striking is the harmonisation. In Schumann's reprise, the climactic melodic note, A, is harmonised with a B in the bass, while Mahler's climactic F similarly takes a bass B. Beethoven and Schubert may also be drawn into the work's intertextual space. The square, four-bar phrases that attain a degree of classical autonomy in bb. 114–25 of the Mahler recall the classicising procedures of late Beethoven, as heard, for example, in bb. 25–40 of the 'Alla danza tedesca' movement of his String Quartet, Op. 130. Schubert comes to mind in the intrusion of parallel minor on major (see b. 11 for example) and in the use of harmonic side-slips (see Ex. 8.3). Something of Handel's *Messiah* may be heard in the first two bars of the melody introduced at b. 46, which recalls the beginning of the accompanied recitative, 'Comfort ye my people'. Above all, Mahler quotes himself. The figure and instrumentation of the stock accompanimental pattern introduced in b. 4, in addition to referring generally to the vamps of Italian opera arias, calls to mind the lead into the concluding strophe of the last song of the *Gesellen* Lieder. The oboe melody in bb. 32–7 (recapitulated in bb. 289–94) is a near-quotation from the second of the *Kindertotenlieder*. Perhaps most dramatic of all is the quotation from the Adagietto of the Fifth Symphony (compare bb. 30–2 of the Adagietto to bb. 310–12 of the *Nachtmusik*). Each passage is a local melodic high point composed over a sustained dominant. Furthermore, the intense, drawn-out, and linearly directed melody of bb. 56–76 of the *Nachtmusik* is strongly reminiscent of the overall profile of the Adagietto's melody, with its illusion of endless ascent.

6. The most considered discussion is in Reinhard Kapp, 'Schumann-Reminiszenen bei Mahler', in Heinz-Klaus Metzger and Rainer Riehn, eds., *Gustav Mahler*. Musik-Konzepte. Sonderband. (Munich: Edition Text + Kritik, 1989), pp. 325–61.

More general signs and symbols are engaged from the very beginning
of the movement. The first main theme (beginning with the upbeat to b. 8)
combines a horn melody in F major with simple tonic–dominant harmony
and broken accompaniment figures in the clarinet, all of which collectively allude to the pastoral genre. (We have already mentioned the role of
mandolin and guitar in creating a serenade atmosphere.) The $\hat{6}$–$\hat{5}$ melodic
element embedded in the clarinet figure may also represent a Mahlerian
take on a familiar melodic *topos*. It colours the final cadence of the
Rückert song 'Ich atmet einen linden Duft'. It also occurs in the closing
bars of both the *Gesellen* Lieder and the *Kindertotenlieder*, and perhaps
most famously, as a simultaneity in the final cadence of *Das Lied von der
Erde*. It is used to enhance the intensity of a couple of melodic turning
points in the *Nachtmusik* (see bb. 203 and 244), and forms part of the clarinet turn figure at the very end of the movement (bb. 389–90), making it
the last melodic sound heard in the movement. Something of the learned
style, here symbolised by the formality of imitative counterpoint, is conveyed by bb. 98–113 and 176–86. The low-style music that begins the B
section of the movement is interrupted by a serious, perhaps even sublime
style in b. 199, creating a typical Mahlerian juxtaposition. Finally, and
from our vantage point, the *Nachtmusik* may be heard to refer to works
not yet written. One such reference is in bb. 373–5, recalling bb. 240–3
of the first movement of the Tenth. In both passages, a local $\hat{3}$–$\hat{2}$–$\hat{1}$ descent,
an embodiment of 'the definitive close of a composition',[7] is presented
without embroidery, thus highlighting the moment of closure.

It is easy enough to identify intertextual references such as the above
– and the list could go on, of course – but it is less easy to establish their
significance. How can awareness of such references be incorporated into a
real-time audition of the movement? By taking the listener 'outside' the
work, a self-consciously 'intertextual hearing' slows down the narrative
urgency by expanding the spatial or 'paradigmatic' dimension of the work.
The worlds of Schumann, Schubert, Beethoven and Mahler, or of the pastoral, sublime and learned styles, create sub-worlds, bringing into aural
view new and sometimes unsuspected relations. All this enables the listener to construct a hearing that is not merely a direct, linear traversal of
two temporal points, A and Z, but a halting, highly variegated journey in
which forward, backward and 'sideways' references force us to revise our
sense of beginning and ending, thus enriching the auditory experience.
Intertextual hearing makes for a less hegemonic narrative; it is more like

7. Heinrich Schenker, *Free Composition*, trans. Ernst Oster (New York:
Longman, 1979), p. 129.

movement through a temporalised network in which the listener builds an intricate web of relations around text and intertexts. In such hearing, the drama of tonality, which Beethoven analysis has accorded foundational status, is recontextualised to play only a minor – though not ultimately dispensable – role in our experience of the *Nachtmusik*.

The narrative of form

To speak of discontinuities and intertextual references in the *Nachtmusik* is to speak, at least implicitly, of form. Yet the discussion so far has dealt with brief moments or short passages taken out of larger contexts. We need therefore to extend it to the larger context, the overall form. Contexts, however, are neither given nor transparent; they are constructed. To construct a context is to intervene mightily in setting up a horizon for perception. Setting up a horizon in turn depends on the nature and scope of the analyst's plot. To accept this ideological or pragmatic bias is to challenge the common view that wholes (often held to imply 'context') matter more than fragments (often seen as denying context).

The formal 'problem' in the *Nachtmusik*, however, hinges on the issue of wholes: what is the overall form of the movement? Does it fit any of our standard categories? De La Grange hears A B A C A . D E . A B A C A, a tripartite division peppered by rondo elements.[8] His first section, A B A C A (bb. 1–98), is neutrally labelled 'Première section' while the second, D E (bb. 99–258), is referred to more qualitatively as 'Développement avec nouveaux matériaux'. The third, A B A C A (bb. 264–362), is a 'reprise'. (Curiously, de La Grange excludes bb. 259–63 and 363–90 from his outline.) Constantin Floros, on the other hand, divides the movement into five parts. He refers to the first section as the 'Main section' (bb. 1–98), the second as 'Development' (bb. 99–186), the third as 'Trio' (bb. 187–259), the fourth as 'Recapitulation' (bb. 259–353), and the fifth as 'Coda' (bb. 354–90).[9] The categories 'development' and 'recapitulation' suggest sonata form, while 'trio' suggests part of a scherzo-trio or 'third movement form'. A 'main section' implies subsidiary sections, thus hinting at rondo form. To say with Adorno that 'all categories are eroded in Mahler, none is established within unproblematic limits'[10] is in one sense to state an obvious truth, one that may apply to all composers who use 'categories'. But it

8. Henry-Louis De La Grange, *Gustav Mahler: Chronique d'une vie*. Vol. II, *L'Age d'or de Vienne (1900–1907)* (Paris: Fayard, 1983), p. 1198.
9. Constantin Floros, *Gustav Mahler: The Symphonies*, trans. Vernon Wicker. (Portland: Amadeus Press, 1993), p. 204.
10. Adorno, *Mahler*, p. 23.

reminds us that categories are indispensable – how else would we know that they have been 'eroded'? – but need to be superseded.

Competing approaches to segmenting the movement arise from the unsolved problem of how to parse an on-going musical discourse whose individual dimensional processes are staggered. Consider, again, the opening 'refrain' or 'motto' (Ex. 8.4). De La Grange locates it in 'bars 1–3' while Floros places it in 'bars 1–4'. The discrepancy is tiny but instructive, for it concerns not only the challenge of balancing the upbeats of phrase boundaries but also coming to terms with closure in different dimensions. These opening bars are enough to suggest that the boundaries of the *Nachtmusik*'s internal segments are likely to be fluid and unstable.

Approaching the problem of form in this movement not from its outer trace but from its inner dynamic reveals a binary impulse. The first, linearly charged and goal-oriented, results in polarised structures. The other, circular, 'solar', and making occasional use of symmetrical partitioning and equal-interval construction, results in network-type structures. Each scheme is defined by repetition, the basic form-building principle. The *Nachtmusik*'s narrative is thus embedded in the path traced by repetition, 'a purely musical residue'[11] that is not subject to the vagaries of the foreground. The fact that the impulse is binary should not leave the impression that the overall formal contour is undecidable. Mahler's serenade is grounded in a circular, non-teleological temporal mode. The discourse is internally directed and turns upon itself. In the process it maps out a narrative trajectory quite different from, say, that of the first movement of the Seventh.

Before we turn to the moment-by-moment unfolding of the narrative of form, let us acknowledge the role played by repetition in designing the movement's outer form. The tripartite A B A' scheme arises from the repetition in compressed and varied form of earlier material. This sort of large-scale recapitulation enshrines a double tendency: on one hand, it works *against* the novelistic principle insofar as it refuses the movement any further expository power by restating large chunks of familiar material. On the other hand, because the restatement contains subtle variations, it provides 'new' information, thus returning to it some expository or narrative capacity. The B section replicates the larger tripartite structure, the main difference being a change of key from B♭ major to F major in the outer sections. Repetition is further evident on local levels. Within the A section, for example, extensive repetition conveys the impression of circular movement, a refusal to get off the ground. De La

11. Adorno, *Mahler*, p. 3.

Grange's synopsis of this section distinguishes between three types of material: the refrain; accompaniment figures; and themes. The refrain occurs four times, the accompaniment figures four times also, while three distinct themes (A, B and C) are exposed. The enduring impression is of a constant return to earlier or 'older' ideas, not necessarily in cumulative fashion – although that process is discernible in the behaviour of the refrain – but in a deliberate and unhurried manner.

We may study the moment-to-moment unfolding of the *Nachtmusik* in the first fifty-five bars. The following outline segments these bars according to what might be called 'sense units' or minimally meaningful musical ideas. (An asterisk marks units that begin with an upbeat. The absence of an asterisk means that the unit begins or ends somewhere in that bar, not necessarily at the end.)

Unit	Bars
1	1*–4
2	4 –7
3	8*–11
4	12*–17
5	17*–20
6	20 –7
7	28*–38
8	38*–41
9	42 –6
10	46*–55

There are ten units in all. By simply numbering them from 1 to 10, I use a somewhat more neutral approach to segmentation. Although each unit subtends a network of ideas and competing profiles, a guiding idea is not hard to discover. It is the succession of guiding ideas that embodies the *Nachtmusik*'s 'narrative'. Such a succession is, of course, constructed by the listener out of a large number of events and tendencies. What follows is one such construction.

Because of its later function as a refrain, Unit 1 is designed to provide a non-transparent point of reference, to be memorable and not easily elim-inated from the listener's consciousness. A number of conflicting gestures meet these prescriptions. The solo violin, for example, symbolises both authority and the absence of authority. As a lone voice speaking from among a crowd, it gains a certain peculiarity. But the unironic thinness of its sound sets up an expectation for something fuller, something more proper, something that would define what Carolyn Abbate calls a 'normal musical state'[12] for the *Nachtmusik*. The playful accompaniment figures of Unit 2 prepare us for song, for the emergence of a central character. Song does indeed arrive in Unit 3, played by the horn. Its annunciatory ascending fourth, followed by stepwise movement and repeated notes: these together suggest a leisurely, unhurried discourse, a contrast to the somewhat charged opening unit. But the theme has hardly run its full course before it is interrupted by the flattened third degree. Another voice, that of the oboe, enters to rescue the narrative (Unit 4), leading the theme to a proper cadence while making appropriate concessions to the parallel minor mode. The narrative starts up again in Unit 5, promising to 'correct' the interruption of Unit 3. It is, however, quickly interrupted by $\flat\hat{3}$. Unlike the previous occurrence in Unit 4, the task of setting the narrative back on course is taken up more communally. First the cellos, then the oboes, then the solo violin take up a version of the refrain melody, leading to a broader cadence in Unit 6. (Note, incidentally, that the last two bars of Unit 6 are equivalent to the first two of Unit 2.) Retrieving the refrain melody from the subconscious and making it participate, alongside its own variants, in the cadence, makes explicit its double meaning as beginning and ending. The somewhat restrained tonal movement across Units 1–6, its frequent touching down on the tonic, underlines the circular element in the narrative.

Unit 7 signifies change, for it begins as if it was the expected consequent to the opening antecedent. But as before, the gesture initiated at the start of Unit 7 is quickly cut off by a strong intertextual resonance (the *Kindertotenlieder* reminiscence played by the oboe and violins starting in b. 32). Getting back on track now becomes the task of the cellos, who play the refrain figure to prepare for yet another beginning. This will be the fourth time that the movement begins again. Like Units 3 and 5, Unit 8 begins with the horn's song, but unlike the earlier units, it overcomes the interruption of $\flat\hat{3}$, thus signalling a new forward impetus in the narrative. Unit 9 provides the expected closure, thus replicating in part the function of Units 4 and 6. Here, however, there are no submerged voices to be rescued. The horn carries through to the cadence in bb. 45–6. Then comes what appears to be a new theme (Unit 10). Its novelty is, however, short-lived. Rising rapidly to the biggest high point of the work so far, it not only brings back the refrain melody in the highest register (solo violin) but

12. Carolyn Abbate, *Unsung Voices: Opera and Musical Narrative in the Nineteenth Century* (Princeton University Press, 1991), p. xii. Abbate is distinguishing between a 'normal musical state' and 'rarer moments of narrating'.

recomposes the $\flat\hat{3}$–$\natural\hat{3}$ melodic progression (bb. 50–2) in the approach to the cadence. This type of recomposition is one reason that the metaphor of organicism is not easily eliminated from Mahler criticism.

We could, of course, extend this blow-by-blow account to the rest of the movement, but this is unlikely to improve the theoretical suppositions of the foregoing analysis. The quality in the *Nachtmusik* that is effectively framed in terms of narrative stems from a specific temporal stance, namely, deferral: when will the movement (properly) begin? where are the points of closure? when will the consequent arrive? And so on. A search for answers to these questions inevitably leads us through a labyrinth of competing temporal modes. I hope to have added some support to the view, set forth most cogently by Adorno, that the metaphor of 'narrative' is a highly fertile one for Mahler analysis. What remains to be worked out – and is only hinted at by Adorno – are the specific technical forms that will enable a faithful translation of that metaphor.

9

'Von heute auf morgen': Schoenberg and the New Criticism

Alan Street

> Mummy, what are modern people like then?[1]
>
> The words of Mercury are harsh after the songs of Apollo.[2]

Within the free republic of the new musicology, there remains, one senses, a persistent neurosis: that today, practitioners are no more than slaves to intellectual fashion. Utopian confidence, prompted by sceptical reaction, consequently fears its transgressions turning into the stuff of parable. Thus moral decay begins with neglect of the Toveyan concordat with the populace and reaches its crux in the breaking of the covenant with the Great Tradition. Such Babylonian excess as is enjoyed through these acts of radicalism will, however, prove as illusory as it does transitory. For in truth, the supposed founding of a new culture amounts to nothing other than the making of bricks for the great interdisciplinary Pharaohs, a condition of servitude itself but a prelude to the eventual destruction of the great academic Temple and the woeful state of Diaspora.

Hyperbole apart, this brief fantasy describes perhaps only the essential tensions perpetually present between orthodoxy and hetero- doxy in any sphere. Yet some truths appear palpably less open to inter- pretation than others, a state of affairs which is strongly enshrined in the nature of Schoenberg historiography. Over the last decade, however, several published studies have begun to expand on the *prima facie* common stock of conservative and revolutionary rhetoric used to depict the composer as chief musical modernist. In *Music and Poetry: the Nineteenth Century and After*, for example, Lawrence Kramer fuses melopoetic structural rhythm with Freudian cathexis to explore the 'tragic view of sexuality' in *Das Buch der hängenden Gärten*.[3] A psychoanalytics of structure also provides the impetus for Michael

1. Gertrud Schoenberg (alias Max Blonda), *Von heute auf morgen*. The original reads: 'Mama, was sind das, moderne Menschen?'
2. William Shakespeare, *Love's Labours Lost*, Act V, sc. 2, lines 931–2.
3. Lawrence Kramer, *Music and Poetry: The Nineteenth Century and After* (Berkeley: University of California Press, 1984), p. 166.

Cherlin's uncanny sensing of purportedly taboo tonal implication in the opening recitative of the third movement of the Fourth String Quartet.[4] And latterly, Julie Brown has reread *Das Buch* according to Schoenberg's willing embrace of a Wagnerian *Weltanschauung*; a strategy of self-sacrifice caught between the horns of a Jewish modernist and Wagnerite anti-semitic dilemma.[5]

Pan-Germanist Wagnerianism, together with Zionism and aestheticism, are among the forms of mythological regeneration by which, Jacques Le Rider argues, one may discern a prefiguring of the postmodern condition within Viennese life at the turn of this century.[6] Successive loss of faith in the triumph of bourgeois autonomy and its enabling instrumental rationalities correspondingly obliged individuals to function more as '"autopoietic systems" in a process of continuous creation';[7] fundamentally fluid and flexible subjects for whom 'the woman and the Jew' might be understood as archetypal.[8] To berate a musicological tradition at this point for its congenital myopia on failing to take better account of such issues would signify little more than a progressive critical blindness now incapable of anything but hindsight. Even so, it remains unclear as to why the shock of extreme alienation recorded in *Erwartung* and *Die glückliche Hand*, as well as the open androgyny of the planned *Seraphita* stage work deriving from Balzac, should not have attracted much wider attention, particularly of late.

A firm declaration on this matter has issued recently from Richard Taruskin. The increasingly uncertain sense of an ending brought on by, for instance, psychopoetic encounters with Bloomian angst, he argues, still betrays a teleological anchorage through continued faith in a self-evident beginning. In this respect,

> the central evolutionary problem is compounded by one of asserted
> legitimacy. Unlike tonality, atonality (the kind that survived) has
> one father. This has given rise to a cult of personality, has intensified
> polarization, and has lent the historiography of twentieth-century
> music a characteristically post-Romantic Caesaristic mode that has
> long been under siege but will not capitulate until those who have

4. Michael Cherlin, 'Schoenberg and *Das Unheimliche*: Spectres of Tonality', *Journal of Musicology*, 11 (1993), 357–73.
5. Julie Brown, 'Schoenberg's Early Wagnerisms: Atonality and the Redemption of Ahasuerus', *Cambridge Opera Journal*, 6 (1994), 51–80.
6. Jacques Le Rider, 'Between Modernism and Postmodernism: the Viennese Identity Crisis', *Austrian Studies*, 1 (1990), 1–11.
7. *Ibid.*, p. 9.   8. *Ibid.*, p. 6.

cast themselves as the victorious father's dynastic heirs have relin-
quished their power bases.[9]

Boulez and Babbitt are named as principal benefactors; but Taruskin's
accusation of elective patrimony extends to all the 'self-defined legatees
on American campuses [acting] as the exclusive custodians of [a classical]
... mainstream'.[10] His disaffection arises in part from what he sees as a
canonising complicity to centralise and extend the 'ad hoc and insularly
German tradition',[11] an inevitably flawed faith, since 'the sense of tradition apparent in Schoenberg's works of the twenties is no longer immediate. Like Stravinsky's, it has been put at an ironic distance by the very
same end run around an "immediate tradition" that had met with dis-
aster.'[12] Its deeper motivation nonetheless concerns what he perceives to
be an ingrained epistemological error: the 'poietic fallacy'. An 'unconscious residue of ... Romanticism' and 'the fatal flaw of most twentieth-
century theorizing on the arts', this 'wholly production-oriented model'
characterises a critical philosophy wherein

> to equate music ... with the techniques of manufacturing music,
> to regard the manufacturing of music as the only legitimate profes-
> sional concern of musicians, and to sanction only such locutions
> as may describe or analogically represent that manufacture, is ...
> merely to practice another politics of exclusion.[13]

So expressed, Taruskin's thesis represents a gloss on the anti-intentional-
ism of Wimsatt and Beardsley: specifically, a prohibition against attempting to settle interpretative questions by 'consulting the [compositional]
oracle'.[14] Raised in the context of ideology critique – of retracing neo-
classicism through its contingent historical circumstances – it is detached
from the wider question of 'what is an author?' and joins instead with his
additional revisionary tactics of resolving both music theory and period
performance reconstruction into the historical continuum generated by
practice. The purpose is the valorisation of action such that composition,
performance and criticism may be viewed in the single sphere of performative demonstration; its apparent weakness the diminishing of

9. Richard Taruskin, 'Revising Revision', *Journal of The American
   Musicological Society*, 46 (1993), 125.
10. *Ibid.*, p. 133.   11. *Ibid.*, p. 133.   12. *Ibid.*, p. 135.
13. Richard Taruskin, 'Back to Whom? Neoclassicism as Ideology', *19th Century
    Music*, 16 (1993), 288.
14. Richard Taruskin, 'The Pastness of the Present and the Presence of the Past',
    in Nicholas Kenyon, ed., *Authenticity and Early Music* (Oxford University
    Press, 1988), p. 146.

reflective thought into the narrow termini of individual sensibility and connoisseurship.[15] A potentially elitist turn amid the general musicological drift of turning the apparently eternal back into the ever temporal, Taruskin's argument remains consistent in seeking to demystify some of the aura surrounding creativity. Hence while willing to concede that learning from the literary theory of proponents like Bloom may help to restore the music-analytical memory, he is insistent that this process should not stop short of the realisation that although poets and composers may 'make history . . . they do not write it. That remains our job.'[16]

Taruskin's attack on the cult of paternity which sustains faith in musical modernism also poses a further challenge to Schoenberg historiography: that membership of the twentieth-century dysfunctional family was ultimately determined by Wagner as 'everybody's appalling father'.[17] Addressing the relationship between Wagner and the post-modern,[18] John Deathridge acknowledges the composer's initial '"strong" belief in the young Hegelian version of the "power of history"',[19] a vociferous advocacy of the radically new which found its apogee in *Siegfried* as allegory of progress. Yet, Deathridge contends, even Wagner could not withstand the final jettisoning of history. Rather, his encounter with Schopenhauerian nihilism occasioned a weakening 'of the notion of the new as a perpetual critical overcoming of tradition',[20] a creative volte-face by which 'the fake Lutheran chorales and amusing parodies of Baroque musical figures in *Die Meistersinger* are Wagner's "post-modern" reaction to the heroic revolutionary phase of the 1850s'.[21] The crises of creative will experienced by Wagner and theorised by Nietzsche anticipate those of Viennese modernity, a conjunction which Deathridge emphasises with reference to Schoenberg. In this respect the subcutaneous classicism in the latter's music in the 1920s and 1930s parallels the decorative use of history in *Die Meistersinger*; each succumbs to a realisation that 'the logic of critical overcoming and radical innovation . . . is a burden the moment it embraces the possibility of failing to break with the past'.[22]

Like Taruskin, Deathridge presents a revisionary view of modernist evolution; one less committed to the sweep of progress than haunted by the trials of autoengendering. Like Taruskin, Deathridge also foregrounds something of the factitiousness involved in historiography of whatever

15. I have argued this case more fully in 'Carnival', *Music Analysis*, 13 (1994), 255–98.   16. Taruskin, 'Revising Revision', p. 138.

17. *Ibid.*, p. 138.

18. John Deathridge, 'Wagner and the Post-modern', *Cambridge Opera Journal*, 4 (1992), 143–61.   19. *Ibid.*, p. 145.   20. *Ibid.*, p. 145.

21. *Ibid.*, p. 158.   22. *Ibid.*, p. 160.

cast. An encounter with the truly self-reflexive narrative of representation is, however, harder to arrange. A promising candidate is nonetheless suggested by Dika Newlin's troping of Berg in 'Why is Schoenberg's Biography so Difficult to Write?'[23] Published in 1973, six years after Derrida's *Of Grammatology* and one year before *Glas*, Newlin would seem to raise the stakes considerably for inscription of the modern by aligning Schoenberg with both generic subject-position and the anterior logic of the arche-trace. Newlin's text itself takes on the guise of autobiography, explaining that since the age of fourteen she has been collecting material 'for the ideal Schoenberg book', 'none, even the most recent', having 'achieved true completeness and depth', although their authors 'may well have been capable of more profound studies'.[24] The prime difficulty is in '*really* writing about the *real* Schoenberg';[25] a problem which is perhaps only to be explained by 'biographers . . . equating a deeper study of Schoenberg's life with a too-close approach to divine things'.[26] She concludes:

> It sounds too simple. But I know . . . that a majority of Schoenberg pupils looked up to him as a super-Father-Figure – maybe even quasi-divine? They were overawed by him, while often resentful of the 'thought control' which he exercised over them . . . . How to avoid being artistically paralyzed by Schoenberg yet at the same time not to reject him – it is a conflict that we all went through![27]

Here the framing of Newlin's sentiments is deliberately ironic. Yet the purpose is not to belittle her convictions, themselves offset by the vibrant marginalia of *Schoenberg Remembered*,[28] but to account more fully for the 'asserted legitimacy' and 'cult of personality' which attaches only to Schoenberg, as Taruskin charges, within the historiography of twentieth-century music. The values invoked by Newlin – responsibility, fidelity and profundity – are ranged between the extreme poles of the real and ideal, over which the inaugurating aspect of law, in effect the Lacanian Name-of-the-Father ('the symbol of an authority at once legislative and punitive'),[29] is granted ultimate jurisdiction. The quasi-divinity Newlin identifies is also supported by several humanising articles of faith among initiates of different generations. For instance, Berg writes of 'the creative-ness of Schoenberg, the "father of atonal thought" as he is generally

23. Dika Newlin, 'Why is Schoenberg's Biography so Difficult to Write?'
    Perspectives of New Music, 12 (1973–4), 40–2.
24. *Ibid.*, p. 40.   25. *Ibid.*, p. 41.
26. *Ibid.*, p. 42.   27. *Ibid.*, p. 42.
28. Dika Newlin, *Schoenberg Remembered* (New York: Pendragon, 1980).
29. Malcolm Bowie, *Lacan* (London: Fontana, 1991), p. 108.

called',[30] Webern of craftsmanship,[31] Keller of originality[32] and Subotnik of integrity.[33] None of these terms of approbation is false as it stands. Yet they each contribute to an emblematic picturing of the composer closer to the abstract than corporeal: of man as idea rather than flesh-and-blood matter.

In one important respect, the impression of a visionary figure approaching his symbolic apotheosis in the form of pure Logos is no more than one might acquire by reading several of the key essays in *Style and Idea*.[34] In other words the images of lonely prophet and embattled moralist are among the gallery of self-portraits Schoenberg himself bequeathed to posterity. For Taruskin, such forms of mediation intended to bridge the void of modernist alienation might seem to perform their oracular purpose too completely. Conversely, Le Rider's interpretation of fin-de-siècle self-begetting raises the possibility that Schoenberg too, like Theodor Herzl, imagined himself a modern Moses of the Jewish people. In actuality, however, Schoenberg drew back from this hubris. As Newlin observes,

> Schoenberg feared that the 'Supreme Commander' would not allow him to complete his great religious works. And what he feared came to pass. 'Yes, even a Schoenberg dared not approach too near, in his conversations with God: "... let not God speak with us, lest we die!"'[35]

Instead, his declared sense of destiny recognises two foci of responsibility: to genius as the summit of individuation and tradition as the validation of collectivity.

Genius, Schoenberg writes, is 'the capacity to develop oneself',[36] its essence that of futurity. The legitimacy of the 'truly new music' meant to ensure Germanic centennial supremacy nevertheless resides in the belief that 'being based on tradition', it is 'destined to become tradition'.[37] Despite its capacity to transcend the cultural milieu, genius thus pays continued obeisance to history. Because, as David Gross makes the point,

30. Alban Berg, 'Why is Schoenberg's Music so Hard to Understand?', trans. Anton Swarowsky and Joseph H. Lederer, in Elliott Schwartz and Barney Childs, eds., *Contemporary Composers on Contemporary Music* (New York: Da Capo, 1978), p. 69.

31. Anton Webern, *The Path to the New Music*, ed. Willi Reich, trans. Leo Black (New Jersey: Universal Edition, 1975), p. 11.

32. Hans Keller, 'Schoenberg: the Future of Symphonic Thought', *Perspectives of New Music*, 13 (1974–5), 14.

33. Rose Rosengard Subotnik, *Developing Variations: Style and Ideology in Western Music* (Minneapolis: University of Minnesota Press, 1991), p. xxii.

34. Arnold Schoenberg, *Style and Idea*, ed. Leonard Stein, trans. Leo Black (Berkeley: University of California Press, 1984).

35. Newlin, 'Why is Schoenberg's Biography so Difficult to Write?', p. 42.

36. Schoenberg, *Style and Idea*, p. 468.   37. *Ibid.*, p. 174.

'tradition was always authoritative and authority always traditional'.[38]
Freedom from material determination might seem to mark a definitive
stage of emancipation from the rituals of cultural memory. But as Donald
Pease explains, the bond between genius and tradition may be retraced at
least to the relationship linking *auctor* and society in the European
Middle Ages.[39] Indeed the role of revered secular authority (for example,
Boethius as musician) sanctioning the allegorical transformation of lived
experience into shared spiritual custom implies a clear premodern precedent for the creed to which Newlin subscribes.

Tradition and authority name a complex of values such as respect
and responsibility dedicated to the preservation of social cohesion. Taken
together, the premodern *auctor* and Schoenbergian visionary appear as
testaments to the prolonged survival of a Judaeo-Christian cultural continuum. Gross's recent study of tradition in decline, however, argues
differently. Instead, he contends, the period between 1650 and 1850 is
characterised by the emergence of a modernity whose advocacy of the
malleability of nature, independence of selves and unbounded futurity
was responsible for ridding tradition of its '"quasi-natural status", and
hence also of its power to bind social life into an organic whole'.[40]
Modernity fulfilled its dream of a self-engendered normativity. Yet the
epochal difference in kind to which the West is now heir knows few of its
promised liberties. Rather its fundamental problems, 'the erosion of the
lifeworld, the growing manipulation of consensus, the atomization of
experience and the disintegration of individual autonomy and subjectivity',[41] are closer to a dystopian inverse.

Gross's account of aesthetic vacillation and restoration within the
modernist avant-garde also reprises elements of the ideas presented here
from Le Rider, Taruskin and Deathridge. The scope of his critique, though,
implies a broader scenario: that due to the usurpation of tradition by the
contemporary centralised state and the commercial market, historicist
and traditionalist patterning has become all but ubiquitous. Facsimile is
of course the very image of a postmodern major generality. But, Gross
advises, 'however refunctioned a tradition may be, it nonetheless contains
flecks of authenticity which need to be seen again in a new light'.[42] What
appears to be needed is the activation of counter-memory: a release of the

38. David Gross, *The Past in Ruins: Tradition and the Critique of Modernity*
  (Amherst: University of Massachusetts Press, 1992), p. 10.
39. Donald E. Pease, 'Author', in Frank Lentricchia and Thomas McLaughlin,
  eds., *Critical Terms for Literary Study* (University of Chicago Press, 1990),
  pp. 106–8.   40. Gross, *The Past in Ruins*, p. 42.
41. *Ibid.*, p. 91.   42. *Ibid.*, p. 113.

refractory energy inherent in non-identity long suppressed – in short, the shock of the old. In consequence, Gross advocates the practice of 'a *genealogical* deconstruction', which 'would dismantle diachronically rather than synchronically'.[43] Beginning with the actuality of refurbished traditions, 'this method would trace layer by layer the constituent elements of those traditions back through time',[44] unlocking 'the present's hold on the past'[45] in order to discover '(1) what a tradition was *originally* at the time of its emergence; (2) what it became *historically* as it unfolded through a chain of transmissions; and (3) what it became after it was refunctioned'.[46]

While wishing to engage with the widest implications Gross raises, I should like to approach these through a brief genealogical survey of key positions within Schoenberg historiography. Indeed the line of asserted legitimacy identified by Taruskin appears to display a broad homogeneity perhaps itself equivalent to the synthetic continuity of a refurbished tradition. Judging Milton Babbitt's role in the formation of a Cold War music theory, Martin Brody notes that Babbitt, 'falling at the cusp joining modernist and postmodern trajectories', engages the 'problems of contemporary cultural construction most compellingly just when those positions are ostensibly freeing themselves of all sectarian cultural biases'.[47] To this end, Brody asserts, Babbitt's 'metatheory embraces a neopositivist's concern about the relationship between concept and percept with a pluralist/pragmatist view of cultural diversity and the immanence of musical values'.[48] Within this philosophy, the key words would appear to be less metatheory and neopositivism, however, than pluralism and pragmatism. Because for Brody, it is through his 'overt anti-ideological [stance] . . . and . . . anxieties about conserving standards of musical citizenship' that Babbitt was able to foster 'an alternative picture of American musical culture to that which opposed Europe and America, Stravinsky or Schoenberg and the "working man"'.[49]

Brody's analysis is detailed and well-reasoned; the claim of ideological transparency, though, seems less certain. For example, to Babbitt, lessening of the distance between continents has meant active critique of the European avant-gardists' strategy of viewing 'the history of . . . con-

---

43. *Ibid.*, p. 116.   44. *Ibid.*, p. 116.   45. *Ibid.*, p. 117.
46. *Ibid.*, p. 118.
47. Martin Brody, '"Music For the Masses": Milton Babbitt's Cold War Music Theory', *Musical Quarterly*, 77 (1993), 164.
48. *Ibid.*, p. 164.   49. *Ibid.*, p. 173.

temporary music as a *tabula rasa*, with its history beginning with them, [as if] . . . the dozen years preceding the end of World War II simply never happened, particularly since what happened in music necessarily happened mainly in the United States'.[50] Darmstadt, for Babbitt, was thus an Old World cabal. And worse, its lingua franca was the mandarin discourse of Adorno; '"analytical" . . . sentences . . . characteristically unintelligible or unbelievable'.[51] Brody concedes that Babbitt would share little empathy with Adorno's view of Schoenberg as the 'self-sacrificing artist who . . . retreats from complacent notions of beauty while "point[ing] out the ills of society rather than sublimating those ills into a deceptive humanitarianism"'.[52] Yet in mounting a 'vehement polemic against historical teleology' by focusing 'on what distinguishes Schoenberg from his predecessors rather than smoothing over the "jagged edges of abruption"',[53] Babbitt still expresses a view that is perspectival. Indeed by advising that primarily Schoenberg 'knew no general principles', 'was not capable of deep theoretical thought', but that 'trial and error showed him a great deal as he proceeded',[54] Babbitt tropes Schoenberg away from his professed metaphysics of creativity towards a stance as try-and-test empiricist. Commitment to a 'communality of shared . . . principles and assumptions validated by tradition, experience and experiment' suggests that Babbitt like Schoenberg ultimately acknowledges the virtues of collectivity and continuity in some form.[55] Yet to minimise the ideological traces of this position is really to reprise what Adorno calls empiricism's 'boast of being "value-free"'.[56]

Implicated perhaps as chief schismatic, Pierre Boulez too has nonetheless paid homage to the traditional function of music in helping 'to establish a cultural community of minds and souls'.[57] Early polemic against Schoenberg's American compositions, though, is undoubtedly forceful: Boulez writes of an 'output . . . bizarrely divided between a

50. Milton Babbitt, 'On Having Been and Still Being an American Composer', *Perspectives of New Music*, 27 (1989), 109.
51. *Ibid.*, p. 109.
52. Adorno quoted in Brody, '"Music For the Masses"', p. 180.
53. *Ibid.*, p. 165.
54. Milton Babbitt, *Words About Music*, ed. Stephen Dembski and Joseph N. Straus (Madison: University of Wisconsin Press, 1987), p. 18.
55. Benjamin Boretz, 'Milton Babbitt', in John Vinton, ed., *Dictionary of Twentieth-Century Music* (London: Thames and Hudson, 1974), p. 44.
56. Adorno quoted in Subotnik, *Developing Variations*, p. 13.
57. Pierre Boulez, 'Through Schoenberg to the Future', *Journal of the Arnold Schoenberg Institute*, 1 (1977), 122.

number of purely serial works and works of "conciliation"',[58] adding
that 'the official musical life of the United States was absolutely not
made for a man like him: his integrity and courage were rudely tested
by its disheartening conformism'.[59] The deeper motivation for these
apprentice statements was clearly still intact two decades later in the
1970s. Then, Boulez insisted that 'strong, expanding civilizations have
no memory; they reject, they forget the past . . . From this viewpoint
our musical civilization shows very distinct signs of decay since at all
levels its emphasis on reclamation . . . shows that it has too many
memories.'[60] More recent commentary appears to temper these beliefs,
yet in a way which reinforces with a Bloomian strength the thrust of
Boulez's most famous polemic. Hence of 'Schoenberg is Dead',[61] he
states that

> what I meant then . . . I still mean today . . . that mannerism *after*
> Schoenberg is absolutely dead in its very beginning; and that inven-
> tion *through* Schoenberg is the only vital solution. [In] . . . many
> ways, a composer of this importance *has to die* through his real
> successors.[62]

Describing the legacy of Hans Keller, Alexander Goehr notes that for
Keller, 'it was an article of faith that composers, at any rate from the eighteenth century onwards, had formulated certain musical practices and procedures. . . . These might be said to constitute a tradition – and a living
tradition.'[63] Gratefully acknowledging Keller's analytical perspicacity,
Babbitt nevertheless specifies the distillation of these practices under the
notions of '"composing with the tones of a motive" and "perpetual variation"' as the real dispositions behind the supposedly informal phenomenology of Keller's performance 'intuitions'.[64] Keller, he admits, was a
defender of the faith for 'the Vienna of Schoenberg and Freud, not that of
Schenker or the Vienna Circle';[65] this is the explanation, then, for his failure to appreciate (with Babbitt) 'the more embracing, singular bases of

58. Pierre Boulez, *Stocktakings from an Apprenticeship*, ed. Paule Thévenin,
trans. Stephen Walsh (Oxford University Press, 1991), p. 286.
59. *Ibid.*, p. 286.
60. Pierre Boulez, *Conversations with Célestin Deliège* (London: Eulenburg,
1976), p. 33.
61. Pierre Boulez, 'Schoenberg is Dead', in *Stocktakings*, pp. 209–14.
62. Boulez, 'Through Schoenberg', p. 123.
63. Alexander Goehr, 'Memoir', *Music Analysis*, 5 (1986), 380.
64. Milton Babbitt, 'Memoir', *Music Analysis*, 5 (1986), 376.
65. *Ibid.*, p. 376.

structured musical individuation through parallelism of processes at a subsuming succession of temporal and structural levels'.[66]

Freudian and Schoenbergian that he was, Keller of course did not quail at the thought of marking out his own terms of conflict and continuity with respect to that tradition. Censure of Boulez for a lack of innate sense of harmonic movement, evident in performance,[67] and traceable to a condition of 'aggressive narcissism',[68] explains how the creative avant-garde might transgress. Equally significant, however, are the newly acknowledged inheritors: Stravinsky less noticeably than Britten in open defiance of Adorno's derogation in the *Philosophy of Modern Music*.[69] Adornian accusations of meagreness and technical inadequacy are therefore turned back into a critical unease with undue facility. Consequently Adorno is diagnosed as a further victim of the Polycrates complex surrounding gift and guilt, though with an insistence that betrays 'the historio-geographical limitations of his understanding'.[70] The assertion of relative cosmopolitanism is a particular coup for Keller. But nowhere so daring as his thesis of the repressed tonal background, only now reprised by Cherlin, within Schoenbergian atonality and serialism. To submit that a latent tonal logic determines a fully chromatic surface would not of itself seem extreme in light of theoretical submissions from Salzer, Travis and Hicken as Arnold Whittall observes.[71] However, for Keller, the concept cannot be properly grasped without an appreciation that the discovery of twelve-note technique actually '*depended* on its harmonic roots remaining undiscovered – in the temporary banishment of tonal implications'.[72]

In Vienna, the 'consistent traditionalism protested . . . against the tradition itself and revolutionized it with the demand that it take itself seriously'.[73] Thus the geographical emphasis of Adorno's decoding of modern

---

66. *Ibid.*, p. 376.
67. Hans Keller, *Music, Closed Societies and Football* (London: Toccata Press, 1986), pp. 200–1.
68. Christopher Wintle, 'Hans Keller (1919–1985): An Introduction to his Life and Works', *Music Analysis*, 5 (1986), 347.
69. Theodor W. Adorno, *Philosophy of Modern Music*, trans. Anne G. Mitchell and Wesley V. Blomster (London: Sheed and Ward, 1987), p. 7.
70. Hans Keller, 'Resistances to Britten's Music: Their Psychology', *Music Survey*, 2 (1950), 233.
71. Arnold Whittall, 'Schoenberg and the English: Notes for a Documentary', *Journal of the Arnold Schoenberg Institute*, 4 (1980), 29.
72. Hans Keller, 'Schoenberg's Return to Tonality', *Journal of the Arnold Schoenberg Institute*, 5 (1981), 7.
73. Theodor W. Adorno, 'Vienna', in *Quasi una Fantasia: Essays on Modern Music*, trans. Rodney Livingstone (London: Verso, 1992), p. 204.

music as 'the surviving message of despair from the shipwrecked'.[74] Progressively burdened by 'all the darkness and guilt of the world',[75] creative strength might now reveal itself to society only in the form of sustained resistance. Therefore 'the late Schoenberg composed not works, but paradigms of a possible music'.[76] Some weaknesses can nonetheless be detected among these paradigms. In the pieces 'which played with tonality, [for example] the *Ode to Napoleon* ... just as in the Piano Concerto, it is impossible not to hear a certain forced, impure quality'.[77] Adorno's echoing of Boulez's judgement against Schoenberg's synthetic strategies implies that resistance must remain the aesthetic call to order for any truly new music. In this respect, 'newness' retains its 'objective social dimension' only as critique.[78] About the palpable achievements of the post-war European avant-garde, however, Adorno was much less sanguine. By the early 1950s 'symptoms of false-satisfaction' seemed endemic to compositional material which had made 'little progress ... since the early twenties'.[79] Observing how 'the best-known serial composers of the younger generation re-enact the traditional drama of the father-son conflict and so prefer to stress their remoteness from Schoenberg',[80] Adorno ultimately judges their self-conscious oppositions with a sceptic's ear. Thus integral serialism is chastised as a capricious form of legalism; an abject submission to system in which 'the merely thought up is always also too little worked out'.[81] Likewise its symmetrical spatial effect remains defective; an undifferentiated totality which cancels the dialectic between identity and non-identity. A 'widespread allergy towards every kind of expression' is also matched by the poverty of medium.[82] Electronic music in particular has so far 'failed to fulfil its own idea' and conjures up little more than the impression of Webern played on a Wurlitzer organ.[83] The final conclusion is therefore inescapable: that 'in the levelling and neutralisation of its material, the aging of the New Music becomes tangible: it is the arbitrariness of a radicalness for which nothing is any longer at stake'.[84]

The introduction of Thomas Mann's novel *Doctor Faustus*[85] would

74. Adorno, *Philosophy of Modern Music*, p. 133.   75. *Ibid.*, p. 133.
76. Theodor W. Adorno, 'Arnold Schoenberg', in *Prisms*, trans. Samuel M. Weber (Cambridge, Mass.: MIT Press, 1983), p. 171.   77. *Ibid.*, p. 168.
78. Adorno, 'Music and New Music', in *Quasi una Fantasia*, p. 255.
79. Theodor W. Adorno, 'The Aging of the New Music', *Telos*, 77 (1988), 95, 96.
80. Adorno, 'Vienna', p. 217.
81. Adorno, 'The Aging of the New Music', p. 103.   82. *Ibid.*, p. 106.
83. *Ibid.*, p. 110.   84. *Ibid.*, p. 100.
85. Thomas Mann, *Doctor Faustus*, trans. H. T. Lowe-Porter (Harmondsworth: Penguin, 1968).

appear to inject an unnecessary degree of incongruity into the genealogical sequence. Nonetheless aspects of matter (not least its borrowing of ideas and identities from the *Philosophy of Modern Music*) as well as manner (the reflexive conflation of time and trajectory) indicate that it represents an apposite case study for Gross's suggested mode of critique. In each instance, Mann problematises the effects of reference over several discursive planes: biography as generic articulation, montage technique as the seeming legitimation of intertextuality and authorial chronicle (*The Genesis of a Novel*),[86] an illustration *avant la lettre* of the endless logic of supplementation. Experiencing a sense of crisis in the novel form, Mann understood *Faustus* as an exercise in calculated construction appropriate to narrative at the stage of self-conscious critique. The particular principle of montage, Mann wrote to Adorno in December 1945, was 'a kind of higher copying than the use of life as a cultural product [or] ... set of mythic clichés'.[87] At the same time as confessing to unlimited borrowing, however, Mann believed his technique still capable of maintaining a conventional distinction between real and fictive, constructing a symbolic entity on the one hand, while leaving its sources '*intact in their original places*'.[88]

Mann's paradigmatic medium is of course music, conceived as 'calculated order and chaos-breeding irrationality at once ... the most unrealistic and yet the most impassioned of arts, mystical and abstract'.[89] Therefore if Faust could be taken as the symbolic 'representative of the German soul, he would have to be musical, for the relation of the German to the world is abstract and mystical, that is, musical'.[90] In this regard Mann's purpose of creating a political and ultimately Christian allegory confronting the specifically German roots of National Socialism appears neutral in the present context. Even the effects of narrative doubling in relation to an allegory of creativity are constrained historically through particular precedents in Diderot, Heine and Wackenroder. As Adrian Leverkühn's fictional biographer, Serenus Zeitblom (himself a double for Mann), writes of the composer's oratorio *Apocalipsis cum figuris*, however, 'the profoundest mystery of this music ... is a mystery of identity'.[91]

86. Thomas Mann, *The Genesis of a Novel*, trans. Richard and Clara Winston (London: Secker and Warburg, 1961).

87. Thomas Mann, *Letters: Volume II: 1942–1955*, trans. Richard and Clara Winston (London: Secker and Warburg, 1970), p. 494.

88. *Ibid.*, p. 495.

89. Mann quoted in Gunilla Bergsten, *Thomas Mann's Doctor Faustus: the Sources and Structure of the Novel*, trans. Krishna Winston (University of Chicago Press, 1969), p. 162.   90. *Ibid.*, p. 162.

91. Mann, *Doctor Faustus*, p. 364.

Throughout the course of the novel, Mann famously depicts Leverkühn exploring a series of well-trodden genres for their conventional and therefore parodic potential. And within these, it is the youthful anti-Wagnerian comic opera *Love's Labours Lost* and the final serial cantata *The Lamentation of Dr Faustus*, an 'Ode to Sorrow' taking back the spirit of Beethoven's Ninth Symphony,[92] which appear to seal Leverkühn's fate with that of the Germanic canon. The Adornian thrust of this representation, as well as Leverkühn's creative proximity to Schoenberg, is nonetheless explained with only varying degrees of precision in *The Genesis of a Novel*. Rather Mann seems finally to have fallen victim to the power of his own fictive invention through a creative tropics of possession with respect to serialism as structural principle. For although Schoenberg's protests brought an ardent denial of portraiture and a published postscript to the novel recognising Schoenberg's intellectual copyright, Mann appears ultimately to have retreated into the belief that 'within the sphere of the book . . . the idea of the twelve-note technique assumes a coloration and a character which it does not possess in its own right and which . . . in a sense make it really my property, or, rather, the property of the book'.[93]

In both concept and detail, *Moses und Aron* is as distinct from the *Lamentation* as *Von heute auf morgen* remains from *Love's Labours Lost*. All the same, Schoenberg took pains to distance himself from Mann and Adorno under Keller's aegis in the periodical *Music Survey*, a defence which turns expressly on the inadmissibility of transferring 'authorship on to someone else'.[94] The case of *Von heute auf morgen* is nevertheless worth considering in its own right. Because unlike any of Schoenberg's later 'paradigms of a possible music', it was actively conceived as a transposition of tradition into the sphere of popular success. *Von heute* belongs to the short-lived genre of *Zeitoper*; as such it was intended to emulate works including Krenek's *Jonny spielt auf* (1926) and Hindemith's *Neues vom Tage* (1929), at the same time demonstrating the potential versatility of serialism. The apparent marriage of high and low cultures was joined, as Stephen Davison relates, by Gertrud Schoenberg's participation as librettist. Writing under the pseudonym 'Max Blonda', Schoenberg's second wife produced a contemporary comedy of extra-marital desire fitting the 'definition of *Zeitoper* almost perfectly [through its reliance] . . . on parody, social satire and burlesque as dramatic tools'.[95] Schoenberg responded

92. *Ibid.*, p. 470.   93. Mann, *Genesis*, p. 32.
94. Arnold Schoenberg, 'Further to the Schoenberg–Mann Controversy', *Music Survey*, 2 (1949), 77.
95. Stephen Davison, 'Of its Time, or Out of Step? Schoenberg's *Zeitoper, Von heute auf morgen*', *Journal of the Arnold Schoenberg Institute*, 14 (1991), 273.

by adding elements of popular and elevated parody: a brief episode which Keller terms a tango (Ex. 9.1),[96] and a literal quotation from Act I of *Die Walküre* (Ex. 9.2). However, neither amount to a presaging of wholesale pastiche or intertextual liberation. Throughout, Schoenberg's wish was to critique the alliance of canonical genre and topical content. Consequently parody and quotation are both firmly enclosed within a familiar combinatorial logic: successive, rather than simultaneous (between I11 and P6 statements, bb. 547–9 and 553–4), in the first ordering of the series used for the Wife's 'improvised' dance (Ex. 9.1), and gradually emergent rather than

Example 9.1   Schoenberg, *Von heute auf morgen*, bb. 547–55

Sie singt einige Takte eines modischen Tanzes und nötigt ihn, mit ihr zu tanzen./She sings a few bars of a current dance number and makes him dance with her.

96. Hans Keller, 'Schoenberg's Comic Opera', *The Score*, 23 (1958), 33.

Example 9.1   (*cont.*)

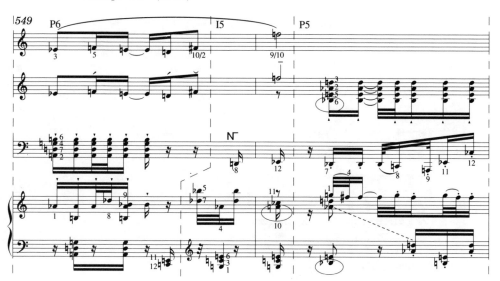

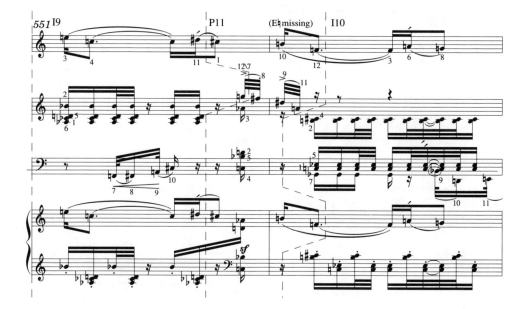

Example 9.1   (cont.)

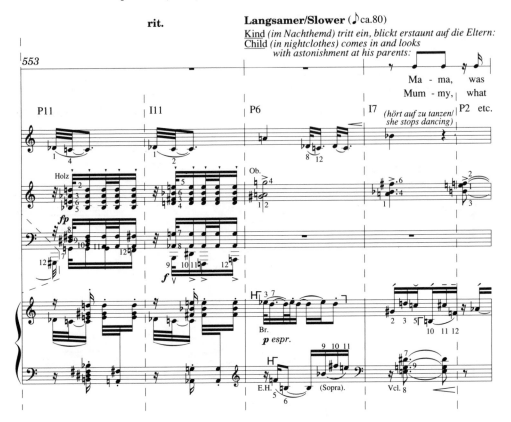

Example 9.2

(a) Wagner, *Die Walküre*, Act I scene 1, bb. 282–300

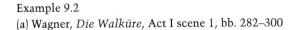

(a)

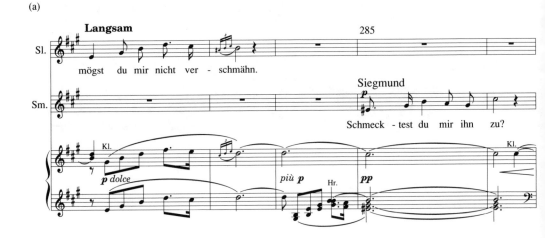

Example 9.2a (*cont.*)

Example 9.2
(b) Schoenberg, *Von heute auf morgen*, bb. 998–1002

(b)

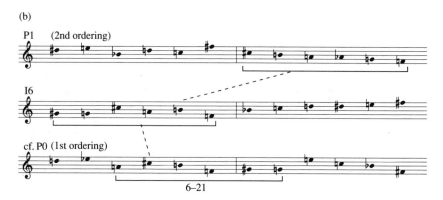

Example 9.2b (cont.)

immediate (between P1 and I6),[97] in the second ordering readopted for the promiscuous Singer's Wagnerian allusion. Taken together, such examples of strict serial policing (missing only the E♮ of P11 in bb. 551–2) seem designed to counter their potentially decadent effect, thereby bearing out Davison's judgement that within the dramatic context, the incorporation of popular idioms into modern music is understood to degrade 'the musical experience just as promiscuity cheapens one's marriage vows'.[98] Hence as Schoenberg had earlier conceded, with reference to the future of opera,

> it is self-evident that art which treats deeper ideas can not address itself to the many. 'Art for everyone': anyone regarding that as possible is unaware how 'everyone' is constituted and how art is constituted. So here, in the end art and success will yet again have to part company.[99]

Assessed at this stage, the genealogical process would appear to reveal a fairly clear separation: between the definitive sovereign wisdom of Schoenberg on the one hand and the competitive striving for legitimacy among his interpreters on the other. For the latter, poietics seem to be exactly what one makes them; subsequent judgement an agony column of Oedipal conflicts and sibling rivalries. But with a deconstructive purpose in hand, one should of course be alert to any strict binary divide. Nor does the idea of a Mosaic testimony misread by so many interpretative Aarons altogether agree with the evidence. A signal case, for example, appears in Schoenberg's late commentary 'Anton Webern: Klangfarbenmelodie' (1951).[100] Schoenberg's attitude to Webern's music is most characteristically recalled in relation to the Foreword to the Six Bagatelles, Op. 9 (1924).[101] Here the key-words of glance, sigh, poem and novel are capped by another: faith. Apprised

97. Only the second hexachord of the series is affected by Schoenberg's scalar reordering, each remaining equivalent to Fortean set class 6–21 (cf. Ex. 9.1). Incidentally, the pitch-class content of the second hexachord of P1 (and, correspondingly, the first hexachord of I6) is anticipated by that of order positions 3–8 within P0 in its first ordering. My thanks to Stephen Davison for his advice in the identification of series forms, particularly with respect to a number of proof-reading errors which exist in the original vocal score as published by B. Schott's Söhne (used here), as well as the Collected Works edition. Corrections on the examples are indicated by the circled notes and should read as follows: b. 550, first beat: A♮, not A♭; b. 550, second quaver beat: B♭, not B♮; b. 552, fourth quaver beat: B♭, not A♭; b. 1000, third crotchet beat: B♭, not B♮.   98. Davison, 'Of its Time, or Out of Step?', p. 289.

99. Schoenberg, *Style and Idea*, p. 336.

100. *Ibid.*, pp. 484–5.   101. *Ibid.*, pp. 483–4.

by Dorian-Deutsch that Webern and not Schoenberg might have been the progenitor of *Klangfarbenmelodie*, however, this is precisely what Schoenberg seems to renounce. Insisting that due credit would have been awarded were this at all true, Schoenberg then proceeds to accuse Webern of habitual secrecy in contradistinction to his own generosity,

> with the exception of the method of composition with tweve-tones –
> that I long kept secret, because, as I said to Erwin Stein, Webern
> immediately uses everything I do, plan or say, so that – I remember
> my words – 'By now I haven't the slightest idea who I am.'[102]

It would be easy to inflate the significance of this statement, perhaps just one final spasm of a past Oedipal rivalry, or even a direct consequence of the challenge to authorship and copyright fought out with Mann. Yet such disparity undoubtedly serves to further obscure the backward path from the promised land of the new music.

Commenting on the dialectical divorce between theory and history that has done much to institutionalise belief in a poietically driven advance, Christopher Hatch and David Bernstein have lately argued (in line with Taruskin) for a renewed awareness of the situated condition of both theory and praxis.[103] Recognising the gains of disciplinary independence for the emergence of theoretical studies, Hatch and Bernstein determine that since 'social forces and biographical facts are vital components of any historical situation',[104] theorists and analysts alike might now benefit from a synthetic sublation of the dialectical process. Invoking the language of German idealism, Hatch and Bernstein together acknowledge a further strand of Schoenberg historiography developing over the last decade. The inspiration for reading Schoenberg back into the European philosophical tradition stems from Patricia Carpenter. Thus her 'Musical Form and Musical Idea: Reflections on a Theme of Schoenberg, Hanslick and Kant' concludes that 'Schoenberg was ultimately conscious of the musical idea in its Platonic sense, like Kant, as beyond sense experience. The musical space is the space of thought; the musical idea is an "idea of intellect", not a perceptual image'.[105] Developing the thesis in

102. *Ibid.*, p. 484.
103. Christopher Hatch and David Bernstein, eds., *Music Theory and the Exploration of the Past* (University of Chicago Press, 1993).
104. Hatch and Bernstein, Introduction to *Music Theory and the Exploration of the Past*, p. 2.
105. Patricia Carpenter, 'Musical Form and Musical Idea: Reflections on a Theme of Schoenberg, Hanslick and Kant', in Edward Strainchamps, Maria Rika Maniates and Christopher Hatch, eds., *Music and Civilization: Essays in Honor of Paul Henry Lang* (New York: Norton, 1984), p. 417.

an analytical context, P. Murray Dineen's 'The Contrapuntal Combination: Schoenberg's Old Hat' has latterly sought to demonstrate the synchronic totality which lies behind the temporal articulation of a contrapuntal structure.[106] Hence the tonal space of a Bach fugue and twelve-note composition are largely homologous. 'Both . . . are abstract and unitary: there is no absolute point of reference, no favoured row form or combination. Prime row and basic contrapuntal combination are deter-mined extrinsically by order of appearance in the piece.'[107] The inclusion of Hanslick in Carpenter's comparison also implies a broader vision of the Germanic history of ideas. Correspondingly in 'Schoenberg and Goethe: Organicism and Analysis', Severine Neff grafts the Goethean concepts of *Anschauung* (intuitive contemplation) and *Urphänomen* (archetype) onto the idealist template.[108] However, Neff senses no dilution or distortion through this extension. Rather 'nothing could be more indicative of the holistic, organic model that is the basis of all Schoenberg's thought, and nothing could be further from the mechanistic, logical positivist model that is the basis of much contemporary theoretical thought on Schoenberg'.[109]

The general tendency observable in this line of thought is of a theology of the Schoenbergian divine giving way to an epistemology grounded in secular rationality. All three studies are fastidious in avoiding the traps of false consciousness which might lead to either a fetishisation of history at the expense of theory or, conversely, the neutralisation of theory concomitant with its conduct at a supposedly safe historical remove. But as with its theological equivalent, there is a strong anti-materialising drive to such a viewpoint; once again the desire for cognitive integrity turns Schoenberg back from flesh-and-blood matter into an idealised essence. No less abstract than the positivist model to which Neff refers, each seems motivated by an unconscious preservation order: what Jean-François Lyotard specifies as the Freudian belief 'that no one can kill *in absentia* [because] . . . to place something *in absentia* is to place it out-side the range of murder, to conserve it, to memorize . . . it, to invest it'.[110] The process of *articulation* in each instance nonetheless answers to Jean Baudrillard's observation that we need at least 'a visible past, a visible con-

---

106. P. Murray Dineen, 'The Contrapuntal Combination: Schoenberg's Old Hat', in *Music Theory and the Exploration of the Past*, pp. 435–48.

107. *Ibid.*, p. 446.

108. Severine Neff, 'Schoenberg and Goethe: Organicism and Analysis', in *Music Theory and the Exploration of the Past*, pp. 409–34.

109. *Ibid.*, p. 409.

110. Jean-François Lyotard, 'Adorno as the Devil', *Telos*, 19 (1974), 137.

tinuum, a visible myth of origin to reassure us as to our ends'.[111] The reality or rather hyperreality generated by so many contending cultural posits is, however, somewhat different. Turned back into the overall semiotic continuum, the effect is again that of 'a visible theology . . . volatilized into simulacra which alone deploy their pomp and power of fascination – the visible machinery of icons being substituted for the pure and intelligible Idea of God'.[112] Cancelling the Name-of-the-Father thus surrenders the creative subject to an epiphany of representations at the same time as the interpreting subject is delivered into a Babel babble of competing voices. In both respects the outcome is a partaking of the radical devaluation of the sign; a submission to the supposedly utopian economy of endless exchange.

This sideslip into the swirl of semiotic equivalence brings Gross's genealogical critique into full focus. The communality between theological, positivist and idealist versions of historiography emerges as an ideological resistance to ideology: a common if not always conscious strategy of depoliticisation marked by an absence of reflexive disclosure. It would be altogether wrongheaded to dismiss these carefully argued positions as exercises in nostalgia. Yet as follows from Gross's argument, they remain preferred points of investment within the most voracious form of abstraction sustaining the postmodern condition: capitalism. Addressing this situation in an article from 1974 with the *Faustus*-inspired title 'Adorno as the Devil', Lyotard advises that heroic modernists like Schoenberg and Adorno have been stripped of the patina of ideality by 'the cynicism and polymorphous perversity of an economy which can absorb any object, any capacity, any expression into the circuit of commodity exchange'.[113] In Schoenberg's case, 'the new music was indeed the emergence of a new deployment, "radical," critical, inside the womb of the old, the classical deployment; but a deployment which was itself liturgical'.[114] Yet rather its truth is contained in the scepticism of serial technique wherein as 'in capitalism . . . everything has value through relation . . . in so far as it is exchangeable'.[115] So expressed, Lyotard's analysis seems to double that of Adorno. However, for Lyotard, 'Adorno's work, just as . . . Schonberg's, is marked by nostalgia.'[116] His failure was to have ignored 'the critique of

111. Jean Baudrillard, 'The Procession of Simulacra', in Brian Wallis, ed., *Art After Modernism: Rethinking Representation* (Boston: Godine, 1984), p. 259.
112. Baudrillard, 'The Procession of Simulacra', p. 255.
113. Peter Dews, *Logics of Disintegration: Post-Structuralist Thought and the Claims of Critical Theory* (London: Verso, 1987), p. 137.
114. Lyotard, 'Adorno as the Devil', p. 129.
115. *Ibid.*, p. 130.   116. *Ibid.*, p. 133.

representation [which] would have led him to a critique of politics, and of dialectics'.[117] For

> to raise doubts about representation is to manifest the theoretical relation . . . as being directed by an arbitrary libidinal deployment . . . sometimes invested in a prevalent fashion, sometimes not. By extending this relation to a number of domains, capitalism brings about the emergence of the libidinal, irrational nature of the apparatus which supports it.[118]

In other words, so complete and so complicit with gratification as deployed through the empire of signs, capitalism attains full congruence with the forces of desire. All-pervasive, the libidinal economy disregards the historical weight of dialectic in favour of a shifting sequence of surface intensities. And what this calls for, counter to Schoenberg and Adorno, is both 'a surface music, without depth, preventing representation [and] . . . a politics-intensity, rather than a politics-tragedy'.[119] But within this post-Nietzschean field of perpetual metamorphosis, Lyotard too is pressed into the early intimation of a final deadlock. Because deprived of the ground of even potential opposition, the metaphysics of libido founders into immobility, its singular intensities trapped into a fundamental amorality and political inertia. Thus 'the positive grasp of the breakdown of values does not permit one to take it for an indispensable . . . moment in the process of reconstitution'.[120]

Having reached this impasse, the present genealogy might do best to either pause and reflect on 'what is an author?', or to simply declare the creator dead. In the first case, this would do well as a reflexive strategy against the interpretative blindness which appears to accept its historiographical sources more at face value than its subject. In the latter, the impression of a subject successively divided, decentred and otherwise manufactured might indicate that in truth, the subject is really no longer there at all. So much provides a disingenuous link to a deliberately deferred encounter with the almost canonical positions of Foucault and Barthes in respect of authorship.[121] For Barthes, deposition of the anterior Author-God dispels both the myth of univocal 'theological' meaning and

---

117. *Ibid.*, p. 128. 118. *Ibid.*, p. 133. 119. *Ibid.*, p. 132.
120. *Ibid.*, p. 127.
121. Michel Foucault, 'What is an Author', trans. Josué V. Harari, in Josué V. Harari, ed., *Textual Strategies: Perspectives in Post-Structuralist Criticism* (London: Methuen, 1980), pp. 141–60; Roland Barthes, 'The Death of the Author', trans. Richard Howard, in *The Rustle of Language* (Oxford: Blackwell, 1986), pp. 56–64.

the secular impulse towards biography as act of homage. Thus scripture becomes the province of the reading *scriptor*; that is, a polytextual fabric delimited by the metatextual interpretation of critics themselves defined as an effect of the writing game they activate. For Foucault, conversely, the effect of such critical displacement-with-a-difference serves to reinscribe precisely the defining cultural practice of the author-function. Authorial naming, by these terms, is a necessity. For the legislative role of the author-function is to unite otherwise unrelated discourses into a coherent realm over which it then maintains sovereignty. To some extent the author is therefore an ideological barrier installed against a flood of aimless polysemy. At the same time, the decisive role of the fundamental author such as Freud or Marx has been to expand the very possibilities of discourse, an act of cultural intervention and individuation re-emphasising the power of the writing agent.

There is much here which would seem applicable to the process of genealogical demystification. From the reflexive exposure of critical construction mediated through language to the possible evaluation of Schoenberg as fundamental author overmastering an inherited discursive context, Barthes and Foucault together suggest an array of tactics and strategies for reading behind the commonplace façades of the authorial subject. None of these are inappropriate for the development of a keener metatextual comprehension. But as Sean Burke argues, no amount of cognitive application can resolve 'the essential problem posed by the author . . . that whilst authorial subjectivity is theoretically unassimilable, it cannot be practically circumvented'.[122] Critical science fixed on the machinations of discursive tropics is thus ultimately obliged to confront the interplay between work and life. Because otherwise the equation of methodological with ontological questions of authorial disappearance begins to distort on grounds of performative contradiction. Finally then, as Burke concludes,

> a theory of the author, or of the absence of the author, cannot withstand the practice of reading, for there is not an absolute *cogito* of which individual authors are the subalternant manifestations, but authors, many authors, and the differences (in gender, history, class, ethnology, in the nature of . . . authorship, in the degree of authorship itself) that exist between authors – within authorship – defy reduction to any universalising aesthetic.[123]

122. Sean Burke, *The Death and Return of the Author: Criticism and Subjectivity in Barthes, Foucault and Derrida* (Edinburgh University Press, 1992), p. 173.
123. *Ibid.*, p. 173.

By these terms, the purpose of a deconstructive genealogy ranged against the effect of illusory cultural continuity belatedly reveals itself: not synchronic surrender in the textual domain alone, but rather active confrontation with the nature of alterity. Otherness, in short, is the difference which makes a difference. For as Gross confirms, 'today no less than in the past we still require powerful encounters with alterity',[124] not least as a means of enabling the potential 'critique of modernity from outside modernity'.[125] To date, the secularised unbinding of the musicological canon has released considerable ammunition from the direction of gender and sexuality, while the battleground of class has remained largely deserted. Among these theatres of critical conflict, however, those of race and ethnicity remain potentially the most volatile. Alexander Ringer's study of Schoenberg as Jew continues a seemingly vital debate in this field to which Julie Brown's analysis of Schoenberg's post-Wagnerian poetics of cultural regeneration adds a significant dimension.[126] In this context, Brown determines that Schoenberg as true artist 'like Wagner's self-sacrificing Jew' felt compelled to 'not only acknowledge his difference, but [also] . . . submit to its implications'.[127] Correspondingly 'it seems inescapable that race was an element of Schoenberg's "revolutionary" musical technique and aesthetics'.[128] By these terms 'the emancipated dissonance . . . may be read as a type of harmonic Ahasuerus, inscribed – whether before or after the fact – as part of Schoenberg's attempt to redeem music from the contaminating Jewish element: separating the "vagrant" chord from the tonal system and allowing it freedom to wander alone redeems that system and ensures its "natural" purity'.[129] *Das Buch* therefore represents the earliest 'symptom of the baptised Schoenberg's acceptance and internalisation of his own damaged discourse',[130] a course of self-discovery in which he sought to fictionalise himself 'as both "new man" – visionary, prophetic hope for the future – and self-sacrificing Jew, wandering out into the wilderness of atonality'.[131]

---

124. Gross, *The Past in Ruins*, p. 84. To this extent, Newlin's faith in the quasi-divine ultimately emerges as an embrace of the most absolute form of alterity: what Gross terms the desire 'for mystery beyond security', *ibid.*, p. 84.
125. *Ibid.*, p. 87.
126. Alexander Ringer, *Schoenberg: the Composer as Jew* (Oxford University Press, 1990). See also Michael Mäckelmann, *Arnold Schoenberg und das Judentum* (Hamburger Beiträge zur Musikwissenschaft: Hamburg, 1984) and Hartmut Zelinsky, 'Arnold Schönberg – der Wagner Gottes: Anmerkung zum Lebensweg eines deutschen Juden aus Wien', *Neue Zeitschrift für Musik*, 4 (1986), 7–19.   127. Brown, 'Schoenberg's Early Wagnerisms', p. 72.
128. *Ibid.*, p. 76.   129. *Ibid.*, p. 69.   130. *Ibid.*, p. 77.
131. *Ibid.*, p. 73.

The implications of such a reading are far from easily assimilable. Overall they appear to add a particularly compelling perspective to the autopoietic thesis explored by Le Rider, Taruskin and Deathridge. Perhaps most important is the sense of creative identity returning, in however sublimated a form, from the eternal not only to the temporal, but also to the territorial: that is, towards the contingent political circumstances of time and place. That Schoenberg's lived experience from the Jewish quarter in Vienna's second district onwards seems to ring true with the authenticity afforded by the concrete boundaries and material formations of social relationships, however, ought not to obscure the fact that this remains one further construction from the viewpoint of the present. As such the awarding of representational status does not evade the lures of consoling myth, but rather stays bound by the realisation that there are potentially as many authenticities as uses.

Critical dissolution of idealised identities and associations into the contingencies of everyday existence carries its own seductions in the form of real world contact. In this respect the virtue of alterity is also its encouragement of reflexivity: the necessary acknowledgement of the observer's own situated condition along with a questioning and even surrender of acquired advantages. In a recent symposium on the relationship between musicology and difference, 'traditional music analysis' is charged with being 'one of the most aggressively universalizing discourses still in common use'.[132] Although analytical modes of the new musicology have so far tended to conduct a critique of the instrumentalism involved in close reading while retaining the normative bias offered by, say, Bloom rather than de Man or Gadamer rather than Habermas, such a comment now seems misplaced. Hence as Philip Bohlman writes, the fear that someone is 'not really talking about "the music"' is increasingly less of the issue analytically than beginning 'to "face the music", that is, to confront it physically and politically, thereby to grapple with music's embodiment of self and Other'.[133] Consequently the older form of testing for (structural) identity is supplemented by a new one. And as in all spheres it remains subject to the reflexive check of 'understanding when different treatment stigmatizes, and when similar treatment stigmatizes by disregarding difference'.[134]

132. Gary Tomlinson cited in Ruth Solie, ed., *Musicology and Difference: Gender and Sexuality in Music Scholarship* (Berkeley: University of California Press, 1993), p. 8.
133. Philip Bohlman, 'Musicology as a Political Act', *Journal of Musicology*, 11 (1993), 423, 435.
134. Ruth Solie, Introduction to *Musicology and Difference*, p. 2.

To this point the revision of any 'rigid theoretical ideal' in response to 'the actual participation of peoples in the making of human life' indicates a form of liberation.[135] But as Edward Said warns, faith in cultural praxis can easily decline into an academic strain of political correctness, merely reaffirming 'the paramount importance of formerly suppressed or silenced forms of knowledge' as well as indulging 'the sanctimonious piety of historical or cultural victimhood as a way of making our intellectual presence felt'.[136] Less desirable still is the thought of enshrining 'a pure politics of identity [in which the] . . . signs and symbols of freedom and status are taken for the reality'.[137] Far from fulfilling the message of modernity, such a tendency tropes it only in the direction of a perpetual roll call of the weak and unbroken logic of displacement among the strong. If the hermeneutics of suspicion is to be superseded, therefore, the new goal must be not merely a strategy of reiteration, but one of reconciliation and restoration; of generosity and duty in which rights and responsibilities are brought to the fore. Thus, as in Aimé Césaire's words, since 'no race possesses the monopoly of beauty, of intelligence, of force . . . there is a place for all at the rendez-vous of victory'.[138]

Said's own commentary on music has shown something of how this general *extra*disciplinary concern might proceed: less a process, as Henry Louis Gates Jr. advises, of technology transfer from the sphere of literary theory than a critical reorientation towards a 'sense of the social and cultural work that music performs [and] . . . the social space it inhabits'.[139] The ultimate significance of work by cultural critics like Said of course hangs in the balance. But the signs within musicology (at least while it remains an independent discipline) are of an ever increasing rapprochement with all spheres of human enquiry. Under these terms, as Philip Bohlman makes the point, ideological inscription through universalising strategies of notation and interpretation stands to be erased by the recognition 'of musicology as a reflexive process, a moving of music into discourse'.[140] For now, however, optimism is hard won while the field is characterised more by crisis, the result of the still 'new responsibility to come face-to-face with the political nature of all acts of interpretation and with the political consequences of excluding for too long the . . . Others we

---

135. Edward W. Said, 'The Politics of Knowledge', *Raritan*, 11 (1991), 20.
136. *Ibid.*, p. 26.   137. *Ibid.*, p. 24.
138. Aimé Césaire quoted in Said, 'The Politics of Knowledge', p. 24.
139. Henry Louis Gates Jr., review of Edward W. Said, *Musical Elaborations* (New York: Columbia University Press, 1991), *Raritan*, 13 (1993), 108.
140. Bohlman, 'Musicology as a Political Act', p. 418.

simply do not see and hear.'[141] In truth, a paradigm shift in favour of auto-critique, as disabling as it may first appear to be, is likely to remain a question of careful and patient negotiation. But then this admission too is germane to the debate. Because the very actions involved in breaking the spell of transcendence in the interests of worldly engagment are themselves consciously out of step with the imperial march of progress. Rather, like history itself, they proceed only gradually, from one day to the next.

141. *Ibid.*, p. 436.

10

Misleading voices: contrasts and continuities in Stravinsky studies

Anthony Pople

Ideas of contrast and continuity have become familiar themes in commentary of all kinds on Stravinsky and his music. The most obvious example of this concerns the commonplace division of his work into creative periods, defined stylistically – an idea which dates back to the 1920s. This division, though deeply engrained in the subsequent critical literature on this composer, has nonetheless attracted at least two kinds of counter: first, from those who, with Druskin, argue that 'whatever "manner" [Stravinsky] favoured, whatever model he selected, he remained unmistakably himself';[1] and secondly, from those who, perhaps through a closer historical study of Stravinsky's critical reception, detect a lack of consistency in the identification of turning-points in his oeuvre which sits uneasily with the decisiveness that is commonly claimed for the composer's stylistic contrasts.

Both of these points of view serve to focus attention, within the stylistic frame, on those works which are held to represent beginnings, ends or transitions. But the focus is nonetheless diffuse. In his *Poetics of Music*, Stravinsky names *The Rite of Spring* as the work which meant that 'I was made a revolutionary in spite of myself',[2] and, though one must observe that the whole trajectory of the self-depiction in this book is intended to (re-)establish his credentials as a traditionalist, it is clear from many of Stravinsky's public utterances that the reception of *The Rite* indeed represented a turning-point for him, albeit one whose effects were to be rationalised in more ways than the merely stylistic. Gerald Abraham, too, writes of 'the post-*Rite* works', which he sees as interesting for their instrumentation, but he identifies 'Stravinsky's individual harmonic

1. Mikhail Druskin, *Igor Stravinsky: his Life, Works and Views*, trans. Martin Cooper (Cambridge University Press, 1982), p. 23. Roman Vlad's widely read *Stravinsky*, 3rd edn, trans. Frederick Fuller (Oxford University Press, 1978) also follows this line.
2. Igor Stravinsky, *Poetics of Music*, trans. Arthur Knodel and Ingolf Dahl (Cambridge, Mass.: Harvard University Press, 1942), p. 10.

271

evolution' as having begun with *Petrushka*.[3] For Asaf'yev, perhaps the most perceptive of early commentators on Stravinsky's music, the 'new instrumental style' began not directly 'post-*Rite*' but with *Ragtime*,[4] while Aaron Copland, whose Parisian training brought him into close contact with the leading edge of the neo-classical movement in music, claims that the inaugural work of that movement, with its 'conscious adoption of the musical ideals of the early eighteenth century', was Stravinsky's Octet, and the inaugural moment was that work's first performance on 18 October 1923.[5] Beside the apparent authority of these ear-witness opinions, the popular view that *Pulcinella* marked the clear beginning of this movement some four years earlier might appear naive, but it ought not to be discounted altogether.

My purpose is not to portray any or all of these commentaries as inept, still less to mediate between them. Rather, I wish to identify the difficulties that accompany a move from the general to the specific in this regard – of moving deliberately, if in these early examples of Stravinsky criticism not yet strategically, from the recognition of an inter-opus shift of style to the identification of a specific opus with such a shift. The achievements of Leonard Meyer and others in recent decades make it incumbent on critics, analysts and theorists to deal effectively with such difficulties, but the ways of handling them from respectively critical, theoretical and analytical standpoints themselves demand attention, not least because their interactions expose the difficulty of articulating any of these three musicological disciplines as standing hermetically apart from the others.

In the past fifteen years or so, a number of analysts have translated the Stravinsky–Abraham focus on *The Rite of Spring* as turning-point into the domain of single-opus studies. Pieter van den Toorn's monograph devoted to *The Rite* has as its subtitle 'The Beginnings of a Musical Language', the language in question being that characterised at greater length in his monumental *The Music of Igor Stravinsky*.[6] A monograph by Allen Forte and a celebrated exchange of published letters between him

3. Gerald Abraham, *A Hundred Years of Music*, 4th edn (London: Duckworth, 1974), pp. 255, 251.
4. Boris Asaf'yev, *A Book about Stravinsky*, trans. Richard F. French (Ann Arbor: UMI Research Press, 1982), p. 226.
5. Aaron Copland, *Our New Music: Leading Composers in Europe and America* (New York: McGraw-Hill, 1941), pp. 100–1.
6. Pieter C. van den Toorn, *Stravinsky and 'The Rite of Spring': The Beginnings of a Musical Language* (Oxford University Press, 1987) and *The Music of Igor Stravinsky* (New Haven: Yale University Press, 1983).

and Richard Taruskin deal also with this work.[7] Each of these three writers is concerned to relate *The Rite* to a broad corpus of music: either seminally (van den Toorn), emblematically (Forte) or teleologically (Taruskin). The evident contrasts between them – expressed through heated language in the Forte–Taruskin exchange, merely by respectful distance in the case of Forte and van den Toorn – amount to contrasts between their referential corpora and between the relationships they identify between *The Rite* and those corpora, perhaps misleadingly surfacing as divergences of opinion about the music of *The Rite* itself. In each case, what amounts to a fairly straightforward (if ideologically loaded) critical point of view has been reworked into an endeavour which separately focuses both the interpretation and its context, transmuting the relationship between the general and the specific into the familiar methodological interpenetration of theory and analysis. Only in van den Toorn's case does the result actually rework the Stravinsky–Abraham line: the others construct, develop or reveal (according to one's point of view) quite different critical positions which revisit an old Schoenbergian fixation about the emergence of atonality from (or against) nineteenth-century common practice and were thus always on a collision course, because projecting the modernist credentials of atonality requires the likelihood of being accused of promoting discontinuity to be programmatically maintained.

Another important distinction between van den Toorn's approach, on the one hand, and those of Forte and Taruskin, on the other, is the rather obvious one that van den Toorn's is a theory of Stravinsky's works only – which is to say that the corpus against which he measures *The Rite* consists in fact of Stravinsky's other music – whereas Forte and Taruskin interpret Stravinsky's music in a not necessarily broader context defined by the works of his supposedly like-minded contemporaries or supposed precursors. (The latter strategy is also that which underlies those few analyses of passages by Stravinsky that have appeared emblematically in the post-Schenkerian tradition.[8]) Another theory, comparable to van den Toorn's in its provision for Stravinsky's works alone, is to be found in

7. Allen Forte, *The Harmonic Organization of 'The Rite of Spring'* (New Haven: Yale University Press, 1978); the letters by Forte and Richard Taruskin are published in *Music Analysis*, 5 (1986) [Forte, 321–37; Taruskin, 313–20]; see also Taruskin, 'Chernomor to Kashchei: Harmonic Sorcery; or, Stravinsky's "Angle"', *Journal of the American Musicological Society*, 38 (1985), 72–142, which defines his own position in greater detail.
8. See, for example, Adele T. Katz, *Challenge to Tradition: A New Concept of Tonality* (New York: Knopf, 1945), Chap. 8; Roy Travis, 'Towards a New Concept of Tonality?', *Journal of Music Theory*, 3 (1959), 257–84.

Edward Cone's seminal article, 'Stravinsky: The Progress of a Method', which transfers the idea of exposed, contrasting discontinuities from the broader historical-stylistic frame to the realm of intra-opus commentary – i.e. to a different 'level' of analytical criticism – reworking it in terms of the alternations of 'musical areas' within a continuous movement or work. This shift of critical/analytical 'level' is quite deliberately undertaken, and is held to defuse a line of criticism which Cone affects to take as pejorative:

> For many years it was fashionable to accuse Stravinsky . . . of artistic inconstancy: of embracing a series of manners instead of achieving a personal style. Today it is becoming increasingly clear that [he] has been remarkably consistent in his stylistic development . . . This does not mean that all questions concerning Stravinsky's methods are now settled. Some of his most persistent characteristics are still puzzling, and as a result is it hard to explain why some of his greatest successes really work. But they do work, and this essay will try to throw some light on how they work by examining one of these characteristics: the apparent discontinuities that so often interrupt the musical flow.

> From *Le Sacre du Printemps* onward [*sic*], Stravinsky's textures have been subject to sudden breaks affecting almost every musical dimension . . . On examination, the point of interruption proves to be only the most immediately obvious characteristic of a basic Stravinskyan technique comprising three phases, which I call stratification, interlock, and synthesis.[9]

Both van den Toorn and Cone use theories conceived for Stravinsky's works alone to emphasise continuity rather than contrast through his career as a composer. But this version of the contrast/continuity theme is potentially dialectical: the 'continuity' of style across periods is argued in the context of received ideas about severe stylistic contrasts (as in the passage from Cone quoted above); while the more commonplace identification of severe stylistic contrasts is (trivially) expounded within the context of a premise of continuity afforded by the fact that the music in question constitutes the creative work of one individual. Whether Cone's identification of synthesis as the culminating strategy of Stravinsky's 'basic technique' fully accomplishes a shift of this proto-dialectic from the

9. Edward T. Cone, 'Stravinsky: The Progress of a Method', in Benjamin Boretz and Edward T. Cone, eds., *Perspectives on Schoenberg and Stravinsky* (Princeton University Press, 1968), pp. 165–6.

inter-opus to the intra-opus level is a moot point. I am inclined to think his use of 'synthesis' in this context more likely to have been a pre-emptive strategy which by evoking ideas of development and unity tried to ensure the credibility of his theory among the community of scholars at which the article was directed. His analyses of intra-opus 'synthetic' resolutions may support this gambit, but their status in relation to the larger continuity/contrast dialectic of style and career – essentially, that they encourage the reader to believe that *something* has been resolved, but do so in a misleading way that jumps across critical/analytical 'levels' – raises more difficult questions, to which I shall return in another context.

At an intra-opus level these issues have a history of their own dating back to Asaf'yev in the 1920s, who saw Stravinsky's 'new instrumental style' as exemplifying a refinement of the sonata principle, and as doing so in an essentially dialectical way, observing that

> In so far as the sense of the sonata is to be sought in the contrast of two opposing themes, there need be no dialectic. Contrast is not dialectic. But the converse: that dialectic implies contrast – is true.[10]

Asaf'yev's insistence that Stravinsky's dialectical approach went beyond the mere contrasting of materials was taken up by the composer himself, though with a different emphasis, in *Poetics of Music*:

> Music that is based on ontological time is generally dominated by the principle of similarity. The music that adheres to psychological time likes to proceed by contrast. To these two principles which dominate the creative process correspond the fundamental concepts of variety and unity . . . For myself, I have always considered that in general it is more satisfactory to proceed by similarity rather than by contrast. Music thus gains strength in the measure that it does not succumb to the seductions of variety.

> Contrast produces an immediate effect. Similarity satisfies us only in the long run. Contrast is an element of variety, but it divides our attention. Similarity is born of a striving for unity. The need to seek variety is perfectly legitimate, but we should never forget that the One precedes the Many. Moreover, the coexistence of both is constantly necessary, and all the problems of art . . . revolve ineluctably about this question . . . Mere common sense, as well as supreme wisdom, invites us to affirm both the one and the other. All the same, the best attitude for a composer in this case will be the attitude of a

10. Asaf'yev, *A Book about Stravinsky*, p. 223.

man who is conscious of the hierarchy of values and who must make a choice. Variety is valid only as a means of attaining similarity.[11]

In this regard, it is interesting to observe that in a recent study which quite deliberately grapples with the critical dimension of the theoretical/analytical refocusing of both the interpretation of musical works and the intertextual contexts of such interpretations, Joseph Straus deals almost exclusively with works from Stravinsky's so-called neo-classical period, alongside those of Schoenberg, Berg, Webern and Bartók.[12] This allows him to circumscribe the corpora against which individual works are analysed through a common-practice understanding of tonality, though he also supplements this strongly Bloomian – i.e. genuinely intertextual – approach with a number of analyses which simply identify interopus remodellings in what might be called a weakly Bloomian way.

The latter approach is a familiar one in discussions of Stravinsky's neo-classical music: it is found even in Taruskin's letter *contra* Forte about *The Rite*, as evidence that the tonal sense of a downbeat sonority may be taken from its upbeat.[13] But the distinction between this kind of citation and genuinely intertextual criticism must not be pressed too far: arguably, Taruskin's 'model' (a Musette by the eighteenth-century composer Chédeville) is given as one of many possible examples, stylistically distant from Stravinsky's score, of the underlying common-practice feature to which he wishes to draw attention, rather than being proposed as a specific model against which Taruskin hears, or expects his readers to hear, part of *The Rite of Spring*. Similarly, Straus's critical purpose is not to align Stravinsky's music with its models, general or specific: rather, he is concerned to distance the music from them but in a dialectical way which depends considerably on the maturity and power of the analytical means through which the 'remakings' of past models are described. Pitchclass set classifications, the charting of row dispositions and the identification of relationships within row-classes have sufficient explanatory force to construct an interpretation of the 'remade' work no less securely than the historically distanced, but in Straus's view inescapable, context. It has to be said that Straus's decision to restrict the occasions on which he tests the strength of atonal and serial theory against the full weight of common-practice tonal theory makes the balance of descriptive power more even. His concentration on the neo-classical works also de-

11. Stravinsky, *Poetics of Music*, pp. 31–2.
12. Joseph N. Straus, *Remaking the Past: Musical Modernism and the Influence of the Tonal Tradition* (Cambridge, Mass.: Harvard University Press, 1990).
13. Taruskin, letter in *Music Analysis*, 5 (1986), p. 314.

escalates the inter-corporal rivalry that so inflamed Taruskin and Forte. Nonetheless, he deals elsewhere in his study with serial compositions by other composers, and it is perhaps surprising that apart from a page on the opening of *In Memoriam Dylan Thomas* he discusses no work of Stravinsky later than *The Rake's Progress* (1948–51).

In a discussion which predates Straus's book by several years, Arnold Whittall has no hesitation in tackling such matters.[14] His strongly Bloomian assessment of the opening bars of Stravinsky's Anthem ('The dove descending') is focused against a non-specific but explicitly common-practice model, which I have adapted in Ex. 10.1. My adaptation is more fully detailed than Whittall's original – deliberately so, because his emphasis is on the intrinsic distance between a piece such as this and any model to which it might relate, whereas my purpose below will be to consider the process of interplay between a developing analytical interpretation and its context. Whittall's overall argument, anticipating Straus, is that the semblance of the old within the new must be seen as precisely that – a semblance – rather than as a straightforward instance, one consequence of this being a crucial distinction between unifiable structures of the kind we associate with tonality and, in modernist music, a form of intra-opus contrast that implies a non-dialectical linkage of materials. For example, in assessing a putative 'fundamental contrapuntal structure' for the first movement of Stravinsky's Serenade in A, in which both upper and lower lines depart from A and then return to the same pitch *via* a single intervening note, Whittall writes:

> I would not myself argue against the contention that these elements are of fundamental importance to the movement, identifying, as they do, its principal pivots. The difficulty I have is in hearing all of them as members of a single, integrated, unifying process, rather than as the representation of one process enclosing a second process.[15]

His analysis of the opening of 'The dove descending' indeed represents 'one process enclosing a second process'. In this reading, a D major harmony arises through linear motion as III in B minor but is prolonged as V in G minor, progressing to the tonic harmony of that key before the linear motion in B minor is resumed. In other words, a straightforwardly prolonged progression from tonic to dominant in B minor encloses a dominant-to-tonic progression in G minor.

14. Arnold Whittall, 'Musical Analysis: Descriptions and Distinctions' [An Inaugural Lecture in the Faculty of Music] (University of London, King's College, 1982), pp. 10–12. 15. Whittall, 'Musical Analysis', pp. 12–13.

Example 10.1

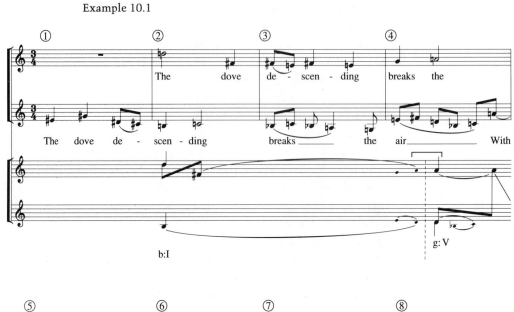

The first point of detail I should like to address concerns the perceived location of a boundary between B minor and G minor tonalities. It
seems evident that the open fifth D–A is the cue which shifts Whittall's
perspective from one tonality to the other: to adapt his description of the
Serenade, this fifth is a 'pivot'; and the fifth F♯–C♯ on the downbeat of b. 6
is the 'pivot' around which his reading subsequently returns to B minor.
But, just as van den Toorn has elaborated on the alternatives of 'radical'
and 'conservative' approaches in listening when confronted by conflicting
patterns of pulse and metre,[16] so there are 'radical' and 'conservative'

16. Van den Toorn, *Stravinsky and 'The Rite of Spring'*, Chap. 3.

approaches to hearing a tonal shift in this passage from 'The dove descending'. Whittall's D–A open fifth represents the 'conservative' pole of a field of possibilities, whereas the D–C–F♯ configuration in b. 2, if heard as an outlined dominant-quality sonority in G, would represent a 'radical' pole, in the terms outlined by van den Toorn for rhythmic perception and analysis:

> in analytical review and hence presumably in perception, ['radical' interpreters] tend to readjust their metrical bearing 'radically' at the first signs of conflicting evidence. On the other hand, the instinct of the more 'conservative' listener is to cling to an established regularity for as long as possible, and often with the consequence that the effect of conflict or disruption is all the more acutely felt.[17]

This conservative–radical domain of alternatives in listening transfers to the intra-opus level the critical uncertainty about stylistic turning-points in Stravinsky's oeuvre, and also their possibly illusory quality. Whittall's identification of 'pivots' makes this clear linguistically; Stravinsky's protestation that *The Rite* 'made [him] a revolutionary in spite of [himself]' can also be understood as describing a tension between, on the one hand, the radical perceptions of his critics – i.e. an early, perhaps premature, interpretation of *The Rite* as a radical work, projected onto its composer who was thereby identified as radical himself – and, on the other hand, Stravinsky's determination that this was 'in spite of himself' – i.e. that he perceived his own stylistic progress in a 'conservative' way. One is also reminded of the naively 'radical' identification of *Pulcinella* as a stylistic turning point a few years later and the subsequent fleshing-out in the Stravinsky literature of a more 'conservative' interpretation which recognises the innovatory nature of *Pulcinella* but maintains recognition of a tension between that style and the 'Russian-ness' of, say, *Les Noces*, until the breaking point is reached – which occurred, in the case of Copland's perception, for example, at the first performance of the Octet.

In the case of the perceptible shift of tonality in the opening passage of 'The dove descending', the whole of b. 3 and the first crotchet of b. 4 constitute the field of tension between the conservative and radical poles of what I have characterised as a domain of possible shifts of perspective. At the radical and conservative poles stand cues towards a G minor perception; in the field of tension, all the pitches lie within the gamut of this tonality (G♮, A♮, B♭, C♮, D♮, E♮, F♯) but the counterpoint is difficult to interpret as projecting any particular harmony – the two notes of the open fifth

17. Van den Toorn, *Stravinsky and 'The Rite of Spring'*, p. 67.

A–E are not attacked simultaneously, for example. Whittall's 'conservative' reading must skate over this passage: its accommodation to a B minor perspective would be awkward in the extreme and is not attempted. Yet an alternative 'radical' reading must also indulge in a certain amount of hand-waving when dealing with these misleading voices (see Ex. 10.2). If the pitches are read as participating in a prolongation of the D7 harmony outlined across the voices in b. 2, then it must be said that the most characteristic feature of the counterpoint is that the harmonic pitches in the two voices hardly ever coincide.

Example 10.2

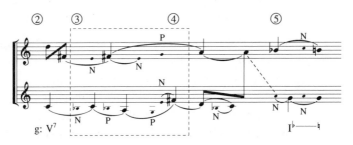

It is perhaps a convenient coincidence that the Anthem's first publication was in a volume of Stravinsky–Craft exchanges among which the composer castigates *The Firebird* as follows:

> the few scraps of counterpoint to be found in it – in the Kastchei scene, for example – are derived from chord notes, and this is not real counterpoint (though it is Wagner's idea of counterpoint in *Die Meistersinger*, I might add).[18]

If the voice-leading in bb. 3–4 of 'The dove descending' constitutes, by way of contrast, an example of 'real counterpoint' in Stravinsky's terms, then its defining modernist, post-Wagnerian aspect is perhaps to be seen in relation to the 'field of tension' and the tonal cues at its temporal boundaries. The configuration of these elements tallies with van den Toorn's suggestion that in a 'conservative' listening 'the effect of conflict or disruption is all the more acutely felt', because only the conservative listening will be open to the tension that arises in bb. 3–4 through the maintenance of an alignment with a tonal gamut that correlates with the initial cue, combined with a failure to confirm it harmonically by virtue of the fact that

18. Igor Stravinsky and Robert Craft, *Expositions and Developments* (London: Faber, 1962), p. 132. The Anthem is found at pp. 154–7.

the voice-leading within the putatively prolonged harmony is out of alignment. A similar recognition of misleading voices is to be found, appropriately enough, in the analysis by Schenker himself of a passage from Stravinsky's Concerto for piano and winds, which arouses that analyst's wrath precisely because the voice-leading is out of alignment with the harmonies within which prolongational motion is assumed to take place.[19]

Although the specific recognisability of pitch configurations as cues in the sense outlined above is open to dispute – indeed, must definitively be so, if the domain of possibilities between radical and conservative perceptions is to be maintained as a principle – both the alignment of notated pitches with a gamut and the extent to which the counterpoint projects or fails to project a recognised sonority are amenable to more rigorous investigation, albeit against the context of such uncertainly cued harmonies. In a serial work such as the Anthem, the series itself may form a useful starting point, as it does here by virtue of the relatively straightforward structure of the work in serial terms (see Table 10.1). The series as presented initially in the alto voice (P5) contains a seven-pc segment that aligns with a 7–34 gamut of G minor (G♮, A♮, B♭, C♮, D♮, E♮, F♯); the remnant has the pcs of a C♯9 chord (Ex. 10.3a).[20] The other members of the row-class that appear in the Anthem may be viewed in a similar fashion (Ex. 10.3b–d).

In the first phrase (see Ex. 10.1), the soprano voice (R5) enters as the alto's non-G minor segment ends, so that both series are in alignment with a G minor gamut until the alto's P5 is exhausted on the third quaver of b. 4. Since the alto then continues with IR11, however, the G minor alignment continues through to the soprano B♮ at the end of b. 5. Then, from the second crotchet of b. 7 to the end of the phrase both series share the C♯9 alignment with which the alto began. Taken in the context of the foregoing discussion, this sequence of events suggests that the passage from the soprano B♮ to the second beat of b. 7 might be seen as another 'field of tension' between radicalising and conservative tonal cues. The example of Whittall's analysis allows us to identify the cue to a radical hearing as the open fifth F♯–C♯ at the beginning of b. 6; although the F♮–B♮ dyad is less clearly the cue to a conservative hearing, the straightforward-

19. Heinrich Schenker, 'Fortsetzung der Urlinie-Betrachtungen', in *Das Meisterwerk in der Musik*, vol. II (repr. Hildesheim: Georg Olms, 1974), pp. 37–40.

20. The five pcs of the remnant also lie within a nine-pc segment (wrapped around the two ends of the series) which aligns with a 9–7A gamut of E♭ minor (E♭, F♮, G♭, A♭, B♭, C♭, C♮, D♭, D♮).

Table 10.1 *Serial layout of Stravinsky, Anthem*

b.	1	2–4	4–8	9–14	15–16 33–34	17–20 35–38	21 39	22–25 40–43	26–29	29–32
S		R5———		IR11	R5———		I5———			
A	P5———		IR11	R5	R5———					
T						IR11———		I5	P5	(R5)
									×	
B						P5	R5___		R5	(P5)

Example 10.3

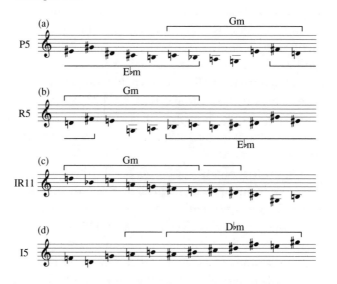

ness of the paired voice-leading through Stravinsky's maligned 'chord notes' is evident from this point onwards, as shown in Ex. 10.4.

All of this calls into question the B minor tonality which plays an important role in Whittall's reading. There, the F♯–C♯ dyad is credible as a cue largely because of its identity with the 'dominant' of the B minor domain cued for Whittall by the B–D dyad at b. 2. But the B minor recognition neither tallies with the preceding notes nor assists in cueing what follows directly: in fact, if recognised harmonically it obscures the D7 outline (D–C–F♯) that is the first, potentially radical cue for the G minor region. As observed above – and as critics of tonal interpretations of music such as the Anthem are liable to emphasise – all such harmonic recognitions are arguably illusory and misleading; but the foregoing discussion

Example 10.4

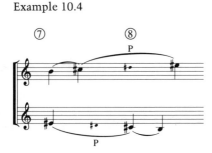

has attempted to work towards a way of discussing such illusion and its consequences more productively. Just as Schenkerian theory speaks of *Scheintonarten* – illusory foreground 'keys' through which a supposedly monotonal work passes[21] – so we may here identify a configuration like the B–D dyad as a *Scheinharmonie* – something which could be interpreted as a harmony but which if so interpreted can be misleading. Schenkerian tonal analysis frequently invokes changes of foreground tonality but treats them as lacking in corroborative contextual implication for (and from) the deeper levels of structure; in a work such as the Anthem, where tonal perceptions themselves are fleeting and uncertain, the identity of certain pitch configurations with tonal harmonies can be accepted without treating all such configurations as equally significant. The contextual corroboration here involves not just the identification of similar or related harmonies close by – as in the case of the tonic *Scheinharmonie* of B minor in b. 2 of 'The dove descending' and its putative dominant in b. 6 – but must take into account the dynamics of cueing, uncertainty and confirmation through which illusions come to be perceived as allusions. In the case of bb. 6–8, the tonal orientation may be taken as F♯ rather than B: the open fifth F♯–C♯ cues a change of orientation largely by negating the foregoing G minor, but is confirmed for the 'conservative' hearing by the dominant-quality sonority on C♯ that emerges a bar or so later. The intervening 'field of tension' fails to confirm the tonic-quality harmony of the 'radical' cue, but at the same time does not step outside an F♯ minor gamut.

Like Whittall's analysis of this passage, the reading summarised in Ex. 10.5 may be said to interpret 'one process enclosing a second process', if the activities within 'F♯ minor' and 'G minor' regions are understood as processes. But the specific concept of 'process' that has been invoked to arrive at this reading concerns the cueing and subsequent clarification of

21. Heinrich Schenker, trans. and ed. Ernst Oster, *Free Composition* [*Der freie Satz*] (New York: Longman, 1979), vol. I, p. 112, §277.

Example 10.5

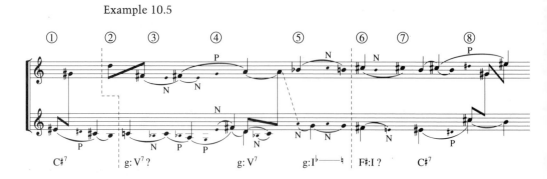

tonal orientations – something quite different from a process-like conception of 'motion within a key'. The latter attribute of common-practice
tonal thought has simply not been taken over as a defining characteristic
of 'tonal orientation' as interpreted here; gamut membership and the (possibly provisional) recognisability of tonality-cueing harmonic configurations have been accorded a higher priority.

Nor is the other linguistic component of the statement tenable. To
say that one area 'encloses' the other seems at first sight to do no more
than concur with Whittall – at one remove from Cone – in identifying
straightforward properties of chronological contiguity and near-contiguity
applying to the segmentation of a sonic continuity that the analysis in
effect proposes. But while Whittall's use of the word 'enclose' is evidently
intended as significantly different to the Schenkerian (and not only
Schenkerian) principle that areas can subsume or subordinate other areas,
it nonetheless retains overtones of hierarchic thinking. In fact, Whittall's
purpose, as shown by the tone of his wider writings on musical modernism, is precisely to indicate that the *possibility* of sub- and superordina-
tion between juxtaposed materials remains available as an interpretative
strategy: his analyses of this principle in action identify the domains in
which such judgements might occur, but deliberately stop short of making them.[22] Whittall's justification for this is that such exposed non-
dialectical contrasts are a classically defining feature of modernism –
implying that the legitimacy of his critical view stems from an assertion
of authorial intent.

This asks difficult questions of, for example, Stravinsky's remarks
in *Poetics of Music*, and it may be the composer rather than the critic who

22. See, for example, Whittall, 'The Theorist's Sense of History: Concepts of
Contemporaneity in Composition and Analysis', *Journal of the Royal
Musical Association*, 112 (1987), 1–20.

wilts under the strain. If, in Stravinsky's self-advertisement, contrast is said to precede unity, Whittall's view might be rather that, in the modernist situation he describes, contrast precedes (arbitrary) interpretative decision – an arbitrariness he is prepared to expose but not to commit. It seems to be an important part of his thinking that such decisions might be made in different ways on different occasions by an individual, in a way which might be seen as humanly necessary but which is critically unnecessary or even undesirable. To see such decision-making as evasive of responsibility suggests that the point of an interpretative process at which a hierarchising imperative becomes inoperable – when the privileging of one among two (or more) elements at one 'level' so as to carry it forward to the 'next' is self-evidently arbitrary – must also represent the end of a critical trail, even if other critical trails remain, as in Whittall's rich writings they evidently do. One point of 'process' which is at issue here is whether an interpretative decision which 'moves on' from a conceptually simultaneous focus on two (or more) entities to the identification of something which acknowledges both entities within a single focus must amount necessarily to a shift of level, or can instead be seen to arise merely from a shift of perspective: is the level of resolution 'meta', or is it – misleadingly, but credibly – simply 'other'?

The attack on hierarchisation which results from an anti-dialectical refusal of arbitrary resolutions, whether at the 'level' of style history – modernism perpetually, definitively, 'against' the past – or, as Whittall has argued, at an intra-opus 'level' in the focused juxtaposition of resolutely differentiated musical materials, may have still more far-reaching consequences. Returning to the first eight bars of Stravinsky's Anthem, it is certainly reasonable to expose as arbitrary an interpretative strategy that would see the 'F♯ minor' area enclosing, let alone subordinating, the 'G minor' area in the manner of a tonal hierarchy of prolongations; but alternative criteria of serial layout and phrasing permit the identification of these eight bars as a unit, within which the 'F♯ minor' area quite clearly begins and ends and the 'G minor' area comes in the middle. The 'critical trail' of hierarchical tonality has dried up, but the availability of another critical/analytical 'trail' allows an analogous judgement of the status of the two 'tonal' areas to be made. Moreover, this coincidence between the 'real' and 'false' trails is unlikely to be overlooked: it might even be argued that the hierarchising power of the 'false' tonal trail is a factor in the interpretative process through which the 'real' trail becomes recognisable. This is another domain of interpretation in which the dynamics of cueing, uncertainty and confirmation remain to be studied. As a first stab, one might suggest that in a reading that combines these perspectives, phrasing

– cued through texture, textual structure and various performance nuances – combines with the misleading quasi-hierarchisable 'tonal' areas to cue a serial layout which might otherwise go unnoticed. Other examples of arguably misleading inter-perspective corroboration would include the interpretation of the Fisherman's Song refrain at the end of *The Nightingale* as 'unifying' an evidently stylistically diffuse work, and the recognition of the palindromic layout of *Agon* as accomplishing a similar reconciliation.[23] It is in the nature of this kind of thing that critical arguments remain exposed concerning whether in each case it is the formal device or the stylistic discontinuity that is the 'false trail'.

But if 'false' hierarchisation is to be exposed as an interpretative strategy, so too can the 'real' thing. It is widely recognised that the critical analysis of music requires a framework through which the construction of hierarchic, unifying and other classically resolutionary interpretations can be more keenly observed. This would include noting the recognition of self-similar processes in ostensibly similar (i.e. potentially hierarchisable) domains – such as various transfers of the Stravinskyan contrast/continuity issue to stylistic and intra-opus 'levels'. The result would be something quite flexible, geared to the analysis of interpretations and their contexts rather than to making statements about musical works *per se*. There is a cultural divide implied in this, because of the assumption that 'ordinary' interpretation will continue – rather as Nattiez's 'neutral level' analyses place themselves 'above' (or 'below') ordinary interpretation – and the fact that this new activity needs 'ordinary' interpretations as cannon fodder has meant that its main line of approach up to now has been the analysis of critical writing (or the criticism of analysis) using deconstructionist methods. The difficulty with this is that unless it successfully promotes a two-tier professional system of criticism and super-criticism it will eventually run out of materials. In the longer term, therefore, such work is more likely to rely for its raw analysable materials on those mainstays of genuinely musical interpretation: performance and listening. The analysis of these may still deal in contrasts and continuities, but at present lacks acceptable working methods – Krumhansl and Schmuckler's study of the perceptibility of the octatonic collection, for example, is simply not credible from the Stravinsky analyst's point of view.[24] Analysts will have largely themselves to blame,

23. See the brief discussion in Thomas Clifton, *Music as Heard: A Study in Applied Phenomenology* (New Haven: Yale University Press, 1983), pp. 250–6.

24. Carol L. Krumhansl and Mark A. Schmuckler, 'The *Petroushka* Chord: A Perceptual Investigation', *Music Perception*, 4 (1986), 153–84.

however, until, with performers, they begin to participate consistently in this divided culture not only as purveyors of super-criticism but also as subjects for the quantity of empirical observation through which 'ordinary interpretation' – against which analytical criticism has already begun to measure itself – can be renewably defined.

11

Immortal voices, mortal forms

Carolyn Abbate

How do Wagner's characters die? Or rather, how do their bodies die on the one hand, and their voices on the other? Odd as the question might seem, this particular red thread can lead to a whole speculative underworld, in which motivic transformation intersects with nineteenth-century views on language acquisition, and where mirroring gestures between voices and orchestra seem to mix the human and the mechanical in ways that anticipate that most traumatic of *fin-de-siècle* inventions, the gramophone.

Immortality and mortality in opera are hardly unfamiliar topoi, though I am not thinking of plot, of 'songs of love and death'. Operatic interpretation, in particular musical analysis of opera, has unconsciously tended to immortalise music and assume greater collapsibility in opera's other aspects. Much about opera collapses, in time. Performance itself is a process of dying away, since the singing and playing of any opera is a unique moment that cannot be repeated. Recordings remind us – more and more – that we are listening to the dead, just as photographs suggest so strongly that their subjects are no more. But beyond this inevitable marriage of temporality with mortality in the phenomenology of operatic performance, even more prescribed aspects of opera will also seem to grow old. Certain Wagner stagings may strive for neutrality or evoke the eternal as opposed to the topical (Chereau was *Gesellschaftskritik*, Emil Praetorius or Wieland Wagner, *Mythos*). But inevitably even mythic stagings are instantly recognisable, as is a singer's coiffure, as products of a particular epoch (though Wieland Wagner had archetypes and emptiness, his shelf life was not longer than Chereau's). Wagner's libretti, in being bound narratively to a time and culture that produced them, seem more subject to ageing than his music. Though taken from the Old Norse, infested with Gods, and filled with mythic archetypes, the plot of the *Ring* functions as an historicising accompaniment to the music, some (Debussy) would say, a burden. And everything lying outside the score – libretto, performances, singers, stagings, conductors – can come to seem like a heavy curtain that is inserted between us and an idealised music. One might even speak of a *déformation de l'amateur d'opéra* that causes many opera lovers to strip opera, mentally, of its materiality (from libretto

288

to soprano). We close our eyes in the theatre, we prefer the invisible voices and perfection of CDs; perhaps we prefer even not knowing the words.[1] Paradoxically, in thus freeing opera (we imagine) from time, history, and the mortality of live performance, we are experiencing opera in its most lifeless form.

Sound dies away

Meditations upon dead sonorities are almost inevitable during performances of Wagnerian *Verwandlungsmusik* at Bayreuth. There the covered orchestra, the closed curtain, and strange carvings on the proscenium (one imagines knobs, dials . . .) transform the stage into a huge antique phonograph, or perhaps a radio set, circa 1925. Where does this music come from? Is anyone alive in there? Mark Twain had already anticipated this fantasy in 1891, when he wrote that Wagner's dead brain, still dreaming away behind Wahnfried, produced the sounds one heard up the hill in the Festspielhaus.[2] Even when the curtain is parted, one tends at Bayreuth to focus on how everyone ends, and what becomes of their voices thereafter. *When* Wagner's characters die is not always obvious, a point worth considering. Tenors, heroes, die unmistakably. This is true of Tristan, Tannhäuser, Siegfried or Siegmund. Clément-like, we could imagine that Wagner, to hammer home some socio-cultural point, makes *certain* we know when men breathe their last. Female characters die far less obviously, and usually it is impossible to say what has happened to them, when, how and why, as with Elisabeth, Elsa or Gudrun, who 'sinks, dying, upon Gunther's body'. Sieglinde, who expires between two operas, shares the fate of certain Wagnerian women who, unlike her, never even appear on stage: the nameless girl described by Siegmund in *Die Walküre* Act I, the twins' mother, or Herzeleide, all of them women whose deaths are conveyed wholly indirectly, through narration. Finally, we neither see nor hear the moment of Brünnhilde's death, since she disappears into the fire while the orchestra rolls on for the destruction of Valhalla, of the Gibichung hall, for the recovery of the Ring, Hagen's drowning. Wagner's music is looking at something other than the heroine. Isolde dies (I would claim) only after all music has ceased to sound.

1. Michel Poizat, in *L'Opéra, ou le cri de l'ange* (Paris, 1986) cites an interview with an opera fan: 'par contre, les opéras que j'ai vus là, au Palais Garnier, eh bien . . . j'ai été deçu. Pour l'instant je préfère encore le disque à la représentation. Je n'ai pas encore vu de représentation qui me plaisait véritablement, qui me prenait vraiment' (p. 31).
2. Mark Twain, 'At the Shrine of St. Wagner', in *What is Man? and Other Essays* (New York, 1917), p. 212.

What, then, should we make of Kundry, an exception among Wagner's women? Her death is very precisely defined for us in scenic terms, but it is also stared at, with some dismay, by the orchestra as well. The last hundred-odd bars of *Parsifal* accompany a set of staging instructions, and can, famously, be understood as a spiral, a tonal sequence starting in A and falling through subdominant harmonies to reach A♭ at the end, A major through F♯ minor to E major, through C♯ minor to B major, through G♯ minor to F♯ major, through E♭ minor to D♭ major, where the juggernaut pauses for a moment as the dove appears above the grail. What happens next is this, 'Kundry, eyes raised to look upon Parsifal, sinks, lifeless, to the ground.' And the entire harmonic pattern breaks. This D♭ triad, for the space of a single measure, is released into a disturbing A minor (agitated string arpeggios) only to recover itself a moment later, and glide on, as prescribed, through B♭ minor, to A♭ (Ex. 11.1). This moment's intense strangeness was recognised by Jürgen Syberberg in his *Parsifal* film; for a second, we see an empty shore, and a receding wave washes sand from an ancient skull. Kundry, we seem to understand, has died absolutely. Nothing of her remains in the music that follows.

Brünnhilde, on the other hand, stays behind in sonorous form even after she has been consumed by fire. So we might understand a notorious effect at the end of *Götterdämmerung*, when Brünnhilde sings 'fühl meine Brust auch, wie sie entbrennt' to a motive that otherwise appears only once in the *Ring* (as Sieglinde's last vocal moment in *Die Walküre*), and when this motive recurs in the high violins in the *Ring*'s final instants. This is a calculated enigma, and from the outset had released speculative energies in the *Ring*'s first listeners (rather like the end of *Götterdämmerung* itself, which still engenders intense interpretative competitions). But already by the mid 1870s a notion of leitmotifs as signifiers for concrete literary concepts was fixed, and speculation about this motivic recurrence was oriented to a semiotic decoding of the theme. Famously, Cosima described Wagner's own understanding of the motive in a letter of 1875, as Sieglinde's 'glorification of Brünnhilde which at the end of the work is taken up, so to speak, by the entirety'.[3] This kind of semiotic precision was typical in contemporary interpretations, and while Wagner's comment suggests the motive's association with Brünnhilde, the motive is more than a literary sign. Better to hear it in less fixed ways: as signing-off (the radio again), as music sung by women who are about to disappear. Hence the eerie effect in the *Ring*'s final seconds, where Brünnhilde seems to survive her own physical death, in the form of her decorporealised voice, speaking through the vio-

3. Letter cited by John Deathridge in *19th Century Music*, 5 (1981), 84. Trans. John Deathridege.

Example 11.1   *Parsifal*, Act III: Kundry's Death

(**Kundry** sinkt, mit dem Blicke zu ihm auf, langsam vor Parsifal entseelt zu Boden. **Amfortas** und **Gurnemanz**

huldigen kniend Parsifal, welcher den Gral segnend über die anbetende Ritterschaft schwingt.)

(Der Bühnenvorhang wird langsam geschlossen.)

lins. Any decoding of the motive into a literary concept like *adoration* is insufficient.[4] And conventional interpretations of *Götterdämmerung's* end for their part may be fulfilling a psycho-ideological function, building a protective analytical barrier, which suppresses other associations called up by the *Ring's* final moments: the realisation that we are hearing the voice of a woman who has died.[5]

What are we to make, then, of two very differently dead women, Brünnhilde and Kundry? In laying out Kundry's death, the end of *Parsifal* reveals itself as pessimistic. One cannot escape dying, escape being brought to a final silence; the orchestra stands outside of the event and seals it in, by mourning Kundry so deeply that the afterlife is revealed as sentimental illusion. This orchestral expression of mourning (the A minor bar), if brief, is unsettling not the least because the gesture pulls us away from all that Christian myth-making (visual and musical) at the end of the evening. It pulls us back into the inescapability of time. Thus Kundry is, within the Grail world, a principle of the historical against the mythical – so the orchestral *memento mori*. Through Kundry the *Parsifal* plot is subject to a historicising principle, so that one could even speak of two conflicting *Parsifal* plots, the Grail-knights' *Bühnenweihfestspiel*, which impresses one as circular and eternally continuous, and the tragic-ironic Kundry tale, that reaches an absolute narrative close. The musical-metaphorical depiction of this contrast is sharp indeed, for the potentially endless tonal circle is derailed by one thing only, the A minor moment of Kundry's death. Yet we cannot assume that the mythic principle, merely because it has the last musical word, has prevailed.

If the *Ring*, to the contrary, allows an escape from absolute death

4. One way of conceptualising this critical distinction between motive as abstract concept and motive as voice is to borrow terms from Peircian semiotics, his distinction between symbol and icon. Wagner's motives are not words, not that which (indirectly, in mediated forms) stands for another object (a word for a thing), but rather that which, in its form, its forms of materialisation, its mode, directly replicates an object (Teddy Bears for bears, Mussorgsky's orchestral bells in *Boris Godunov* for the bells of the Moscow cathedral).

5. Readings of *Götterdämmerung* often display a manner of *Schutzhermeneutik* designed to draw the reader's attention away from Brünnhilde's image, as if the radical social implications of Wagner's feminine eschatology were too much to bear for modern man. See, for instance, Warren J. Darcy, 'The Metaphysics of Annihilation: Wagner, Schopenhauer, and the Ending of the *Ring*', *Music Theory Spectrum*, 16/1 (1994), p. 1ff.; and John Daverio, *Nineteenth-Century Music and German Romantic Ideology* (New York, 1993), pp. 178ff.

expressed in equally metaphorical-musical terms, immortality is nonetheless bought at the price of the body's dissolution (Brünnhilde's, the soprano's). In this sense, the conversion of singing body into pure instrumental voice is an *acoustic* allegory that replaces a more familiar *scenic* allegory that typical of Wagner's earlier operas. Indeed, the original ending of *Siegfrieds Tod* in 1848 still resorts to the image. Up until the first publication of the *Ring* poem in 1853, Wagner had planned to end *Siegfrieds Tod* with Brünnhilde and Siegfried rising from smoke and ashes to ascend into Valhalla. In the 1853 poem, this final transfiguration à la *Fliegender Holländer* was eliminated. Thus transmutation of a living body into a transcendental essence, still expressed visually in *Siegfrieds Tod*, was transformed in *Götterdämmerung* into audible form. And bold Siegfried is, now, nowhere to be found.

Mirror effects

Brünnhilde's voice is echoed by instruments, and, hardly for the first time in the *Ring*, the orchestra thus metamorphoses into an acoustic mirror. Although this *topos* of an 'acoustic mirror' now has other resonances, having become common coin in contemporary film theory,[6] it was there long ago in the *Ring* text, specifically in Sieglinde and Siegmund's conversations in *Die Walküre* Act I. References to 'mirrors of sound' which enable the twins to recognise one another are a librettistic homage to the musical phenomenon of voice-orchestral echoing. But Siegmund and Sieglinde's recognition scene, besides playing with a poetic metaphor of mirrored voices, also sets the terms of an epistemological hierarchy, in which sound conveys a great truth, while image can be insufficient or misleading. Siegmund and Sieglinde principally discover each other's identity not through recognising a face, but by sensing an unmistakable quality of voice; as Sieglinde says, 'ach still, laß mich der Stimme lauschen; mich dünkt's, ihren Klang hörte ich als Kind. Doch nein, ich hörte sie neulich, als meiner Stimme Schall mir widerhallte im Wald.' Their antithesis, Hunding, dull, congenitally unreceptive, is condemned to reason from strictly visual clues, and he senses their resemblance not through their faces *in toto* but in something even more meanly and merely optical, something that 'looks out of their eyes'.

Wagner played with echo effects between voice and orchestra from the beginning of his career, but the effects in the early operas have a quali-

6. The phrase was popularised by Kaja Silverman in her eponymous book *The Acoustic Mirror: The Female Voice in Psychoanalysis and Cinema* (Bloomington, 1988).

tatively different thrust. The notion of an orchestra that could sing, *Orchestergesang*, 'chant d'orchestre', was a familiar concept in nineteenth-century Romanticism, though what was understood by the term was an orchestral idiom that is gesturally vocal (instrumental recitative, and so forth). But how does such a technique differ from constructing an orchestra that seems to possess its own subjectivity? Wagner tended to use orchestral-vocal effects to replace characters' voices that have been temporarily silenced by an emotional overload, as in accompanying Elsa's 'stumme Gebärden' in *Lohengrin* (a technique Wagner could have learned from Auber's *La muette de Portici* or many other French romantic operas). How do such orchestral replacements of voice differ from a mirror effect, in which the orchestra seems eventually to attain its own subjectivity? Another way to ask would be, when does the instrumental voice become unsettling rather than merely sentimental? In *Lohengrin*, the orchestra represents a voice that hasn't yet begun to speak, and as soon as Elsa sings, her orchestral representative dissolves. In *Die Walküre*, the cello motives that express what Siegmund and Sieglinde cannot linger through an entire act, until finally sung in the 'Spring Song' at a point when the twins are prepared (though only allegorically) to declare their love. But significantly the orchestral voice remains even after they have gained their own, and out of pure substitution a process of exchange, of constant mirroring, has now been born.

Musical exchanges between orchestra and voices are something else; here the orchestra is not replacing a failed voice, but working over material already sung, as in the clarinet postlude to Elisabeth's final aria in *Tannhäuser*. In this case these echoes remain intensely formal (the clarinet repeats a whole strophe from the aria, as if what is being imitated with solemn care were not *Elisabeth* or her *voice*, but a structure). Otherwise the 'Song to the Evening Star', where the cello's repetitions are interjected upon the heels of the voice, where fragments of vocal melody, short motives, are immediately echoed instrumentally. In the *Ring* the relations between the singing voice and its resonance within the orchestra are even more intimate, more breathlessly decided, and under the surface of the mirror lurks an unsettling creature.

But why *a creature*? One is accustomed to thinking, for instance, of *Das Rheingold* as full of helpful leitmotivic *symbols*. But this is a great misapprehension, one that has damaged our capacity to perceive something frightening in Wagner's work. *Das Rheingold*'s motives originate (with rare exceptions) in the singing voices. Repetitions of these motives in the orchestra are not comments on the action but iconic representations of human voice, *of singing per se*. *Das Rheingold*'s orchestra is thus not a commentator but something more disturbing, an echo chamber, collective vocal chords that are set humming to sounds just sung. Any *a priori* analytical orientation towards semiotic decoding of leitmotifs will make us dull, deafen us to the moment when mechanically vibrating chords become an eardrum, and an eardrum becomes something that can hear, and sing back. This fantasy of orchestral vocal chords set vibrating is far more compelling in Bayreuth, because of the brass players' location and an ensuing acoustic trickery that occurs in no other opera house. The brass section is so far beneath the stage (and, in horizontal location, upstage) that anything scored for brass sounds as if it emanates directly from the stage world. Thus the few motifs in *Das Rheingold* that are not first sung by characters seem to be sung by *things*. When Alberich lifts up the Tarnhelm to gaze, fascinated, at its beauty, the Tarnhelm itself emits muffled minor-key chords. When the Ring first glitters from under the water, it shouts in a trumpet voice. And whenever the full orchestra (strings and winds with brass) takes up such material, the sound comes from another *locus* entirely, one clearly in front of the stage.

Vocal chords, humming, singing: all words that convert a mirror (something inorganic) into a subject, anthropomorphised, endowed with a soul. This metamorphosis occurs within the *Ring*'s very first scene, as the orchestra quickly begins catching vocal motives, at first only to echo them fairly exactly, as in the first instrumental imitations of the Rhinemaidens' 'Rheingold, Rheingold', or of Woglinde's 'der Welterbe gewänne zu eigen wer aus dem Rheingold schüfe den Ring'. When Alberich snarls 'so listig erzwänge ich mir Lust' and the orchestra repeats Wellgunde's 'nur wer der Liebe Lust entsagt', the instruments reinvoke the particular earnestness of her voice. More unsettling, however, is the famous transformation music between scenes 1 and 2. Beginning with a direct echo of the Ring motive as sung by Woglinde, the orchestra suddenly begins for the first time to improvise, to savour the motive, see if it can be said in different ways. At the end, the motive has been wholly transformed, and an object shimmering far backstage, Valhalla, takes up the motive and sings it back, changed once more.

In the transformation music Wagner translated into sound a typical Romantic conceit, one that found expression in numerous grammars and language treatises at the turn of the century. Children were seen as acquiring language when they finally learn to depart from pure imitation of maternal sounds into improvisation, since the capacity to improvise suggests the child has begun to grasp language as a medium, variable, something that possesses cognitive content. Crossing that border, in modern psychoanalytic theory, is often interpreted as one point at which the infant separates itself from the mother, and recognises itself as a subject. Perhaps the most famous literary description of language acquisition in the nineteenth century was that in Mary Shelley's *Frankenstein* (and here it is worth recalling that her monster, unlike Boris Karloff's, became fully articulate, even elegant in his vocal mannerisms). In the novel, the monster flees Frankenstein's laboratory and, after long wandering, finds permanent shelter in a tiny woodshed, from which he is able to eavesdrop on a poor family inhabiting the adjoining cottage. He begins by imitating their sounds without comprehension. But one day, suddenly, he realises that they are constantly making variations upon acoustic themes, and with this realisation comes the idea that their speech can be understood. He learns language, acquires a voice. At that moment, he later narrates, he also gained his soul, and, with speech, the power to torment his creator, hissing, 'I will be with you on your wedding night.'[7]

The creature that lifts its head during the *Rheingold* transformation music is no monster out of the laboratory, but rather a virtual subject clothed in sound, called into existence through Wagner's sonorous fantasia on language acquisition. From then on, the *Ring* orchestra will be capable of absorbing music from the voices, imitating and mocking, changing. But what is most critical in this voice–orchestra polyphony is that a previously stable relationship between voice and body has been called radically into question, because while a subjective voice has been conjured into being before our ears, this voice no longer comes from a material body. Voice has lost its capacity, to paraphrase Rousseau, to guarantee its human origins. Wagner's destabilisation of this voice–body relationship – his invention of what one might call a haunted orchestra – runs parallel to a turn in philosophy of language, and in Romantic literature, in which for the first time after 1800 automata and speech-machines with their disembodied voices inspire increasing uneasiness. Such phenomena were gradually demonised, at least by novelists and poets, over the course of the nineteenth century.

World-breath, and sighs that unfurl sails

Finally, however, not the *Ring* but *Tristan* introduced mirror effects that led to a radical separation of voice from body. From the extremes of *Tristan* Wagner would later draw back, although *Tristan* nonetheless made possible the end of *Götterdämmerung*, and the rescue of

7. See Mladen Dolar, '"I shall be with you on your wedding-night": Lacan and the Uncanny', in *October*, 58 (1991), 5ff.

Brünnhilde's voice out of the apocalypse. For *Tristan* betrays a deep uncertainty about the origins of voice and its natural association with the human or material. This uncertainty is realised in many small ways, for instance, in those odd recurring quotations that pepper Act I (Tristan's 'wie lenkte ich sicher den Kiel zu König Markes Land', mimicked by Brangäne and Isolde, Brangäne's 'kennst du der Mutter Künste nicht?' thrown back by Isolde, and others). Like an acoustic carnival mirror-house, they multiply to confuse original source with echo.

But before any of the principals have sung a note, a disembodied voice is set as warning sign over the whole work. A sailor sings a song; he is high up in the mast, and invisible, his voice unfixed in space,

> Westwärts streift das Schiff, / ostwärts streift das Blick. / Frisch weht
> der Wind der Heimat zu, / Mein irisch Kind, wo weilest du? / Sind's
> deiner Seufzer Wehen / die mir die Segel blähen? Wehe, wehe du
> Wind, / Weh, ach! wehe mein Kind. / Irische Magd, / du wilde,
> minnige Magd!

With this first gesture, Wagner was transmuting one of Tristan's adventures from Gottfried's *Tristan*, an adventure that takes place before time depicted within the opera, and that joins disembodiment to song. Tristan, mortally wounded by Morold, arrives in his boat at the coast of Ireland, so weak that he cannot lift himself from his cot. He floats along until the boat is seen by some Irish sailors, who at first assume it to be drifting, abandoned. Then, they hear a voice; this voice resounds over the water, singing a 'beautiful' and 'happy' song. They cannot locate the voice, and because they cannot *see* the body that produces it, they make a false interpretation of its meaning, as the song of a strong and healthy man. Gottfried thus reminds us of Tristan's talent for excellent deceptions (one of his legendary characteristics). Yet he also grants us an exquisite parable about the troubled epistemology of disembodiment, for the narrator warns, could the sailors but *see* Tristan (reconnect object and sonority), they would realise how *untrue* a voice they were hearing, would hear the lie in Tristan's song. All this leads to a meditation on music, how one assumes music cannot lie, yet might be capable of conveying a lie when separated from the human body of the performer.

Images of disembodiment creep into Wagner's *Matrosenlied* on higher levels, in other registers. A strange question is posed in the centre of the song, 'is it the wind of your sighing that unfurls my sails?' Where does voice come from? A part, an indisputable sign of the body? Or imperceptible music, something that manifests itself to us as wind? Can voice have a physical force (hurry the ship to Cornwall) even though we cannot see or grasp it? Song, breath, and wind, here poetically bound, all lead back to an invisible mouth, their point of origin. At the end of the opera the image of an unseen sighing woman, whose voice becomes wind, becomes inaudible music, *Weltatem*, the voice of a sighing world.[8] Once more, Wagner borrowed his metaphysics from Gottfried, but hid them by transformation. One of the most peculiar passages in the epic allegorises Isolde's power over men as a silent, secret music that seemed to flow from her eyes to fill the space around her. A bizarre image, this is the poetic source that shimmers behind the opera's uninterpretable final moments, where Tristan becomes the eyes, the lifeless body from which unheard music streams, while Isolde sings her secret music, at last, out loud.

If the sailor's song disembodies voice, it does so in a third fashion as well, with the collusion of the orchestra. At the end of the *Vorspiel* to Act I, Wagner wrote a melody, scored for cellos and basses, played in heavy spondaic steps as a transition to scene 1. This instrumental bass voice *anticipates* the voice of the sailor, an immediate fore-echo of his question 'sind's deiner Seufzer Wehen, die mir die Segel blähen' (Ex. 11.2). As the

Example 11.2   *Tristan*, Act I
(a) *Vorspiel*, end
(b) Sailor's Song

(a)

(b)

8. Friedrich A. Kittler, 'Weltatem: Über Wagners Medientechnologie', in *Diskursanalysen 1: Medien*, ed. F. A. Kittler, M. Schneider, and S. Weber (Wiesbaden, 1986), pp. 94ff. In Bédier's novel *Tristan* (1902), the image of the sighing-breathing woman is explicitly connected to Isolde, in a passage which describes a statue, made by Tristan in the image of Queen Isolt, 'au milieu de la voûte ils dressaient une image dont les proportions et la figure étaient rendues avec tant d'art que personne, à la voir, n'aurait pu douter

melody sounds, we see nothing, darkness, a heavy curtain going up. There is no visible body, no woman with 'mute gestures', not even a human terrain into which this voice could be projected. In this mirror-house of sound, the orchestra has spoken first, and the human voice will mimic. And because the human singing voice is no longer the primary subject, caught by the orchestra, the instrumental voice wins tremendous force. What was once an object that reflects has become the first source of sonority and subjectivity, while human beings become shadow and echo.[9]

Epilogue

Sitting at Bayreuth, listening to Siegfried's *Rhine Journey* played by a giant gramophone, one begins to wonder why gramophones (or radios, phonographs, CD players) are frightening, inevitably gloomy in their design and colour scheme. In *L'Opéra, ou le cri de l'ange*, Michel Poizat cites Jules Verne's novella *Le château des carpathes*, where sound technology becomes the basis for a particularly modern ghost story. Here we are told of a famous singer, engaged to an impressionable young hero, whose voice is caught in a black box by a demonic admirer. She dies at the moment of being recorded, and the mysterious inventor ultimately tortures his rival by luring the young man to a castle in the Carpathian mountains, and bringing the dead woman 'back to life' by playing the recording. For Poizat, Verne's novella indicates a new fetishisation of voice towards the *fin-de-siècle*.[10] But why is recording itself seen as a sinister technology (Verne hardly conveyed the same aura in writing of submarines, another of his prophetic ideas)? This is a point Poizat passes over, silently, though associations of sound recording with death became a typical literary conceit. Thomas Mann, for instance, comments in *The Magic Mountain* upon

que la vie ne fût dans tous ses membres . . . de ses lèvres s'échappait un souffle si doux que son parfum remplissait la salle comme s'il eût été composé de toutes les herbes les plus précieuses . . . l'image était si semblable à la reine Isolt . . . qu'il semblait qu'elle fût là en personne, aussi fraîche que si elle eût été vivante'. Joseph Bédier, *Tristan* (Paris, 1902), pp. 309–10.

9. Such an instrumental voice, unlocalised in any body, is analogous to the 'voix acousmatique' of film theory; see Michel Chion, *La voix au cinéma*, (Paris 1982), pp. 116–17, 'La fantôme est, dans les traditions, un non-enterré ou un mal-enterrée . . . c'est exactement la même chose pour l'acousmêtre, quand il s'agit d'une voix pas-encore-vue, et qui, ne pouvant ni entrer dans l'image pour s'y fixer sur un des corps qui y évoluent, ni occuper la position en retrait du montreur d'images, est condamnée à errer à la surface.' On the terrifying nature of such voices see Slavoj Žižek, *Looking Awry: An Introduction to Jacques Lacan through Popular Culture* (London, 1991), pp. 125–8.

10. See Poizat, *L'Opéra, ou le cri de l'ange*, pp. 138ff.

the funereal aspects of a phonograph lined in black velvet, resembling a coffin, out of which the sound of Hans Castorp's favourite records pours forth.[11]

There is something unmistakably strange about these machines. I remember vividly my grandmother's phonograph, circa 1945, a miniature theatre in walnut, with damask curtains shrouding the turntable. That silently cruising tone arm, those knobs switching off without human intervention, clearly bespoke the supernatural. Voices come from behind curtains, and nothing is alive in there. Meditating further in this direction, one would return to issues in language philosophy, musical metaphysics, histories and myths of automata. But for the moment (at Bayreuth), one starts listening to Wagner in other ways, how intensely the instruments sing back at the voices, how human sound is transformed into an instrumental sighing whose origins remain undisclosed. In the Festival year 1876, machines for preserving voices were still waiting in the wings of history. But as early as 1853, Wagner took an image of human voices captured by a monster, and engraved it into the music of the *Ring*.

A version of this essay appeared in German as 'Mythische Stimmen, Sterbliche Körper', in Udo Bermbach and Dieter Borchmeyer, eds., *Richard Wagner: Der Ring der Nibelungen. Ansichten des Mythos* (Stuttgart, 1995), pp. 75–87. I am most grateful to Roger Parker and David Levin for their comments on the English text.

11. In a meditation on music and recording technology, Friedrich Kittler describes the trauma loosed upon the literary and philosophical world of the *fin-de-siècle* by Edison's invention of voice recording technology; see *Grammophon. Film. Typewriter* (Berlin, 1986).

12

'So who are you?': Webern's Op. 3 No. 1

Dai Griffiths

One is then very sad when the kind of propagation of theory that went on . . . takes over from the development of actual new work. It's a very long and difficult job, to see how, in the very detail of composition, a certain social structure, a certain history, discloses itself. This is not doing any kind of violence to that composition . . . I do want to say that I think it has been extraordinarily damaging, especially since theory – so-called – is much easier than this actual analytical work. It's an extraordinarily easy intellectual practice. Whereas this other analytic task is difficult, because the questions are new each time. And until the last few years there was this very complicated business of finding your way around what was called Theory. It failed to understand what kind of theory cultural theory is. Because cultural theory *is* about the way in which the specifics of works relate to structures which are not the works.[1]

Theory: lyric poetry and society

'And to whom, gentlemen, do we owe the revolution of 1789 if not to Louis XVI!'

The French author Gustav Doré's joke, a simple confusion of cause and effect, is a rather crude example of how things not present can infiltrate the actual. Adorno's 'Lyric Poetry and Society',[2] first broadcast in 1957 during his time as a 'rather engaged disc-jockey'[3] – an article described by Edward Said as 'one of the most compelling pieces on lyric

1. Raymond Williams, in conversation with Edward Said, 'Media, Margins and Modernity', in Raymond Williams, *The Politics of Modernism: Against the New Conformists*, ed. Tony Pinkney (London: Verso, 1989), p. 185.
2. Theodor W. Adorno, 'On Lyric Poetry and Society', in *Notes to Literature, Volume One*, trans. Shierry Weber Nicholsen (New York: Columbia University Press, 1991), pp. 37–54. Also trans. Bruce Mayo as 'Lyric Poetry and Society', *Telos*, 20 (1974), 56–71, prefaced by Bruce Mayo, 'Introduction to Adorno's "Lyric Poetry and Society"', pp. 52–5. All page numbers included in the text refer to Nicholsen's translation.
3. Thomas Y. Levin, 'For the Record: Adorno on Music in the Age of its Technological Reproducibility', *October*, 55 (1990), 23–47.

poetry and lyricism I've ever read'[4] – uses the joke as an absurd reduction of his thesis that lyric poetry depends to some extent on the society which it excludes. I want to take this idea as a platform for creating a fiction around Webern's Op. 3 No. 1, a song which sets a poem by Stefan George. I will engage with how, in Raymond Williams's terms, 'the specifics of works relate to structures which are not the works'. This, a perennial anxiety in reading music in analytical detail, in that it can't see the wood for the trees, can offer a fecund perch from which to view the question of identity in the Webern song, and even beyond.

In 'Lyric Poetry and Society', during a brief reference to the lyric poetry of Stefan George, Adorno refers to the settings by Webern, in terms which are already social and political:

> [The] eccentric boldness [of the poetry of Stefan George] was rescued from the frightful conservatism of the George circle only when the great composer Anton von Webern set them to music; in George, ideology and social substance are far apart.[5]

Just how Webern's settings constitute the redemption of George's failure to reconcile 'ideology and social substance' is not drawn out in this essay, and neither is it at issue in Adorno's essay on Op. 3 itself,[6] but the idea of modernist music's enacting such a rescue is familiar elsewhere in Adorno's aesthetic theory.[7] The dissonance between text and music is something to which I shall eventually return, but, be that as it may, the presence of George's text in Op. 3 No. 1 keeps the poetic issues alive and well. 'Socially motivated behind the author's back',[8] in Adorno's terms, Webern's setting represents a turning inward of an extreme kind, one which provides a metaphor with which to analyse the song.

'Lyric Poetry and Society', although a note to literature, nevertheless contains many issues which are pertinent to, or reminiscent of, musical discourse, particularly the unusual and singular discourse of song:

1. Concerning *language*. An attention to language and form is cen-

4. Edward Said, interview in Imre Salusinsky, *Criticism in Society* (New York and London: Methuen, 1987), pp. 143–4.
5. Adorno, 'Lyric Poetry', p. 50.
6. Theodor W. Adorno, 'Anton Webern: Lieder op. 3 und op. 12', in *Der getreue Korrepetitor: Lehrschriften zur musikalischen Praxis* (Frankfurt am Main: S. Fischer, 1963), pp. 101–26.
7. Theodor W. Adorno, *Aesthetic Theory*, trans. C. Lenhardt (London: Routledge and Kegan Paul, 1984). See also Lambert Zuidervaart, *Adorno's Aesthetic Theory: The Redemption of Illusion* (Cambridge, Mass.: MIT Press, 1991).
8. Adorno, 'Lyric Poetry', p. 43.

tral in the essay, which encompasses an idiosyncratic kind of close reading, of Mörike and George – the word 'gar' in George's 'In windes-weben'
(pp. 50–1) (set by Webern as Op. 3 No. 2), for instance – and sees Adorno
'insisting on the power of those heterogeneous fragments that slip through
the conceptual net'.[9] While Adorno insists that language is not 'absolu-
tized as the voice of Being' (p. 43), it is through language that poetry
conveys both emotion and rational concepts (p. 43).

2. Concerning *ideology*. Adorno holds strictly to a definition of
ideology as 'untruth, false consciousness, deceit' (p. 39) (the fifth of
Eagleton's sixteen possibilities[10]), and is opposed to ideology criticism *per
se*: 'the greatness of art lies solely in the fact that they give voice to what
ideology hides' (p. 39). However, at a few points in the article Adorno is
prepared to bring in the issue of class origin. Mörike is 'as aware of the
empty and ideological aspects of elevated style as of the mediocrity, petit-
bourgeois dullness, and obliviousness to totality of the Biedermeier
period' (pp. 49–50); while George's aristocratic stance 'is not the pose that
the bourgeois, who cannot reduce these poems to objects of fondling,
waxes lyrical about' (p. 51).

3. On *subject and object*. This is a complex theme which, if in any
sense broadly similar to Eliot's notion of the 'objective correlative', reads
as an altogether more charged conception. The subjectivity of both poet
and reader are involved; as is the objectivity through which a subject
expresses itself:

> The unself-consciousness of the subject submitting itself to lan-
> guage as to something objective, and the immediacy and spontaneity
> of that subject's expression are one and the same: thus language
> mediates lyric poetry and society in their innermost core. (p. 43)

4. On *intention*. As with Wimsatt, the 'intentional fallacy' receives
short shrift: 'the social interpretation of lyric poetry as of all works of art –
may not focus directly on the so-called social perspective or the social
interests of the works or their authors' (p. 38). Even so, in attempting
rather to 'discover how the entirety of a society, conceived as an internally
contradictory unity,[11] is manifested in the work of art' (p. 39), Adorno is

---

9. Terry Eagleton, *Walter Benjamin or Towards a Revolutionary Criticism*
   (London: Verso, 1981), p. 141.
10. Terry Eagleton, *Ideology: an Introduction* (London: Verso, 1991), p. 1.
11. An echo here of the 'torn halves of an integral freedom, to which however they
    do not add up' in Adorno's letter to Walter Benjamin of 18 March 1936 in
    *Aesthetics and Politics: Debates between Bloch, Lukács, Brecht, Benjamin,
    Adorno*, afterword by Fredric Jameson (London: Verso, 1977), p. 123.

ready to bring in biographical and historical detail when germane, always as part of a wider conception.

(5) On *history*. Although the article dances through these highly disparate critical perspectives, the underlying foundation is clearly, and in a perhaps surprisingly linear manner, historical. Lyric poetry is understood by Adorno to have reached a particular kind of 'unqualified authenticity' in Goethe (with examples taken from *Wandrers Nachtlied*). From there through Mörike to George, lyric poetry – its immediacy, 'something which flashes out abruptly' – is in the industrial world essentially a 'paradox', with Baudelaire appearing to occupy a particularly delicate balance.

There is little in the last point that a musician might want to disagree with. A certain critical view might insist on the music produced between Mozart and Brahms to be a kind of authentic pinnacle of tonal music, with Debussy occupying Baudelaire's tightrope. What music history might be thought of as lacking is the automatic conjuring of a social context[12] largely because music, familiarly, unlike poetry and visual art, lacks the automatic ground in social connotation either of language or of representation. But song is in this respect a lacuna, because of its overt and clear association, underlined perhaps in the case of Webern's setting of relatively contemporary verse, such as that of George. The analytical question begins to sharpen: do we continue to understand a song as mere film music around a text – a game of pure music – or do we insist upon understanding, as I have already asserted, that the issues of poetry continue to haunt the setting? (What seems to me temptingly pointless is to 'be a musicologist' about poetry.) It is the latter insistence which I suspect separates a 'composer' view[13] from a 'theorist' view. John Carlos Rowe, in discussing the shift from the word 'form' to the word 'structure', describes the latter as approaching the state of being an 'abstract, constructed, even *fictional* model'.[14]

The centre of Adorno's argument is that it is from the society outside that even the most complex poetry will derive its language – albeit in

12. See Richard Middleton, *Studying Popular Music* (Milton Keynes: Open University Press, 1990), pp. 11–16, for an attempt to construct such a model.
13. 'Whatever the end in view, all analysis is directed to revealing the mind and intentions of the composer and the compositional process, and the extent to which any analytical method genuinely succeeds in doing this is a test of its validity.' Robert Sherlaw Johnson, 'Analysis and the Composer', in John Paynter, Tim Howell, Richard Orton and Peter Seymour, eds., *Companion to Contemporary Musical Thought* (London: Routledge, 1992), p. 715.
14. John Carlos Rowe, 'Structure', in Frank Lentricchia and Thomas McLaughlin, eds., *Critical Terms for Literary Study* (The University of Chicago Press, 1990), p. 30.

George's case a highly rarefied and precious form – and that the society so excluded continues to impinge. Things are present by their absence: 'conspicuously absent', as we might say. Lyric poetry always implies the presence of what, in order to create its happy immediacy, it has chosen to reject, so that in recognising what it describes we too are discovering a second nature, 'not only convention', as Bob Hullot-Kentor says, 'but a new nature'.[15] The first person, the 'I' of lyric poetry has 'lost' nature, and 'attempts to restore it . . . through immersion in the "I" itself'.[16] Adorno argues, in a remarkable passage, that in one line of Goethe ('Warte nur, balde'), almost miraculously, a 'second immediacy' is 'promised', and becomes 'full truth'.[17] So too the 'I' of lyric poetry always implies, for both reader and poet – and, as we shall see, for composer and singer – another identity:

> It was always bourgeois: the shadow-side of the elevation of the liberated subject is its degradation to something exchangeable, to something that exists merely for something else; the shadow-side of the personality is the 'So who are you?'[18]

**Analysis: Webern Op. 3
No. 1**

> Dies ist ein lied
> Für dich allein
> Von kindischem wähnen
> Von frommen tränen . . .
> Durch morgengärten klingt es
> Ein leicht beschwingtes.
> Nur dir allein
> Möcht es ein lied
> Das rühre sein[19]

It may be that the identity of the person addressed in lyric song is itself historically conditioned and that, again with Raymond Williams's concern in mind, by asking a vast, and possibly *fictional* question like

---

15. Bob Hullot-Kentor, 'Introduction to Adorno's "Idea of Natural History"', *Telos*, 60 (1984), 109.   16. Adorno, 'Lyric Poetry', p. 41.

17. *Ibid.*, pp. 41–2.   18. *Ibid.*, p. 42.

19. Stefan George, from *Der siebente Ring*. Translated the poem runs: 'This is a song / for you alone./ Of childish longing, / Of pious tears . . . / Through morning gardens it sings / Light-winged. / For you alone / this song is made to bring you peace.'

Example 12.1   Webern, Op. 3 No. 1, 'Dies ist ein Lied für dich allein'

that, it in fact leads us to something quite precise in the analytical context. This is not doing any kind of violence to that composition. The you
of the 'Ständchen' in Schubert's *Schwanengesang*, the you of Webern's
'Dies ist ein Lied', the you of Bob Dylan's 'I Want You' shifts as does the
analytical premise of each song. Wolf, Schoenberg, Pfitzner: different
compositional premise, different audience relation, different you. How we
conceive that relation can vary as the metaphors with which to describe
the relation of voice to accompaniment, and more.[20] So we might think of
Webern's 'you' contained in the singer's mind. Offstage. In the audience.
In a distant country to which a letter will be sent . . .

Or, and analytically I am being perfectly realistic, is not the song's
'you' there, onstage, *inside the piano*? I like the picture this metaphor
engenders, of a singer actually talking to a piano. I think the metaphor
captures the inner torment of the vocal line, and also the way that an audience for this music is essentially voyeuristic, music's becoming a her-
metic deal between composer and performer. There is a crucial moment
here in the history of the connotation of 'setting' a poem: moving from
'set' – to adumbrate, to put to music (pre-Schubert); through 'set' – to
stage-set, to contextualise, to provide film music (the golden age:
Schubert, Schumann, Brahms; Adorno's 'technical illusion of universal
cogency'[21]); to 'set' – to ensnare, to use poetry as pretext for technical
construction which means, effectively, and in time, thinking musically in
terms of a chromatic 'set'. This is the moment of a deal struck between
the Wagnerian premise of texted music with the brevity and precision of
late Brahms. In the relation of music to poetry, this is literally a long story
cut short, a cinematic glance read into a poem, one expressive sigh into a
whole novel, a whole story: Schoenberg's is the crucial metaphor.[22]

So, Op. 3 No. 1 could be possibly a confession made to a piano-priest;
but, in the fiction which follows, it is the recollections made to a piano-
psychoanalyst (such as the very psychoanalyst to whom Webern found
himself uncomfortably talking in Vienna, some three or four years later).

20. The 'vehicle' of the metaphor may vary according to the writer's attitude.
    Examples – narrative, dramatic and cinematic – are found in, respectively,
    Edward T. Cone, *The Composer's Voice* (Berkeley: University of California
    Press, 1974), pp. 1–19; David Lewin, '"Auf dem Flusse": Image and
    Background in a Schubert Song', *Nineteenth Century Music*, 6/1 (1982),
    47–59; Sean Cubitt, '"Maybelline": Meaning and the Listening Subject',
    Popular Music, 4 (1984), 207–24.   21. Adorno, 'Lyric Poetry', p. 45.
22. Arnold Schoenberg, 'Anton Webern: Foreword to his *Six Bagatelles for String
    Quartet*, Op. 9 (1924)' in *Style and Idea*, ed. Leonard Stein, trans. Leo Black
    (London: Faber, 1975), p. 483.

What is more, the couch scene takes place before an audience, present only as onlookers, creating the rich field of relations illustrated below.

SINGER   PSYCHOANALYTIC/POETIC OTHER
                                    ('dich allein')

'confession'   voyeurism

        Dream material

PIANO   AUDIENCE ('dich allein')
piano analyses   voice owns text
voice material

MUSIC–TEXT ANALYSIS   PSYCHOANALYSIS: TEXT ANALYSIS

This topography can be understood as the site of thematic analysis: references from the text which voice passes over to piano create a dialogue between the two which is both textual and musical. The piano part, the unsung hero of Op. 3 No. 1, is an ambiguous phenomenon. It has a double voice, one concerned with its function as accompaniment, film music providing a backdrop for voice; the other where, as analyst, it engages voice in dialogue. The dual function of piano can be expanded as follows:

1. In order to represent piano as film music, setting scenes, linking scenes, the music's montage and its dissolution, and so on, there is need for a language of inclusion. Pitch-class set theory[23] would present one such picture drawing attention to a possible nexus bunched around the configurations 6–34, 5–28 or 4–Z15, constructions of whole-tone plus one semitone. Against this are the smaller Forte numbers, suggesting that along with the nexus are small cluster groupings, sometimes inversionally balanced. All this detail is bound to challenge severely any notion of tonality, however residual or fluctuating.

2. In order to represent piano as speaking voice, picking up from voice, pitching questions and working through answers, there is a need for a language of selection. This is the site of a text-driven motivic analysis. In this, sometimes not everything is of the essence, and the proliferation of structure in piano's inclusive voice is in a kind of dialogue with the phenomenological realism of its selective voice (particularly at the song's

---

23. Allen Forte, *The Structure of Atonal Music* (New Haven: Yale University Press, 1973).

central section).[24] From this is constructed an account of Op. 3 No. 1 as
not only a musical design around words, but as text-music. In this reading
singer and pianist are not happily smiling over towards each other: rather
there is a dialogue over musical direction and the music's relation to the
poem. Smaller metaphors are introduced under the enclosing fiction:
ownership of text is worked through the economic imagery of who is paying for and thus controlling the session; proximity to the text is voice's
great asset, and she parades her knowledge, lording it over the mute piano;
piano however, always sceptical and knowing (vertical as well as horizontal), encloses the vocal part, and regards her as some ventriloquist's
dummy: in this of course she is gendered, while piano remains I, you
or they.

Webern: Op. 3 No. 1

*[Scene: Vienna 1910. Psychiatrist's consulting-room. 'Voice' is lying
down on couch, 'Piano' is seated at her side, taking notes as she speaks.]*

> PIANO: (chord) We are ready to begin. (Here's some pitch material
> with which you may spin out the usual hysterical nonsense. My low
> E♮ has nothing to do with you, and is just my way of reminding you
> who's paying whom in this session, and who's in charge.)
> VOICE: *Dies* – I don't really want to tell *you* this, but an appoint-
> ment's an appointment, and I paid in advance – I'll take D♮ down to
> D♭ thank you. (It'll take you a while to see what I have in mind with
> D♭, and how it will act to unlock my memories later. So much for
> who's boss, as no doubt you're as usual thinking. Just remember
> who's paying whom here.)
> PIANO: Ah, D♭ you say. Interesting. Let me just take down:
> 'Dies . . . ist'.
> VOICE: *ist ein Lied* – I emphasise 'Lied' for reasons entirely known
> by me alone – *für dich allein* (Stefan's words: such lyricism, that 'suf-
> fering distance', a song from a poet to a distant beloved. *My* distant
> beloved: naturally, nothing whatsoever to do with *you*.)
> PIANO: (mumbles) Dies ist ein Lied – you must mean G♮ here – für

---

24. When Adorno does get round to looking at notes, his readings remind me
    of those in Thomas Clifton, *Music as Heard: A Study in Applied
    Phenomenology* (New Haven: Yale University Press, 1983). See especially
    Clifton's interesting reading of Webern's Op. 10 No. 1 (pp. 231–6). See also
    David Lewin, 'Music Theory, Phenomenology, and Modes of Perception',
    Music Perception, 3/4 (1986), 327–92.

dich: for *me*?! (Another day, another analysis: I've brought in my
pitch extremities more comfortably to contain this drab outpouring,
and I think I'll play around with some clusters – B♭/B♮, E♭/E♮ – to see
what she makes of them. I of course build my material on some
attempt to fathom what she's telling me: E♭ and E♮ are at pitch from
syllables 'ein' and 'al-' of 'allein', while B♭ completes 'allein', at pitch.
B♮ is my neat deduction from what I've been told. She doesn't seem to
want to go higher in register today: could be the weather, or maybe
we're in for the regular build-up to high hysterical pitch again, God
preserve us.) Do continue.

VOICE: *von kindischem wähnen* (a perfect fourth which neatly
inverts your presumptuous elongation of my 'Dies – Lied' from
diminished to perfect fourth in b. 2.)

PIANO: *'kindischem'*? (oh no: childhood memories.) Please just
give me time to think about this 'kindischem': I think this may
prove of importance in the dream analysis. (Meanwhile, I take everything she's gone on about in her first line and make of it an expressive
vertical, including my own B♮. So. My, how I'm wasted on these
whole-tones. When I think of what von Pappenheim gets for *her*
money.) It seems that in saying 'kindischem' back there you seem
to have touched on D minor (the chord in b. 4). But it could have been
a slip of the tongue (a point of musical spelling).

VOICE: *von frommen* (a transposition of a tone – the shrinks are all
the same. You mention childhood and off they go. You come in here
in a kind of lightheaded, airy mood and all they do is bring it down to
dull, objective detail. Well, I'm just talking sense; following 'dich
allein' – 0146: is that what they call it? – and working through 'von
kindischem wähnen' – C♯, D♮, F♮, G♮ – to 'von frommen tränen' – E♭,
E♮, G♮, A♮. Anyway, they're all my beautiful melodic lines, and *at register*. And listen out for Stefan's lovely rhymes.) Are you about ready
that I may continue? (Come on, slowcoach!)

PIANO: One moment please. (Another whole-tone chord. What
these bored housewives don't realise is that I have to sift through vertically as well: without this they would end up sounding like some
ranting nun, if they don't do so already.)

VOICE: *tränen*

PIANO : A perfect fourth C♮–F♮, which is of course, of *my* suggestion (D♮– G♮ b. 2). Now, as I was saying, 'kindischem' (up an octave).
Interesting (transposed up án octave), but very interesting indeed
when I decide to combine it with your current reference to 'tränen'.
This makes it into 'kindischem tränen', does it not? I add, for your

amusement, the low E♭, to show how 'kindischem' creates a different tonal order to your waffling, the recollections of your first line. E♭ is a different whole-tone grouping, with A♮ and F♮, from that of 'dich allein' and 'Dies'. (Also, that E♭ is way too low for her even to notice, I mean it's just a rumbling low note for her, and reminds all the onlookers who's boss round here.) Also, I hope you understand, lady, just how subtle my authoritative E♮ was to start with. You think E♭ is as low as I can go, do you? Wait (I studied analysis at the highest level . . .)

Dissolve (PIANO seen still worrying over the melodic content of 'kindischem', back at vocal pitch, with its own sixth harmony, so creating, as it as analyst would say, an 0145 cluster formation) and cut.

To sum up, bb. 1–5, as text-music, appears as follows.

VOICE: *Dies ist ein Lied für dich allein*
PIANO: scene-set   Dies ist ein Lied für dich (?)
                (low E♮ establishes piano control)
VOICE: *von kindischem wähnen*
PIANO: kindischem
VOICE: *von frommen tränen*
PIANO: kindischem kindisch . . . (dissolve and cut)
                tränen
                (way too low E♭ re-asserts piano control)

Scene Two: Flashback. VOICE and PIANO joined together in enactment of dream material. Melodically linked with VOICE, PIANO provides rippling semiquaver accompaniment which presents melodic material in diminution. The phrase 'gärten klingt es' is crucial, interpolated into piano L.H. at b. 7 while R.H. presents fragmentation. An unusual formation (4–18), it is there in the first vocal phrase, A♭ D♭ D♮ F♮, but perhaps better thought of as taking from piano b. 4, C♮ F♮, with E♮ C♯ inverted and heading upwards instead. Piano also extracts from it a D pedal which fits into the bass argument outlined above. Its 'way too low' C♮ links similarly to E♭ in the first scene. Voice transposes its second phrase up a semitone from the first. With 'ein leicht beschwingtes', VOICE enters into PIANO's earlier clustral concern over E♭ and E♮.

As text-music, it is necessary to think analytically of this in different terms from the outer sections. Piano does not go '*morgengärtenmor-*

gengärten' and so on in quite the same realistic fashion as before. It might best be left (in this context) as something along the lines of 'rippling semi-quavers'.[25] One effect worth noting as text-music is this from b. 7:

VOICE: *ein leicht beschwingtes*
PIANO: gärten   klingt es (kindisch-) **t(pc)7**

Otherwise, the central section is best thought as a dream-like, misty, dissolved and surreal flashback.

> *Dissolve and cut. PIANO provides link, this time through trans-posed 'für dich allein' (4–Z15, t9), with many memories: D pedal, D♮–G♮ 'wähnen', and F♮–C♯ from 'kindischem'. The C cues VOICE return ('Nur') at register. Play it: it is a rich, referential sonority. PIANO can be justly proud. Period . . .*

PIANO: And so I now see how 'kindischem' held the key to what you were thinking of. You may now continue.
VOICE: *Nur dir allein.* (Your time-consuming pause has rather detracted from the rhythmic unity of my return with my other phrases in the first section. Thank goodness that 'dir' is at least and finally among my unaccompanied words.)
PIANO: (Still harping on with 0146 I see. So predictable, the early atonal miniatures. Roll on the twelve-note pieces, say I.) *Dies ist ein Lied* (in my now generally accepted version) *für dich allein.*
(Meanwhile see how I have brought back E♭/E♮ in tenor, now with D♯ instead, Webern so fond of these little notational niceties. Also I'm cleverly recalling G♯/B♮ down in the bass, in celebration of the fact that she eventually arrived at B♮ next to G♯ for 'klingt es', part of that funny 'gärten klingt es' business. Penultimate pitch to appear in the vocal line, so helping to close the chromatic, as we analysts say. C♮ just there at 'Nur', the last pitch, picking up no doubt from my C♯/C♮ way back in bar 4.) Go on.
VOICE: *möcht es ein Lied* (Let's be honest: anything for a quiet life, and anyway the session's almost up. I see my vocal ranges as much more a matter of obligatory registers and the like, and so quite inde-pendent of the shrink's pedal notes. Who cares about those, anyway? I can hardly tell the really low ones. And in the end it's my lines that tell the story: I'm in charge of the words round here.) *das rühre sein*

25. A precise rhythmic analysis is contained in Elmar Budde's dissertation, published as *Anton Weberns Lieder Op. 3 (Untersuchungen zur frühen Atonalität bei Webern)* (Wiesbaden: Steiner, 1971), Ex. 49.

(rhyming neatly – Stefan such a perfectionist – with my earlier 'für dich allein').

PIANO: (Sad, really: so tuneless, so limited.) I'll play out with beautifully augmented interversions of 'für dich allein' which I have guided towards being the nexus for today's interesting material. The chords and final dyad refer to one of your favourite whole-tone scales. I declare the session now closed.

[Lights fade, and PIANO walks VOICE offstage. Just before lights out PIANO turns round, looking mystified, a look of forgetfulness.]

PIANO: (By the way, what happened to my low register? Am I now 'dich, allein'?)

[Lights out. End.]

To sum up, the third section is recapitulatory, and works like this:

VOICE: *Nur dir allein* (wähnen, tränen, -gärten: **R**)
PIANO: Dies ist ein
           (bass) klingt
VOICE: *möcht es ein Lied*
PIANO: Lied für dich allein
           . . . es . . . klingt
VOICE: *das rühre sein*
PIANO: für . . . dich . . . allein

Three provisional conclusions

This analysis represents Webern's Op. 3 No. 1 in a textual form. Concerning the relation of the song to its method:

> the diversity of critical and analytical responses to this aspect of Webern's art exposes differences in hearing and understanding that make a general consensus about the nature of his achievement difficult to imagine.[26]

Concerning the method itself:

> A sceptic might point out that . . . it is only natural to respond to *these* works in a theatrical mode. Fair enough, and I do not want to promote a priori any one mode of perception as universally 'better'

26. Arnold Whittall, 'Webern and Multiple Meaning', *Music Analysis*, 6/3 (1987), 333.

than any other. Only I believe we are in some danger, these days, of ignoring the more productive modes of perception; I think we underestimate seriously the extent to which those modes are alive and active even in situations where their pertinence is not so immediately apparent . . . situations where we think of ourselves as 'readers', not as speakers, writers, and directors; as 'listeners', not as players and composers.[27]

Finally, concerning the relation of the analytical method to a wider theory, turn back to the first page of the essay, its first reference.

27. David Lewin, 'Music Theory', p. 386.

Index